What th are Saying...

I see Reverend Harry Williams as doing what makes it count. He puts it before us and says to us, it's real now, because we are living it. And man, are we living it! His book helps us pick up the pieces and get it going! Thank you, Harry. You're all right with me.

Reverend Cecil Williams
Glide Memorial Church, San Francisco

As a mother who lost my youngest son, George C. Scott, to gun violence at age 24 more than 19 years ago, and a nephew, Timothy Scott, 23, in 2007, I know intimately the pain, heartache, depression, and other results of senseless violence. I strongly believe the faith-based community, especially pastors and church leadership, must lead the way in interrupting inner city violence. Jesus Christ went to the people to help heal brokenness; to reduce harm, danger, and biased attitudes; and to increase love, peace, and harmony. Like Christ, it's time for pastors and congregations to be committed and involved in the movement to stop the killing and start the healing. That's why I encourage you to read Rev. Harry Williams's book, *Street Cred*. O.G. Rev does more than just preach about the movement, he *is* about it!

Mattie Scott, Executive Director
Healing 4 Our Families and Our Nation
SF Mothers In Charge Chapter Leader
SF Brady Campaign President

Peace to the universe! This is Mr. Biggs of the legendary Afrika Bambaataa and the Soul Sonic Force. I'd like to send peace and love to my brother Harry Williams, better known as the Incredible Mr. Freeze, and one of the architects of this thing we named "hip-hop." A gigantic part of the old-school hip-hop revolution, Brother Williams went from rapper to minister; this is a brother that really have something to say about the streets. May God bless you, Mr. Freeze. ... I mean Minister Williams.

Mr. Biggs, Afrika Bambaataa
and the Soul Sonic Force

Reverend Harry Williams is a champion for those who have no voice. He is a precious pillar of the Oakland faith community and an invaluable ally to Oakland's disenfranchised youth. Reverend Williams has chosen to do the hard but necessary work of confronting urban violence and human sex trafficking where it is happening – in the streets of our cities. We are thankful for Reverend Williams' service and steadfast commitment to the City of Oakland and its residents.

Annie Campbell Washington, Oakland, California,
City Council Member – District Four

I remember pulling up to a red light one day in the hood and watching O.G. Rev, a.k.a. Harry Williams, being threatened by a pit bull. He was moving like lightning. I drove around the corner to see if I could offer him a ride, but Rev was gone! I laughed my behind off. I respect Rev because you're likely to see him in any location in the city of Oakland. I have driven past him walking through the worst hoods in the city, most often by himself. He's the type of preacher who will take a chance if it means reaching a soul. I never miss his Tuesday night Bible study at Glide Memorial Church in the San Francisco, Tenderloin.

From the very rich to the very homeless, Rev can communicate God's word to everybody. He's real out here in these streets, and people respect him for that. We're not related by blood, but we're family just the same. My daughter and I love this preacher!

Bernadette Williams, East Oakland resident

Harry Louis Williams was once an original MC, a fixture in the troubled and dangerous streets of the South Bronx; a neighborhood surrounded by crime and despair, poverty and addiction, cold steel and urban blight; a neighborhood that would give birth to an underground pastime that would eventually grow into a hip-hop nation; a global voice of hope and forum for injustice and corruption. Harry had a voice and was a New York City original known as "The Incredible Mr. Freeze." That voice still resonates. His words still carry weight. From street cred to spiritual clout this man is a true original who rose from the streets where it all began – The Bronx, New York.

Bronxstyle Bob, One of the original Zulu Kings

I met Harry through hip-hop. He put me on the first record I ever heard my voice on. He went by the name "The Incredible Mr. Freeze," and he took a liking to MC Delite and me. I loved the brother so much that we went to many, many hip-hop events together and met rap greats, from DJ Hollywood to Will Smith. It's amazing to see his ministry. He's literally a hip-hop pioneer, so he knows the streets, their struggles, their pains. He has a mission and a purpose, and I'm glad to be a part of his journey.

Daddy-O, Record Producer for Mary J. Blige, Queen Latifah, Steel Pulse, and the Red Hot Chili Peppers

Where there is a diversity of people there will also be a diversity of beliefs and lifestyles.... Rev Harry specializes in diversity. While defining urban ministry, professor Jeremy Del Rio quotes Jeremiah 29:7: "Seek the welfare of the city ... in its welfare you will find your welfare." He explains, "This is a word spoken by the prophet to a people in exile, a people who find themselves in a place they don't want to be." Rev. Harry specializes in ministering to those in exile, in environments where people don't want to be. O.G. (of God) Rev is by no means timid in reaching out to people, wherever they are at. He speaks/raps the language of the streets and understands the social issues that plague the blacks and browns in "exiled," underserved communities. Harry, you are our modern-day prophet. I'm inspired by how you live the word. Be blessed and encouraged.

Angela Wells Kidd, Resident of East Oakland

When we speak about the anointed, it is critical to place Reverend Harry Williams in that conversation. He sacrifices man-made churches (that may not serve the people) for God's sanctuary, which means speaking truth to false prophets/profits. Reverend Harry manifests the Word of God in this must-read, thought-provoking book filled with practical, humble wisdom.

Cesar A. Cruz, Co-founder, Homies Empowerment

My ninth-grade students had the honor of meeting and talking to Reverend Williams after reading his novel, *Straight Outta East Oakland*. Months later, they still talk about how wonderful that experience was. It is rare that students get to meet authors of the books they read, let alone an important figure in the community. Rev Williams is unlike other authors; he has many special gifts that will touch and inspire the youth. He not only talked to my students about the book, but he rapped to them about his life growing up and encouraged them to write their own stories. It is definitely rejuvenating to hear how much they love the book, since they often complain about how they don't like to read. My students and I truly appreciate Reverend Williams' way of telling our truths in his stories and letting us know that a better society is possible!

Nhi Troung, Arise High School, East Oakland

Rev. Harry Williams is a true urban soldier for Christ! Not just an ordinary Sunday morning preacher, he walks the talk on a daily basis. I've seen this for years. He is not a shot-in the-arm, here-today-and-gone-today kind of preacher! He is consistent in his love for Christ and His people!

I have read all of his books so far. He is an amazing writer. I love everything he has written. I am very sure that his new book will wake us up! Lord, wake us up! Thank you for using Rev. Harry to give us a shot of adrenaline.

Mattie Johnson, President of the Allen Temple Baptist Church Streets Disciples, Oakland, California

O.G. Rev means the world to me. I took a chance and went to his Bible study at Glide Church. I was running from crazy at the time because I was so depressed and scared. My life had been flipped upside down after serving ten years in the military, eight years in law enforcement, and home-ownership for eleven years. I had lost everything, and I had legal woes and an acute illness. Feeling broken, I kept coming to Bible study. There I felt comfortable enough to share my pain and to cry. Reverend Harry Williams always encouraged me to share my interpretation of the Bible, and now he and our Bible Study group are a family.

Gloria Berry, San Francisco Bay Area Community Activist

When I think of Jesus and His mission, how He went from the temple to the hood, and what He fought and stood for, I think of Harry Williams. He is definitely a street soldier. He places himself with people in places that only Jesus himself would go, taking the gospel to the street. Twenty-first century black Jesus, Harry Williams.

Teri Harpo, Leader of the Glide Memorial Church Recovery Ministry – San Francisco, Tenderloin

Harry Williams is a wise, courageous, and compassionate guide through our chocolate cities with a focus on the precious humanity of our neglected and abandoned fellow citizens. Don't miss his powerful book!

Dr. Cornel West, Author of Race Matters *and* Prophesy Deliverance!

STREET CRED

A Hood Minister's Guide to URBAN MINISTRY

REVEREND HARRY LOUIS WILLIAMS III

Soul Shaker Publishing
Oakland, California

Download the official
Street Cred Study Guide
free by writing to
streetcredmanual@yahoo.com.

Soul Shaker Publishing
Oakland, California
www.RevHarryWilliams.us

Cover and interior design
©Tamara Dever, TLC Graphics, TLCGraphics.com.

PHOTO CREDITS
Front cover photo, back cover and interior cross photos, author photos
©Matt Beardsley, MattBeardsley.com; Graffiti photos ©Erin Stark

ISBN: 978-1-5335-9498-3

Dedication

About a year ago, fools kicked in my back door when I wasn't home. Usually it takes only five minutes to clean you out, but this time one of my neighbors heard the thud of a boot against my door and came running. He confronted the thief. Now, that was a courageous act! You see, just two weeks prior, a citizen of East Oakland had been shot in the gut because he responded to the noise of a break-in. In this case, had my neighbor not intervened, the thief would have escaped with the one thing in the apartment that I would have considered irreplaceable. You're holding it in your hands. This book would not exist as you see it if my neighbor, Kenny Wilson, the unofficial mayor of East Oakland, had not acted. This book is dedicated to him.

Foreword

Please forgive me if – after 35 years in the inner city of Chicago, in a mile square with 60,000 neighbors, where we led the city in stolen cars one year (2,330), had 1,300 fires another year that burned out apartments of 27 families from my church in arson-for-profit schemes and gang conflicts – I'm a bit hesitant to endorse many books on urban ministry theology, theory, or practice. But not this book. Harry Williams is the real deal. He has the "cred" from a life in Harlem, Modesto, and Oakland. I went to school in this book as Harry, "the Rev," took me inside the realities of life between the twins: drugs and guns. He tells stories, reminding us he is the outsider. He chose to be there. For him the incarnation of Jesus is both model and message. His stories have practical and Biblical content. Along the way he reminds us there are many kinds of pastors and churches. Jesus makes so much sense in the midst of chaos and violence as Harry takes the stained glass off the gospels, which confirms what I found in Chicago and other cities in decades past. His descriptions of politics, policing, and dollar flow in the ghetto ring true to those who have been there. His "homies" are names, not numbers or categories. The violence is graphic, but Harry models so many sensitive ways to share Jesus and hope in the "hood." I love the way Harry commends colleagues who do ministry alongside him and often differently.

Because most of my doctoral students in urban ministry these days are Asians, Africans, and Latinos, I see this book describing Harry's work on the streets as a prophetic word about the ways cities are changing abroad. Of course, we'll use this book in the United States, but Crips and Bloods are not all that different from ISIS in the Middle East in how they operate. Ghetto violence increases abroad, but traditional mission personnel have not been prepared to engage violent cities on other continents. Harry Williams will be a valuable resource for an urban world on six continents going forward. I am delighted to commend it.

Ray Bakke
Author of *A Theology As Big As The City*

Preface

 In Jesus, God put skin on and moved into the neighborhood to live among us. And it wasn't just any neighborhood. Jesus came from Nazareth, a stigmatized, despised place from which people said "nothing good could come." As you read the Bible, and as you read this "gospel" of Harry Williams, you can't help but be convinced that God has a fondness for the margins and a suspicion for the centers of power and privilege. From Nazareth to Oakland, a war is being waged over the destinies of our youth. And Harry Williams is on the front lines, insisting that hope does not trickle down. Hope must be unlocked, unleashed as we break the chains that hold people down. Williams reminds us all that the best healers are wounded healers – that the worst sinners can become the greatest saints, and that real power doesn't come from the titles we hold but from the testimonies we live. If there is one thing the church needs today, it is street cred. And here is a guide to help us recapture that – a faithfulness that does not just have its head in the heavens; it also has its feet on the ground. Harry Williams is a pastor of the streets – just like Jesus was. *Street Cred* is nothing short of a fresh and daring call to follow Jesus and to bring God's love "down to earth."

Shane Claiborne
Author of *The Irresistible Revolution: Living Life As An Ordinary Radical*

Contents

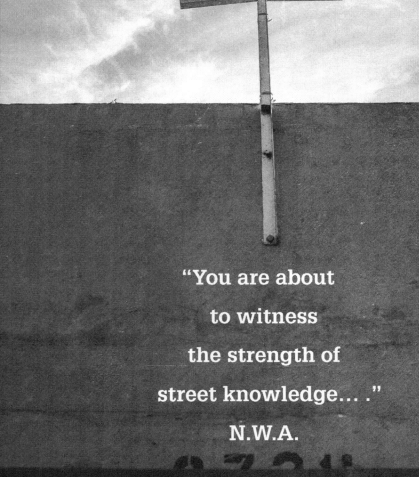

"You are about
to witness
the strength of
street knowledge... ."
N.W.A.

Introduction

It all changed for me when the phone rang at about 6:00 p.m. on September 17th, 2005. A young man had been murdered in a section of West Oakland, California, known as "Dogtown." The call was from a preacher I knew. "A number of clergy are headed over there," she said. "Would you like to go?"

I didn't know what good I could possibly do, but I said "Yes."

Thirty minutes later, we were pulling up to the crime scene. It was dusk. Spectacular dark clouds with a crimson lining, like blood-stained cotton, floated above us. Oddly, the mourning grounds had a distinct carnival atmosphere. Television trucks with satellite dishes lined the street, TV lights brought daylight to the scene, and reporters clamored for involved or interested parties to provide sound bites.

I watched one of Oakland's most revered pastors philosophize into a news anchor's outstretched mic, wringing his hands as he made his points. Other clergy and local politicians milled around, vying for the attention of the press and anxious to get their air time. The winds of fall pushed me farther down the street past a row of aging shotgun houses. Wild pit bulls howled in the urban wilderness. Hard-eyed neighbors crouched on porch steps, whispering their skepticism to one another as they stared warily at the strangers down the street. The people in the round, white collars hadn't yet ventured this far; there were no TV cameras at this end of the block.

A cluster of young men in their late teens stood in a semi-circle sharing a bottle of Hennessey. I climbed the three steps from the concrete to their porch, stuck out my hand, and introduced myself. I stood in solidarity with their pain. They were more than willing to talk.

Turned out the deceased kid's name was Michael. He was a high school honor student who had fostered dreams of attending college. He had never been any trouble to anyone. That morning Michael had walked out of a crowded Victorian house owned by his relatives to get a breath of fresh air. In the predawn hours, some unknown person approached him with a heavy gauge automatic weapon and opened fire. A tragedy indeed, but that's not what had drawn the heavy press coverage to a dark corner in one of America's most dangerous cities. What made it "news" was the sad truth that the 15-year-old's dad had been shot to death just three months earlier, ironically in that same location and in the same way.

While the neighbors and I were conversing, an ancient blue Toyota raced up to the front of the house then dove to the curb like a killer whale with a harpoon in its belly. The young fellows who had been talking with me took a quick step back in unison. Panic flashed across their faces. Someone in the car rolled down the passenger-side window. His menacing facial expression was an unveiled threat. Others peered up from the crowded car, also "mean-mugging" my new friends. Not a word was exchanged, but the message had been delivered – and received. As the Toyota accelerated down the street, racing through its gears, we heard the car's passengers laughing.

"Who was that?" I asked, choking on air heavy with exhaust fumes.

The most talkative of the bunch whispered, "That's the bad people."

I won't elaborate on whom I assumed the bad people to be, but you can imagine.

I shook hands again with the young brothers and continued down the block until I reached a group of women sitting on the hood of a red Maxima. Loud hip-hop music with extra bass blasted from the car's stereo speakers. The pungent aroma of marijuana was in the air. These folks too were sipping alcohol to dull the pain.

"Were any of you related to the deceased?" I asked.

One young woman said, "Yeah, I'm his auntie."

"I'm sorry for your loss," I said. "Is there anything I can do?"

She stared right through me for 10 silent seconds and then blurted out, "Yeah, you can preach my nephew's funeral."

"Me?"

Some of the most famous preachers in Oakland were out there that chilly night. Why would she ask a street preacher without a congregation or a church building to perform the eulogy?

By this time, one of the city's leading pastors had made his way down the block, looking for family members. When he reached the deceased auntie, he just put it out there: "You can have the homegoing service at my church." Now, that made sense. The pastor would have the opportunity to preach a high-profile funeral bound to be covered by the press, and the family wouldn't have to undergo the heavy financial burden of renting a space for the services.

It made perfect sense to me, but, apparently, not to the aunt. She looked over at me and, with some gravity in her voice, said, "I want you to preach the funeral."

I handed the woman my card, then walked away still believing that the aunt must have mistaken me for one of Oakland's more prominent ministers. After all, I did fit the stereotype: a short, chubby black man toting a big, black book. Before long she'd figure out her mistake, I reasoned, and that would be the end of it.

But early the next morning she called me. Indeed, she wanted me, an unknown preacher and a total stranger, to eulogize her nephew. She gave me the name of the funeral home and told me what time to be there.

Homicide funerals are perverse functions, extravaganzas where inner city youth often dress and act as though they were going to a party. In the days following, young mourners would ask each other "Were you there?" as though it had been a rock concert.

On the morning of this funeral, ghetto soldiers and their families began to fill the parking lot 15 minutes before the service was scheduled to begin. Many wore specially designed T-shirts with the face of the deceased printed in multi-color across the chest. Still others wore white dress pants with the lost teenager's name printed down the leg in pastel blue. Plastic-encased images of the deceased youth, created by and sold at T-shirt shops, hung from the necks of other teens (some young people collect these things like baseball cards). Girls in mini-skirts shared pews with elders dressed in black. Many of the young people were angry, tattooed, agitated, and high. A few appeared afraid. One young man had the words "He Won't Be The Last One" printed on his shirt.

This was the first homicide funeral over which I had presided, and so I was kind of counting on some help from the battalion of preachers who had been out on 30th Street to show their angst and support for the community. In fact, only one of them showed up – and he was late. So, with the help of the funeral director, I did the best I could. Even at that, the funeral was America's version of Auschwitz, complete with screams, cries of grief, and moans from the flesh basement of devastated dreams. It was all bad.

In the middle of the service, a grandmother jumped up from her seat and cried out, "Oh Lord, when will the killing end? When will we be able to stop burying our babies?" I, too, pleaded, not so much with God as with the young mourners. I begged them not to go out and wreak retaliatory havoc on their enemies. I pleaded with them to keep their guns in safety mode, especially the kid wearing the shirt that said, "He Won't Be The Last One."

After I had spoken the closing prayer, the funeral director opened the casket to allow those who wished one final view. I took the first glance. Michael, the child in the casket, was 15 years old but looked even younger. After I'd said my prayer, the funeral director produced a clear plastic mask, a protective device similar to what a basketball player with a broken nose might wear. The funeral home official slipped it over the young boy's face.

A burly man with a thick mustache leapt up from the center of the room and hollered, "No mister! You take that off." A rumble from the crowd moved the funeral director to do just that. I was puzzled as to why he would want to cover the boy's face with a mask, anyway. And then I saw. When the multitude of loved ones lined up to say a final goodbye, a good number leaned into the casket and kissed young Michael's cheek. When it was done, the funeral director slowly lowered the lid to leave the man-child – our future – in darkness.

A father slaughtered and then three months later his son killed in the same spot. Clearly, urban America is in the throes of genocide. Ironically, the eyes of the nation are not focused on the devastation that ravages its inner cities.

One day, as a friend and I stood on the corner of East 85th and International Boulevard in East Oakland, he spelled out the changes that had transformed the neighborhood into a hood. (This was back when my friend was in the free world; now he's serving life in San Quentin Prison.) He said, "Rev, there have always been gamblers, hustlers, and pimps in the hood. The difference was that once they kept their dirt out of the sight of old people and kids. Back in the day, the game had rules. One of them was that if I were looking for you and I happened to see you in an area where there were kids, you got a pass that day. Today these cats will pull out a gun and take aim, even if their rival is standing in the middle of an elementary school playground surrounded by 6 year olds. If one of the little ones gets hit, the only thing these young fools can say is, "Oh, well... ."

The problems of the hood have mutated like diseases that defy traditional vaccines. Years ago all eyes would have been aimed at the church doors for solutions. That day is past. Most inner-city churches use a paradigm that hasn't changed in 60 years. A visit to many a local church is like entering a time capsule: the suits and ties, the elaborate floppy hats, the songs, the paper bulletins, the verbal gymnastics, the canned sermons, the organ and piano. All have remained the same. Robes and sashes have never gone out of style here, and yet the world around the building has changed dramatically.

The prison industrial complex has stolen away so many of our family members. Crystal methamphetamine is being sold on junior high playgrounds. Guns are easier to find in some hoods than chewing gum. Our communities have turned into food deserts, void of stores that sell fresh fruit and vegetables. A myriad of crises that didn't even exist 10 years ago face the hood today.

And still the elders insist: "Give me that old-time religion!" Unfortunately, there are consequences attendant upon that insistence on things of the past. Traditional churches are losing the interest and attendance of their youth. Once-vibrant ministries are filled with gray heads. It's not the message of the gospel that has become antiquated, but the medium through which it is communicated. The old-time religion has grown, well ... old.

I called a friend a few days ago, and during our conversation she asked me to check out a sermon on the Internet preached by a talented young minister. The young man was preaching on a rostrum populated with some of America's most highly noted African-American preachers, not one of them under 50. When the young pastor began to preach, he borrowed the techniques and delivery styles of his elders. He was like a religious comedian imitating the accents and time-cultivated routines of honored guests at a roast. The ministers on the rostrum howled in delight as they traced their own styles within his message. Although he was young (perhaps 30), he was preaching from the same blueprint pastors had used since the dawn of the Great Reconstruction. The preaching heroes behind him, cheering on his pitiful display, were also imitators, borrowers of a tradition born when people drove to church in Ford Model T automobiles, warmed themselves by potbelly coal stoves, and looked at the radio as the greatest single innovation of the century.

Our faith communities have failed to evolve with the times. Many of the warriors still willing to do battle are using obsolete weapons. They're tossing spears at an enemy who's pushing the red button on the spiritual equivalent of nuclear warheads. As a result, our churches are imploding in slow motion, and our hoods are dying.

I have a friend who lives in the East Bay Hills, high above Oakland, California. When we talk to each other on the phone, the signal sometimes drops, and the call abruptly ends. Minutes later, she'll call back to say, "I went through a dead zone while I was driving," meaning that the electronic signal that makes phone communication possible was obstructed by the hills as she maneuvered her car to her destination.

Jesus said that the Spirit of God would lead us into all truth. However, our insistence on dusty church culture and threadbare tradition has interrupted the signal that comes from the Holy Spirit to the house of worship. In some locales, the effectiveness of the inner city church has almost fallen off the map. To our disgrace, apathy and malaise have taken the places of evangelism and activism. Yet, in the face of empty pews on the inside and chaos on the outside, we still cry "Give me that old-time religion!" It's as if we're rolling downhill in a car that's run out of gas. As we race toward disaster at the bottom of a hill, we look at each other, shrug, and say, "Well, at least it's still moving."

A generation of young people has never been impacted by the message of the gospel or the ministry of the church. How do we reach them now?

Meet Dashaun "Jiwe" Morris, one of the most well known Blood gang members in the world. I copied these words from Jiwe's Facebook page. They are insights into his life. He told me it was all right to share them with you.

"... If you ain't got thirty-three dead homies, four due to suicide; missed two of your four kids' births because you were in prison; gave your mama gray hair from her worrying if you gonna make it home tonight; watched your childhood friends die every week and eventually get accustomed to it; if you ain't ever slept in cemeteries so that you could still prove to your dead homie you was never leaving his side; if you never played Russian roulette four separate times; if you never dumped 5 pills along with a 5th of whatever, light and dark, then went hunting with three of your killers in a stolen whip [car] and the following morning can't remember s— from da night before; if you've never been slapped by nine different moms who came to the the hood and slapped your face because they felt they left their child in your hands and now he's dead; if you never had a mother cry in your arms to help get bail money for her son that's locked up for murder and aggravated assault robberies; if you have never been to a funeral to bury a 14-year-old homie of yours and got the whole hood looking up to you, waiting, itching for the call to move on the hood that's responsible then don't tell me s—."

The people in Jiwe's world are screaming out for a path to relevant faith. They have souls and destinies. They're thirsty for faith. But how do you touch people like this young brother? How do you reach people in his predicament? Well, keep reading and I'll tell you. In fact, I'll do one better than that. I'll let *him* tell you.

Some of you are already angry with me, and I haven't even gotten you to Chapter 1. No worries. A little anger can be a good thing! Let that rage propel you to make the change that our hoods desperately need. You won't always agree with me as we journey together through the coming pages, and that's fine, as long as you start prayerfully working on your own solutions to issues that I raise.

Street Cred: A Hood Minister's Guide To Urban Ministry offers a boots-on-the-ground insight into many of the issues that confront people in the hood and will allow you, the reader, to see the roots of the crises. *Street Cred* will serve as a touchstone for dialogue on the pressing issues that challenge life in the inner city and how people of faith might respond.

This book will explain how the neighborhood became the hood. It will provide you insight into the social ills that have bedeviled America's inner cities for decades. *Street Cred* will lay out the unique issues that confront our hoods. It will present a challenge to the urban church and people of goodwill who want to make a difference. In between all of that, I will show you how my eyes were opened to the struggle as well as introduce you to some of the bravest street-level activists you will ever hope to meet.

Street Cred is not an intellectual position paper crafted for discussion at a pink tea and bow tie luncheon. It's a grassroots manual written at ground zero of a war zone by a minister who has been there; as they say in the streets "fo' real." You'll be hard-pressed to find another book written from this unique vantage point.

For Activism
Not Entertainment

Recently, I had a very real conversation with a resident of one of the most crack and meth saturated communities in North America. I said, "Tell me Fred (not his real name) why do most churches ignore the fact that human beings are being trafficked in front of their buildings or that gangs are actively recruiting little kids in the neighborhoods where they worship?"

Fred said, "It's like this, at some point those churches had to make a decision. Are we going to wage spiritual warfare or choose peaceful coexistence with Satan? They are not going out into the hood en masse to interact with the lost souls on a regular basis because they have already struck their deal with the devil."

Are you part of a church that has no major emphasis on evangelism or social justice? Is your church like an elephant farm, where folks just stay in one confined place stroking each other's backs and critiquing new trends in Christian thought? Be forewarned that this book might not be for you. "Peaceful coexistence" is not what we're aiming for here. This is a book for people who are interested in being standard bearers for the Kingdom of Christ.

What Gives Me the Audacity?

How could I find within myself the sheer audacity to make such statements? For the past 15 years I've fought for the freedom of people who were on the verge of being incarcerated, and I've helped people paroled from prison to re-create their lives. I founded a ministry to help women tied up in the webs of domestic violence and human trafficking. I've helped the homeless find housing, led the addicted to recovery, and counseled the gang member to put down his gun. I've been in these streets talking peace while other voices were calling for war. I've led many, many people to faith in Christ. Ask anybody.

This is Real Life Talking… .

One night, I was sitting on the edge of my bed interviewing someone for this book when I heard five gun claps. Later, I found that I had heard someone being executed hood-style just a few feet from where I lay my head. I've worked on this book while police helicopters hovered overhead. I have a notebook with ideas on how to save different individuals' lives on one side and book notes on the other. This book is real.

Most of the books I've thumbed through about urban ministry start with sentences that read, "Then Rauschenbusch said," or "Then Neibuhr said… ." In this book you're likely to read, "Then Thunder Mack said," or "Then '07 Street Killa said… ." This is real life talking.

The Uncut Truth

Years ago, I served formerly incarcerated people as a case manager, which is something akin to a social worker. One of the young men I mentored was a street legend. He had been incarcerated multiple times for everything from armed robbery to bank fraud. He was trying to turn a corner in life and, for the most part, was doing great. However, the streets had begun to whisper that he was beginning to make some wrong decisions. I felt it my duty as a minister to point out the errors to him before he had fallen into a hole too deep to climb out of.

I called him aside one day and said something approximating this: "Brother, in the confluence of time there are forks in the road that present themselves. It has come to my attention that you have careened to the left at such a juncture. Now, what might we do to correct this error in navigation?"

He looked at me as though I had two heads on my shoulders. He said, "Rev, just keep it real. Don't put a cut on it."

What is a "cut"? Before a kilo of cocaine leaves the jungle, it's diluted with a white powder called "cut." Every time the package changes hands, another blend of milk sugar, powered milk, Manitol, Pseudocaine, baby powder, or formaldehyde is stirred into the chemical mix. By the time it reaches the consumer, it might have been "stomped on" 15 times. The user might be snorting or smoking a mixture that is 1 part coke to every 50 parts something else. At that point, it's really not even coke anymore.

And so it is with the truth. If I start diluting its intensity to avoid hurt feelings, the message might be meaningless by the time it touches your fingerprints. Too many lives are at stake, too many destinies are in the balance, so I'm not going to put a cut on this, and I'm going to ask you to follow my lead. Sooner or later, you're going to find something in this book that needs to be shared with someone else. Don't dilute it. If you're too shy to say it with the same candor I've used to express it, just quote me. Don't put a cut on it.

How to Use This Book

Before you begin to study the chapters in this book, bow for a word of prayer. Ask God to expand your vision. Then, with a yellow marker or a pen, highlight or underline things that strike you as particularly significant or that deserve notation, further reflection, or study. Write questions and comments in the margins. Next, read this book a second time with a Sunday school class or a group of good friends. You can even download the official *Street Cred Study Guide* for free by requesting via e-mail at streetcredstudyguide@yahoo.com. As they say in the streets, "Get in where you fit in." Plot your own plan of action for healing the hood.

Got that? Cool.

Now, welcome to *Street Cred*.

Chapter 1

The Day the Great Divide Was Pointed Out to Me

 The Church is not a building. It is a gathering of worshipers who come to live out the Christian faith experience within the given context of a geographic community. Too often, the church is shut off from the very people who populate the hoods where its building exists. This fact was put into blunt terms to me by an inmate in a maximum security correctional facility.

And how apropos for him to share this reality with me. You see, each of the men inside this particular California penitentiary was born and raised in a community dotted with churches. Some of the inmates are even church members. However, except for a few churches with prison ministries, these brothers have been forgotten by the local church. Forget Matthew 25's admonition to visit the prisoners. Except for God's all-seeing eyes, these people remain out of sight and out of mind. Let me take you deep inside the belly of the beast to meet them.

Home of the Forgotten Ones

Gangsta rap paints prison as the Valhalla of the gods, the warrior camp where real men are made and tested in the flaming pit of adversity. Hip-hop artists brag about the "bids" they have served at the state-run social club. Well, I've been behind bars to preach the gospel and to minister to the imprisoned on a number of occasions, and I never once saw anything in there that would make anyone want to journey beyond the razor wire for an extended-stay vacation.

Eyes flit back and forth, testing, judging, measuring. Inmates cluster together with affiliated prison gang members. Cats who drove expensive European automobiles and sported alligator shoes on the outside walk with their heads down in no-name sneakers through dim halls stale and ripe with body odor.

Most of all, it's the fear that impresses itself upon you. Terror surrounds you like fog in the human warehouse, though people fight to suppress it. In the streets, they say that "anybody can get it." That's doubly true in here. In the streets you can run. You can hide at your girl's house. Shoot, if things really get hot, Mama can put you on the first Amtrak smoking for down south.

But after you've been sentenced and tossed into the bottomless pit, the running is over. Now you're trapped inside the same concrete squares and rectangles with the enemies who prayed for a chance to kill you on the outside. People get stabbed and chopped up by homemade knives all the time in prison. As rapper Chuck D of Public Enemy once said, "Welcome to the Terrordome."

Jesus Lives in Prison

There is only one room of freedom in the mansion of mayhem. Most of the times, when I go inside, I'm headed there with a Bible tucked beneath my arm. God is not an elitist. God is anywhere that people choose to experience God's presence. You can feel God's Spirit when you walk into the auditorium where the prison church services are held. Some of the most committed Christians I've ever met are praying, playing music, or leading church services behind the walls. I love those guys and they love my hood sermons, the ones with hip-hop lyrics peppered on top of the scriptures. After awhile, the names of the prisons, the visits, even the sermons tend to run together in my mind. However, I do remember one incident distinctly. I was hard at work preaching. My damp, white, button-down shirt clung to my rounded belly. Beads of perspiration popped out on my forehead. It felt like I was trapped in a vise, like someone was squeezing words out of my diaphragm. I listened to myself holler, "Repeat after me! Lord, you love me." The audience response was so heavy and loud I could hardly make out the words.

"Forgive me, Lord!"

The audience repeated the words, ever louder.

"Come into my heart!"

Thunder.

"Be the Lord! The boss! The shot-caller of my life."

The 50 men at the altar stretched their hands forward to where I stood on stage. They repeated my words in rhythmic cadence.

I dabbed away the cold sweat that flowed from the flesh on my forehead as though from behind a burst dam. I had just preached out my lungs and my soul. A sea of hand-claps overpowered every sound in the building – except for the jackhammer beat of my heart. At that very instant, I had the thought that always seeps into my mind at the end of a successful sermon: "I wish my late mother had been here to see me today." The worship band followed my prayer with a raucous number that had the brothers up and clapping their hands to the drums and bass guitar.

I made my way down the podium steps. When I reached the bottom of the staircase, I became aware that, though it was broad daylight outside, triple-stage darkness engulfed those of us inside. Even the huge overhead lights could not make the dim dissipate. An aura of heaviness hovered over the packed auditorium.

Each of the men on either side of me as I moved toward the exit wore blue denim trousers and a blue denim shirt. Some of the pants said CDC (California Department of Corrections) on the side in bright canary yellow. We were deep in the belly of the concrete slave ship.

I would be leaving in a few hours, but some of these men will never leave here. Even when they die, they'll be pushing up daisies somewhere beneath a tree in the backyard.

Of course, there's always an element of danger when you preach behind the walls of a prison. Fact is, though, I never worry about danger because when it's my time, it's my time. Besides, my experience is that the brothers and sisters behind bars are the most hospitable, kindest people you're ever going to meet. They remember your sermons forever!

God Speaks Through a Prisoner

As I made my way through the auditorium toward the exit that afternoon, I felt the sting of open palms as the brothers slapped my damp, sweaty back. Those cats treated me like a hero, as though I had just scored the winning run in the World Series.

Husky male voices hollered, "Right on, brother!"

"You kept it real in the field up in here, preacher!"

"That's what I'm talking about!"

I waded through the sea of worshipers with both eyes set on the door at the back of the chapel. Suddenly, an O.G. (original gangster), flanked by two hard-looking prison soldiers, stepped out of the shadows into the aisle, blocking my path. The O.G. had purposely positioned himself in a spot where our paths would intersect. An open Bible rested on the palms of one of his hands. He was not smiling. My ghetto antennae instantly popped up.

I could see there was something on his mind, and that concerned me. I started thumbing through the sermon notes in my mind. My first thought was that my message must have stepped on his sneakers. Whether I preach on the cell block or the hood block, I tend to be blunt. I reason it like this: Why speak German when you're in Japan? Still, my candor rankles people sometimes, even in here.

"How you doing, brother man?" I asked.

He barely acknowledged my greeting. "Reverend, God spoke to me about you when you were preaching."

My left eyebrow cocked skyward. I never take such words lightly. Because of God's call on my life and my life's journey, I know that God is far more likely to speak a word to me from a state prisoner than from the president of the Rotary Club. God knows that I'm going to give this man my complete and undivided attention. We're on the same plane. We're tied together through history, blood, and destiny. I'm going to hear him.

"Really. What did God say to you?" I asked.

The man cleared his throat and read from the book of Malachi, chapter 5, verses 5 and 6. "See, I will send the prophet Elijah to you before that great and dreadful day of the Lord comes. He will turn the hearts of the parents to their children, and the hearts of the children to their parents, or else I will come and strike the land with total destruction."

The brother closed the book and then gave his own commentary. "Reverend, you are waist deep in hip-hop culture, but at the same time you're a Baptist preacher. God is going to use you as a bridge over the great divide between the young generation and the older generation."

Then he peered deep into my eyes and asked, "Reverend, do you believe that God is speaking through me to you?"

I did. And I told him so.

The Chasm

The great divide, that's what he called it. And he should know. He lives as far away from the loving embrace of a local church as Earth is from Pluto. Churches raise up missionaries and send them to tropical locales all over the world. But few churches are raising up ministers and subsidizing efforts to get inside here and preach to the big homie. He lives on the far side of that divide.

You don't have to go through a metal detector at a prison to understand that the church is divided from the community. Just get in your car in the church parking lot, drive in a four-block radius around the building, and then figure out how many of the people you just passed have never been inside your building. How many people from the housing projects or the trailer parks are regular members of your church? Why don't they come? My new friend described it correctly. There is a chasm, a class and cultural divide that intimidates people who do not have a good suit, freshly shined shoes, or a prestigious job.

The brother in prison said that we needed a bridge. That means that somewhere there is a chasm that we haven't been able to cross. The chasm to which my new friend was referring exists between the hood and the local church.

In 1990 C. Eric Lincoln and Lawrence Mamiya published an exhaustive history of the black church entitled, *The Black Church in the African American Experience.* The two esteemed scholars wrote before hip-hop culture, particularly gangster rap, had exploded internationally; before Crips and Bloods had gone international; before the beast called "incarceration" had risen up on its hind legs to decimate entire communities; before gentrification became the threat it is today; before crystal meth had shown up in the black community; before many of the dark situations haunting today's hood even existed.

The last chapter of their book was entitled "The Black Church and the Twenty-First Century: Challenges To The Black Church." The authors prophesied: "The demographic movement of middle-income blacks out of the inner city areas and into residential parts of the cities, older suburbs, or into newly created black suburbs, has meant a growing physical and social isolation for the poor.... Black pastors and churches have had a difficult time in attempting to reach the hard-core urban poor, the black underclass, which is continuing to grow.... The challenge for the future is whether black clergy and their churches will attempt to transcend class boundaries and reach out to the poor, as these class lines continue to solidify with demographic changes in black communities."[1]

Jesus called his followers to be fishers of men and women, but centuries later something has gone wrong. We no longer have the bait that will draw the fish. Post Civil Rights Movement churches now rarely speak the language of people who still live in the inner city. Many of our churches are like forts. The sheltered and the well-off race into gated sanctuaries of safety, segregating themselves from the people in the communities around their buildings. At best, even when food bags are dispensed at holiday time, members maintain a "we" and "they" distance. This relationship is not only unbiblical; it's unsustainable.

When it All Ceases to Work

I visited a church some years back at the invitation of a good friend. The choir lifted up traditional hymns. I jumped to my feet and clapped my hands. I love the old songs. My Pentecostal roots started to show. When I focused on the goodness of God and the miracles that had happened in my life, I had to shout and jump up and down. You could hear me hollering outside in the streets,

I'm sure.

As the service quieted down, I noticed two young sisters walk through the door with their younger brother. Whereas most of the "church people" wore suits and floppy hats, this family wore jeans and sneakers. They sat toward the back. (I know this because I almost *always* sit in the back of the church, and that Sunday I was, in fact, sitting behind them.)

The choir chose a rousing rendition of "Amazing Grace" for the pre-sermon hymn. I looked ahead of me at the young boy, who might have been 12 or 13 years old. His head bobbed up and down, more or less to the rhythm of the music. I was impressed. He's feeling this, I thought to myself.

Soon enough the pastor, a lady preacher, came to the podium. The young man sat back now, his elbow on top of the pew bench. His head rested on his hand. He seemed to be nodding to the timbre and rhythm in her voice. I can still hear her shouting: "And then the man asked me, 'Preacher, how many angels can dance on the head of a pin?' And I thought for a minute and asked him, 'How many pink jelly beans can fit inside a Mason jar?' And I told him to turn to Ecclesiastes chapter 2, and then he said… ."

I ventured a peek at the young fellow. He was still vigorously nodding at the preacher. I thought to myself, "Well, isn't this something?"

And then the preacher took a deep breath, leaving about three seconds of silence. During that brief vacuum I heard something. It sounded like hip-hop drums. And then I noticed the wire running up the length of the boy's arm and coming to an end beneath the hand underneath his ear. The wire ended plugged into an iPod. He had not been nodding at the choir or the preacher at all! He was bobbing his head to hip-hop beats!

So what was going on here? The truth is that if that

pastor was really thirsty to reach young people, or for that matter, folks in that community, period, a number of things would have to change. And that *does not* include the message! That never changes.

What *does* change is culture, and that most certainly includes the culture of the black community. Just consider the negative changes that have taken place within the black community over the past 25 years!

When our Savior ascended into heaven, He charged His followers to go out into "all the world" to proclaim the gospel. If we're actually going to live out Christ's Great Commission in the hood, something needs to change – and it's not the message!

What We Need is Street Cred

Years ago, a young fellow passed by me wearing a T-shirt emblazoned with the phrase: "Street Cred Is Everything." Often street cred is defined as a reputation gained by having committed violent actions or by being a bona fide member of a criminal organization. But the meaning is broader than that. Street cred is an attribute gained for one's loyalty and steadfast devotion to beliefs held and practiced in the hood. To have street cred is to be considered true to one's creed, devoted and willing to take it to the limit to accomplish one's ends. To have street cred is to have the respect of the "real" people on the block. It is to be the ultimate communicator in an area where uzi submachine guns and grenades are not considered off the table. To have street cred is to be an insider. It is to possess the authenticity that translates into respect. Street cred gives one the ability to powerfully influence a hood.

With that in mind, consider what it would mean for a pastor or a church to have genuine street cred. It's what's required to bridge that chasm.

Chapter 2

Change: Easy to Spell – Hard to Do

 The coffee shop had been empty. I picked the best view of the television screen and focused on the basketball game. In comes an older gentleman. He buys his food and then heads in my direction, balancing half of the restaurant menu offerings on his tray. Even though there is no shortage of unoccupied chairs, guess where he chooses to sit. You got it. Right next to me. And what's more, it wasn't enough that we apparently needed to sit elbow to elbow, the stranger wanted to talk, too.

"It's not fair," he said. "It's not fair."

"What's not fair?" I asked.

As it turned out, he owned a once-prosperous taxicab company. I say "once-prosperous" because Uber, an up-and-coming, do-it-yourself pick-up service was pushing his cash cow into extinction. My dining companion was using his energy and dwindling resources to fund lawsuits in hopes of stopping the possible from becoming the inevitable. For, if Uber and other car cooperatives continue to experience success, my new friend will soon be sitting next to me on the local public bus. Will he win in his efforts to stop progress and technology? I doubt it. The only constant in life is change.

Change or Die

The hood is dying. Poor-quality education is destroying the lives of current and future generations. Gang life has become widespread and pervasive. Too many young people have been hit by bullets – aimed or stray. Urban unrest due to police brutality is on the rise. Nine out of ten kids on the block where your inner city church is located probably couldn't define the word "resurrection" for you. The only time many of the folks who live in the hood have been inside a church was for a homicide funeral. Gentrification is displacing people who have lived in your church community for generations. Fewer and fewer people are being exposed to the gospel of Jesus Christ. Where is the local church in this conversation? Most of the time, it is silent. And it will continue to be mute and irrelevant until we change.

Change in the Body of Christ

Change is often uncomfortable; sometimes it's downright painful. Change might threaten the positions of people who have held leadership in your church or community organization for decades. And yet, it's obvious and undeniable that we have to change our approach to ministry.

Pastor, is your inner city church filled with ghetto soldiers in sagging jeans whose very tomorrow might depend on your words, or do you cater to people who smell like perfume and drive late-model Benzes? Perhaps you see the latter and you're troubled in your spirit.

Change or die. The time for street cred is now!

Human Lives and Souls Rest in Your Hands

If we love God and humanity, we must live with the reality that people who claim to be Christians – pastors, deacons, members – have failed America's inner cities miserably. We like to point fingers at politicians or "sinners" when, in truth, the dropped ball has landed at the church's doorstep. If gunfire in the hood where you worship has interrupted normal life and you haven't created a refuge and a sanctuary for families who are at risk, then there is blood on your hands that hand sanitizer cannot cleanse away. If you haven't made the all-out effort to speak to those cats in the back of the social club playing dominoes, stop saying, "It's not my fault." Because it is!

If God has blessed you with three good pairs of shoes and someone across town weeps because their socks are touching the concrete through the holes of their paper-thin soles, stop saying, "It's not my fault." Because it is! If you are a member of an affluent church in the suburbs and you realize that somewhere there is a church or an organization trying desperately to help homeless families, yet you are more apt to buy that double latte than send an envelope with two dollars to help out, then stop saying, "It's not my fault." Because it is! Either accept your complicity in their suffering or start thinking about how you can bridge the gap. There is nothing in between.

The church's witness to the hood has been corrupted by apathy, complacency, and an unwillingness to shift with the times. If we do not change this thing that we love, the church will die in its effectiveness altogether. We need street cred in our communities to survive.

Chapter 3

Viewpoint is the Key

 I'm sure you've heard the phrase, "You can't understand my journey until you've walked a mile in my shoes." Nowhere is this more true than in urban ministry. Each human being possesses a mindset developed by a social location – where you live, who you know, what you're taught, what you observe. Your parents, schoolteachers, community, aunties, uncles, and numerous role models – good or bad – have helped you forge a set of lenses through which you see your world.

When I visited Senegal, West Africa, our tour guide instructed us to never wave at anyone with our left hand. Also, we were never to hand someone an object with our left hand. It was considered a grave insult. In America, I do that all the time. It would have been easy for me to ignore the tour guide who had lived in Senegal all of his life. I could have said, "Man, that's crazy! Ain't nobody doing that back in Jersey!" But I didn't. I took his advice and tried to see the world through his lenses.

Some of you are blessed to live where you are more likely to hear the hoot of owls than the roar of gunshots, so your reality will be far different from what you will be asked to envision in this book. However, unless you can stretch to see the world through the lenses of people who live in another reality, you will never acquire true street cred.

Two Beginnings – Two Destinations

I once boarded a crowded BART subway car headed from San Francisco to Oakland. When the doors shut, I took a wall and then fell into that state of semi-consciousness that causes one to stare blindly around the car, never actually focusing on anyone or anything in particular. But that afternoon I saw something that struck me. Seated in baby carriages directly across from each other were two children. A little boy with red hair was seated in a state-of-the-art baby carriage, complete with a UV sunshade and paparazzi shield. The wheels looked as though they had been simonized. Silver spokes sparkled. The carriage had three wheels like a tricycle, and it was built for speed.

Across the aisle, a black child in worn blue pajamas frowned at his red-headed counterpart. Somehow he hadn't fared as well. His carriage looked as though it had been rescued from a trash heap. The food tray was crooked. Smashed peas clung to the dingy surface. Dirt was caked around the spokes. Filth coursed in and out of the grooves where the nuts and bolts intersected.

His young mother pushed her little brown child out of the train car when we pulled up to an urban area. The red-headed kid was bound for the suburbs. Perhaps Mommy would take him to cool off in the family pool before dinner. When he's old enough to go to school, it will be no surprise if Mom and Dad treat him to a first-class private school education. About the time he finishes college, he'll click on the television and see the little boy across the aisle. Of course, he won't recognize him. And as the police lead the young black man toward a police car, the redheaded man will say, "What's wrong with these people? We all had the same chances in life! Why do these people constantly seem to be choosing the roads that lead to prison?" He won't say it out loud, but he'll think himself somehow … well, better, more highly evolved. In some dark place of his subconscious, lodged between the floorboards of his mind, that view will exist. And should he ever go to the urban mission field, he'll carry it with him where it will stain everything he touches. Until he learns and understands the reality of the hood, he'll never have street cred.

Welcome to My Hood

Last year some wonderful friends invited me to visit them in another state. As the car drew near to a beautiful two-story, suburban house at the end of the cul-de-sac, their son said, "Harry, welcome to my hood." Brett was 11. A smile spread across my face when I heard those words spill out of his mouth.

Brett's "hood" is a tree-lined curve at the end of a suburban cul-de-sac where the advent of a single automobile passing the front window is an event. Deer sprinted through the woods in back of the five-bedroom mansion he shares with his parents and baby sister. It's doubtful that Tom, Brett's dad, has to tuck a .45 automatic in his jacket pocket to increase the odds that he'll return from that milk run to 7-Eleven. In fact, while I was visiting, a neighbor came by to say that she'd walked through the open front door earlier that day when no one was home to borrow birthday candles from the kitchen drawer.

This house, those people, and their full refrigerator help to create a set of lenses through which Brett sees the world. His loving parents; the well-educated, highly motivated schoolteacher at his private school; his adoring grandparents; his neighbors; his concerned pastor; Officer Bob, the policeman who patrols the community and asks about his grades; and the church people who tell Brett that he can be anything, all form his reality.

Brett's reality may be your reality. No shame in that. In fact, if you were born into a home where you were showered with love, were raised in the church, and had access to a good education, you really should get down on your knees to give God praise. But after you get back on your feet, realize that the people in the urban mission field whom you desire to reach grew up with another set of lenses. They grew up in a world where a teacher might look at them like zoo animals, a world where commuting church members are not going to invite them to church because they don't want them in their Sunday school rubbing shoulders with their little scrubbed-face Eliza or Fauntleroy.

In the hood, you were born into a world where the local pastor, who lives in another county, most likely doesn't know what you go through and really couldn't care less, and where Officer Bob might be a feared, callous, brutal individual who is more likely to beat in your skull with a night stick than ask about your grades.

When the World is Upside Down

In 2008, the film *Crips and Bloods: Made In America* was released. This film about gang life begins with a shot of Los Angeles that shows the city skyline turned completely upside down. It was more than an artistic device. Forest Whittaker, the director, was making a point about the urban world and the lenses though which it must be seen to be understood.

Now, if you grew up in Brett's hood, I'm going to challenge you to do the best you can to trade lenses with the hood kid who lives in a world where everything is upside down. This book will make no sense to you if apply middle-class sensibilities and a law-and-order mindset to a world where all of that is broken or nonexistent.

Chapter 4

My Personal Search for Street Cred

 My dream when I completed seminary was to become a pastor of a traditional church, where the clergy are expected to preach the sermons, kiss the babies, and run the bingo game. If my wish had come true, you would not be reading this book. You see, my insights about the hood were crafted by the things I saw and the people I met beyond the walls of the traditional church building. I saw the need up close, personal, and firsthand. I shook hands with it and hugged it.

Welcome to Killer Cali

The first time I ever smelled crystal meth cooking was when I moved to Modesto, California. Someone must have been operating a meth lab near my residence because each morning when the rooster crowed, you could the smell the sick, sweet scent of what resembled burning plastic.

I was exposed to one more thing for the first time in Modesto: gang culture. It was just as prevalent there as meth. Terms like "Killafornia" or "Killer Cali" are more than slang. The state came by these titles honestly. California is the undisputed home of gang banging. Killer Cali is the well of sorrows from which drive-by killings sprang up as a hood pastime. Killer Cali is where children have to sleep in bathtubs to escape gunfire, where the souls of families are shattered by stray bullets, where 12-year-old kids tote that iron, and where playgrounds are under fire. Killer Cali is where homicide is a hobby, where families are split over gang allegiances, where the color line isn't black and white but blue and red, where the affiliated glare at each other with hate so unspeakable that it cannot be measured in words, where a child who commits his life to the set at age 14 can hear the judge holler "Life!" by age 24. I have been to funerals for both shooters and babies lying in miniature caskets. For this is Killer Cali, and it's no joke. Please believe that.

Street Soldiers

Back in 2000, I got a phone call from the senior pastor of the Modesto church that was planning to hire me once I completed my seminary studies. He whispered, "A family of red raggers has moved in across the street." I found that comment intriguing. What's a red ragger? I wondered. I didn't ask at the time, but it didn't take very long after the wheels of my jet plane touched the ground for me to figure it out.

For most of us red is just a color that looks good with black or white. But in the hot, dusty streets of California's Central Valley, I noticed that many of the young Latinos wore red pants, red shoes, red belts, red shoe laces and even red fitted caps which were often stamped with the insignias XIV or 14. Young men and women wore red bandanas dangling from their pockets and threw up strange hand signs. Everywhere I looked, I saw Mongolian hairstyles – shaved heads with pony tails hanging over the backs of their wife-beater T-shirts. These were Nortenos (translated: Northerners).

The Nortenos are the street soldiers for a prison gang called "Nuestra Familia," Spanish for "our family." Prior to the late 1960s, incarcerated Mexican-Americans from the Bay Area and other Northern California locations found themselves scorned and mistreated by the southern Mexicans who controlled an incarcerated army known as the "Mexican Mafia." The Mexican Mafia is in league with the Surenos, or Southerners, street gang. The Surenos exist in greater numbers than the Nortenos. (We're talking thousands in both groups.) They control the southern portion of California. Surenos wear blue and identify with the number 13 and the letter M (the 13th letter of the alphabet and the first letter of the words "Mexican" and "Mafia).

In 1969, a war broke out in a correctional facility after a member of the La Eme (the Mexican Mafia) allegedly stole a pair of shoes from a Northern California Latino. This incident, known as the "War of the Shoes," intensified the conflict that existed between the two groups. The Nortenos became an enemy to be reckoned with. A line had been drawn in the California sand. Traditionally, everything north of Bakersfield has been considered Norteno turf (though northern migration patterns have somewhat compromised that boundary). Modesto was a Norteno stronghold when I lived there.

The war between the Surenos and Nortenos is an everyday reality, not only in urban areas but in rural towns and upscale California cul-de-sacs. I remember talking to a man with a large bandage on the side of his head. "I'm not a gang member," he insisted. "I just happened to be wearing the wrong color shirt, and they jumped on me like a pack of wolves. Look at what they did to my face!"

Gang warfare is generational. When I first arrived in Modesto, I saw a heavily tattooed grandmother pushing a baby carriage and sporting red house slippers. Another time I met a mother and father who had wrapped their infant in a red blanket and placed a red beanie on the crown of his little head. They had cloaked that baby in his destiny. Just as young English royals are born to one day assume the mantle of the king's throne, this tiny tot was being groomed from Pampers to eventually walk the yard at San Quentin.

A Paradigm-Altering Encounter

The neighborhood where I ministered in Modesto was so poor it didn't even have sidewalks or a proper sewage disposal system. Mothers tugged half-emaciated children behind them, babies still in pajamas even though it was midday. The crowded local bus smelled like stale corn chips. I had lived in some impoverished communities in New York City; however, none of them compared to "Motown," as some call the part of Modesto where the hungry and the homeless live under bridges in the center of town.

I used to do my laundry across the street from the church building where I worked in West Modesto, killing two birds with one stone as I edited my Sunday sermon while my clothes were in the rinse cycle. One afternoon I had taken a seat in the glow of the television set. Not the most ideal spot, but I live by a rule I had learned in New York City as a youth (and you'd do best to memorize it while we're at it): Never sit with your back to the door.

It wasn't hard to tune out "The Price Is Right," but I couldn't ignore the two teenagers who sauntered into the laundry. Neither had a bag of clothes to wash, and they weren't there to play video games. They sat across the room, cracking jokes at each other and roughhousing. I noticed that one of the young fellows was wearing red sneakers. A red bandana dangled from his pocket. Every once in a while he'd stare in my direction. I thought little of it and went back to reading the book of Ephesians.

After folding and bagging my clothes, I walked out the front door and headed in the direction of the nearest bus stop. Whistling and thinking of things other than the red raggers, I noticed a blur out of the corner of my right eye. I was being followed. The inner alarm system that had developed during my years in the hood began ringing. I looked right and left, but there was nowhere to run. The young man with the red sneakers was half jogging, half running in my direction, and he was gaining on me very quickly.

What had he seen in me that might make me a target? In this poor neighborhood, my visit to the Laundromat could have been enough. You have to have money to wash clothes there. Not much money, but in the Land of Desolation, you don't need Donald Trump dollars to attract interest. I was walking in a place where hope is a skeleton with its bones picked clean by rats and vultures. When people are hungry enough, nickels and dimes – sometimes even pennies – will make you a target.

Carrying a giant laundry bag (and a few extra pounds around the middle) made trying to outrun the situation futile, so it didn't take long for him to catch up to me. The young man in red moved into my personal space. Our eyes locked. The world ceased to spin, and then he spoke. I will never forget his words. "Man of God, I saw you reading that Bible in there. I'm lost. I'm thinking of killing somebody – or myself. Can you tell me something?"

I looked beyond the sagging pants, the hood posture, the gang signifiers, and in that moment I saw a lost, hurting soul who could have been my family member. "What's your name, man?"

"They call me "Silent Loc," he said. (I changed his street name here to protect him.)

Inside my soul I prayed for the right words to say to Silent Loc. I said, "Loc, do you know that God loves you, and that God has a plan for your life? You are somebody.

And you're going to be an even greater somebody! Can I pray for you?" He moved in closer. "Do you mind if I place my hand on your shoulder?"

"Go 'head," he said.

And so I prayed for him right then and there. I closed my eyes and prayed that God, the great engineer of the universe, would show him hope, a future, and a destiny. I prayed that doors would open for him. I prayed for his soul. I prayed for his life. Ten seconds after I said "Amen," my bus arrived.

Silent Loc took a great breath like he'd just been rescued from drowning. His smile was genuine as he reached out to shake my hand. From the bus I watched as he headed down Sutter Boulevard in the direction he'd come from. I never saw him again. I don't know if he was changed that day, but I sure was. The veil had been pulled back, and for just a brief moment I saw as God sees. Here was a young man who had been failed by his parents, his teachers, his community, and the church that met a half block from his house. He was roundly shunned as an outcast. And there he stood on a desolate street quite literally crying out for God's help.

I'm reminded of a Sunday school song we used to sing when I was a boy. The refrain said: "I will make you fishers of men if you follow me." Silent Loc was jumping out of the ocean hollering, "Hey, somebody catch me!" If we, as God's people, ever honestly answer that call, we'll need a *much* bigger boat.

You see, there are so many just like Silent Loc wandering the streets of our towns and cities, hunting for unconditional love, searching for connection, for family, for somewhere – anywhere – to belong. These lost souls are searching for something to believe in that's bigger than themselves. They're seeking adults who won't look down on them or turn away from them. In their darkness, these searchers are open to not only God's word, but anybody's word. The question is: Who will get there first? You and me with a Bible or the O.G. shot-caller with a pistol and a bandana?

Jesus said, "The harvest is plentiful but the laborers are few." Nowhere is this truer than in America's inner cities. Jehovah's Witnesses capitalize on that fact. Each Saturday morning, they walk the streets of the American ghettos, briefcase in one hand, *Watchtower* magazines in the other. Mormons do the same thing. People are starving for Jesus or any scrap of knowledge about Him; sadly, few born-again Christians have the will or the courage to walk into the ghetto to bring the gospel truth.

The Body of Christ in the Badlands

Two evangelical churches stand within a half-mile of my front door. In the near ten years I have lived in this neighborhood, I've never received an invitation to either of them. Sometimes members walk past me on their way to a service, slowing just long enough to allow me to admire the cut of a suit or the shine on an alligator shoe. At other times, I pass by members congregating in front of a church door, smiling and laughing. I wonder, "Am I invisible?" as they stare at me with eyes that don't see. None of these people know the state of my soul. Why don't they invite me to visit their churches?

If they don't think that I – about as non-threatening an individual as you'll ever meet – am worthy of an invitation, what must they think of a young person with facial tattoos or sagging blue jeans?

Years ago, we all owned bracelets that said WWJD, an abbreviation meant to remind us of the question, "What Would Jesus Do?" That was and still is a good question. What would He do in the world I just described to you?

The need is so great. It is so great.

Chapter 5

In the Mean Streets

 I left Modesto in 2002 and took a teaching position at a small Christian college in Oakland, California. The section of East Oakland where I relocated had a terrible reputation, yet it defied the definition of a hood that I had developed over a lifetime. I had been born in New York City where 30-story, brown-brick housing projects pierced the sky and thousands of people lived suspended in space on a single block. Back in New York, "ghetto" meant the deafening roar of the overhead subway, the stench of urine in hallways, heroin addicts nodding in doorways, and a crush of people that reminded one of the future world depicted in the classic film, *Soylent Green*.

This section of East Oakland was different. I found palm trees spreading shade over modest single-story houses and manicured lawns. Brothers congregated on street corners on hot nights, trash talking and hollering at the girls. The air was spiced with the scent of Cali weed and raw profanity.

Welcome to the Hood

One evening, I gave my world history class a short break. My motives were not completely altruistic. I planned to go home to grab a sandwich. As I made my way to the college's front door, a bearded young man with horn-rimmed glasses and a frown on his face moved in my direction. Before I could grab the door handle, he stepped in front of me and asked, "Professor Williams, where are you going?"

The pitch in his voice was elevated. His head slumped. He started rubbing his hands together as if he were either cold or nervous. Now this is odd, I thought. Why is this cat asking a grown man where he's headed? What's got him so on edge? It wasn't in me to be rude, so I replied: "I'm going to walk home. I live only a block from here."

"No, sir! No!" he said. His voice had elevated four notches. He inched forward until we stood almost nose-to-nose, and then he whispered, "I've got a car, Professor Williams. I'll drive you."

My, this young man is peculiar, I thought. Not knowing what else to say, I shrugged and said, "Okay, thanks. I'll ride with you." And off we went.

I saw something blazing in the young man's eyes as he steered the car into the middle of the street; it was raw, naked terror. He looked to the left, then to the right, and then he squinted at the rear view mirror. He chattered incessantly, telling me how dangerous these streets were. I did my best to assure him that I had lived in war zone neighborhoods before and that he shouldn't worry about me. But he was not at all convinced. "But you don't know how it is out here," he said. I was soon to find out.

It Gets Real

That Friday night, I was lying in bed watching television when I heard something akin to a sonic blast outside. BOOM!!! The explosion was so loud it drowned out the television.

"What was that?" I shouted out loud to the empty room, but quickly realized it was the roar of a sawed-off shotgun.

Next I heard the clap of a smaller-caliber weapon, perhaps a .9 millimeter Luger. I rolled from the bed and stretched out on the carpet. (This is what you do when the shooting commences.) The saying goes: "Bullets ain't got no name on 'em." They don't differentiate between intended targets and innocent bystanders, even those inside homes or cars. Outside, it sounded like Fallujah at the height of the Iraq war. Sirens whined through the streets and soon a police helicopter hovered overhead, shining a spotlight on my apartment-building courtyard. You could hear the whirling of its propellers in the Bay mist and fog above the two-story building. The sirens and lights didn't deter the shooters at all. It was on and cracking. Clips were unloading. Dead shells were dropping. Gunshots crackled and bullets whizzed through the air. It seemed as though it would never stop.

The police set up a perimeter in front of our building. The ghetto vulture hovered on the air right above my building, its swirling blades blowing candy wrappers and old cigarettes through the air and across the ground. It was midnight, but the spotlight made the parking lot as bright as noon. The police were shouting. There was confusion below. Would the cops be able to overcome the street army that was letting loose on our hood? And if not, what were we to do? Who do you call when the police find themselves outmanned and outgunned?

We lived through the night. The next morning I walked tentatively to the neighborhood store. There, across the street in a public park (little more than a pie slice of asphalt with sliding boards and swings) sat rows of wilted flowers and a banner with the deceased's street name, birth date, and death date. Candles, Remy Martin bottles, and a black-and-white picture of a young black man with a fabulous smile lined the fence. Above all that was posted the advice: "KEEP IT LIT UP THERE IN HEAVEN!"

Welcome to Cokeland

They said of my hood, "one way in, one way out." Narrow one-way streets cut circles in and around it like a maze. If you don't know that area and the wrong people are chasing you, call the coroner. Many days I saw police cars wind through those streets, prowling like a huge black snake. They came through in battalions, yet they seemed no match for the drug gang with its surveillance and high-tech machinery that had allowed them to run that real estate for generations. Drug fiends from all over Oakland came to that hood to cure their thirst. I remember seeing a man speed down the street, steering wheel in one fist, crack pipe in the other.

It was here that God had called me to work out my soul salvation with fear and trembling. What did it mean to minister to this world? A world where people settle disputes with heavy metal machinery. A world where parents hand kids pistols, along with the advice: "It's better to be caught with it than without it."

As I walked through those streets, I couldn't help but wonder, who keeps a weapon under their bed that could blast a hole through the side of a barn? Why would you need such a thing? What state of mind is a man (or woman) in when they can take something with that much force and firepower and point it at another human being's face? Exactly who is capable of such an act? You wonder, does this person know that not only might they take out the hunted, but there might be collateral damage ... say, children or elderly people who just want to sleep safely through the night? And what's it like to live in a neighborhood where killing and dying have become as ordinary as, "What? Cornflakes for breakfast again?"

What did the Great Commission look like down here in the land that time had forgotten? Oh, there were plenty of churches here, but just like in my present day hood, not a single church member ever approached me with an invitation to visit their church or to hear the message of the good news of Jesus Christ.

Taking it to the Street

Soon, the Friday evening shootout was just a memory. Things were going well at the Bible College. I taught and mentored many young men and women who were dedicating their lives to Christian service in not just Oakland but inner city communities all over the world. One afternoon, one of the college administrators approached me and said, "Reverend, would you be interested in teaching the evangelism class?" When I hesitated to clear my throat, he misread me and said, "Oh, now Reverend, nobody is actually expecting you go out into those streets. Your job would be here in the safety of the building. I just need someone to offer advice to the students as they go out into the streets."

In the movie, *The Untouchables*, a grizzled old policeman, portrayed by Sean Connery, mutters, "God hates a coward." I know that's not true, but if there is one thing I surmised, it was that students who want evangelism tips probably wouldn't have had much respect for an instructor who was too chicken to do what he was assigning them to do. One should never ask others to do what she or he is unwilling to do. (Seems like that should go without saying, but I've seen some bizarre things take place in ministry.)

We had a couple of distinct advantages in reaching out to the gang that constituted a second government in our neighborhood. First, we had a captive audience. Drug dealers ply their trade in a set geographical area that they might have captured by violence. Because of the fiercely competitive nature of the game, the drug gangstas might find themselves at war if they take their business two feet beyond a designated boundary line into another gang's territory. This business model meant that we would always know where to find them. They couldn't run from us when we approached them.

Second, all of us lived in the same neighborhood. It wasn't hard to get to know not only these young men and women who were selling crack, but their parents, their baby mamas (and daddies), even their children. We were a very visible part of the landscape. We dressed like them, and we spoke to them not only about Christian faith but also about the Oakland Raiders and the latest hip-hop releases. We became their friends.

Sometimes members of the gang requested prayer. But make no mistake; this was not the glee club. This was organized crime. They call this life of crime "the game," but it's anything but a game. They also call it "the life," but it's not living. It barely constitutes surviving. The crew had the local police under intense surveillance. Somehow they knew when cruisers were headed in their direction. I'm assuming they had people with police scanners and binoculars looking out from second story windows. Young lookouts stood in doorways, their eyes flitting back and forth. For some there the drug game was the family business going back generations.

Guns and Cocaine

Early on, something became clear to me. The people who import metric tons of heroin and cocaine into this country don't stand on street corners. Bay Area rapper E-40 said it better than I ever could in his song, "The Ghetto." He asked: "How did it get here? We broke! We don't own no planes, trains, or boats!"

The people who make real money from the drug game do their business in hotel suites, saunas, villas, and yachts. The smart ones never get within miles of the actual business. They can afford to send their children to private school and pay for health benefits for their families. They'll never lay a naked fingerprint on a kilo of raw cocaine. You'll never see them in the hood unless their limo gets lost on the way to the Oakland Coliseum. And what of the firearms? AK-47s are manufactured in Russia. Uzi submachine guns are made in Israel. How do they wind up in places like East Oakland, California?

Prison or Death

The people that my evangelism class students were charged with reaching existed at the polar opposite of the game. Selling drugs at street level is far riskier and a thousand times less lucrative than flipping kilos. People were out on the street corner selling drugs bare-faced and not making enough to purchase a used Volkswagen. Several street-level dealers often are working out of the same package, meaning they are selling drugs on consignment for someone higher up the chain.

Street hustlers live under constant police scrutiny and harassment. Hand-to-hand drugs are often sold to strangers. How can one know, except by instinct, whether he or she is selling drugs to an undercover police officer? Hitters on the block with pistols tucked in their belts or coat pockets were the muscle that protected the crew from jackers. If you weren't down with the gang that controlled the situation in that hood and you came out there to sell drugs, you could expect them to rob you or worse.

The Hood Retirement Plan

I still remember one of the young men who worked the afternoon shift. I can see him in my mind's eye even now: stocky, gum chomping, Navy pea coat, gray woolen hat on his head. He hardly blinked as he stood on that corner

watching every car that rolled by, squinting at every pedestrian. "What up, O.G.?" he asked as I drew close.
"Whassup wid it?" I asked.

He wasn't going to solicit a sale here. He knew who I was. It was about this time that people had started calling me "Rev," which has become a nickname for me here in Oakland ever since.

"Young man," I said. (One of the perks of passing 40 is that it gives you the privilege of calling young men that name.) "Tell me something. Why are y'all out here on the corner risking your lives?"

He never looked at me. He never took his eyes off the cars, the foot traffic, anything that could potentially represent danger or money.

"O.G., it's like this," he said. And then, for just a fleeting moment, he looked me dead in the eye. "All of us have been to the pen. I got a record now. I can't work at Target. I can't get a job at Best Buy. This is the only thing I can do to put Pampers on my baby's bottom. If it was another way, I'd take it. But until that comes along, I gotta do what I gotta do."

In talking to those young men and women on the corners, I discovered that most didn't live the lifestyle packaged in hip-hop videos. They were taking penitentiary chances for pennies. Most weren't making what would amount to minimum wage out on those corners. And they all knew the hood retirement plan and benefit package by heart. They would huff and sigh from boredom when I repeated it to them, probably because parents and police had worn it into the ground. Prison, the wheelchair, or death – those are the rewards of the life they're leading.

One of the young hustlers on that corner wore a Cheshire cat grin and boasted a charismatic personality. He also had the lowest, most dangerous job on the block. He made hand-to-hand sales. Whenever I could catch his attention, I started talking about Jesus and what Jesus wanted to do in his life.

He would laugh and back away, showing me the palms of his hands. "Hold it! Don't holler at me, Rev," he said once. "You need to get at them down the block. Dey da real killas." His eyes sparkled. His tooth-filled grin spread from ear to ear. A black turban adorned his head. "He's having too much fun out here to be doing what he's doing," I thought to myself.

Each year, the now defunct *Oakland Tribune* published an edition that contained the faces of the previous year's murder victims. A couple of years after I moved away to another East Oakland neighborhood, I opened up to that page. There was a postage-stamp image of the young brother with the black turban. Only he wasn't smiling in this image. He was dead.

Lord, Lord ... How Did We Come to This?

The whirring of police helicopter blades are a part of the landscape in the California hood. In my neighborhood, they call them "ghetto vultures" because they tend to circle high above dead bodies and bloodshed. So why was the vulture circling above my head, I wondered one hot, summer day as I walked toward my apartment building. As I grew closer, my heartbeat quickened. The helicopter was not flying aimlessly around the hood hunting, it was circling directly over my building. A battalion of police had my street cut off on both ends. A sharpshooter on a rooftop pointed his rifle barrel in the direction of my neighbor's front door. A paramilitary squad ran up the steps of another neighbor's house and proceeded to bash in the windows with their rifle butts. Two of the men in black trotted up the steps toting a battering ram. With one pop they were inside.

Moments later, two young men were led out from the house to a wagon. This wasn't television, where you can just change the channel if something comes on that jangles your nerves. This was real life. This was my block, my neighbor. And if my neighbor had really wanted to make something of it, there would have been a shootout that would have put us all in danger. The cops had body armor and helmets, but there was none of that stuff for the people who resided on the block.

As I think of my neighbor being led off in chains, never to be seen again by me, questions form in my mind: How did we come to this? How did we get here?

Blue Rage, Black Redemption, by Stanley "Tookie," Williams gave me some insight into those questions. Few people who have walked the streets of the hood have had more street cred than Williams, co-founder of the Crip gang.

"Throughout my life I was hoodwinked by South Central's terminal conditions, its broad and deadly template for failure. From the beginning I was spoon-fed negative stereotypes that covertly positioned Black people as genetic criminals – inferior, illiterate, shiftless, promiscuous, and ultimately 'three-fifths' of a human being, as stated in the Constitution of the United States ... . Like many others I became a slave to a delusional dream of capitalism's false hope: a slave to dys-education; a slave to nihilism; a slave to drugs; a slave to Black-on-Black violence, and a slave to self hate ... . To die as a street martyr was seen as a noble thing."[1]

Williams saw a conditioning that began in slavery as part of the reason why blacks kill each other at alarming rates. He believed that the images of blacks found in popular culture have created great damage in the black psyche.

But this is only part of the reason for the destruction and negativity that exist in America's ghettoes. Other factors are at work as well.

Hood Economics

I used to live down the street from Leroy's Quik Mart. When I hear the name "Leroy," I think of an African-American man with a slight southern drawl. And that might well have described the man who *used* to own that store. Leroy sold the store about 30 years ago to a family from the Middle East. Leroy used to hire kids from the neighborhood to stock his shelves and sell his merchandise. Today, even though 92 percent of the store's clientele is African-African and Latino, the new owners will never hire them. Thousands of dollars a week changed hands in Leroy's Quik Mart last week. The new owners give that money a one-way ticket to the suburbs. This cash cow full of extortion-level prices is financing an Ivy League education for the owner's children. My heart breaks as I watch the kids from my neighborhood wandering jobless but dropping money on the counter of the Quik Mart when they come across a dollar or two.

Blacks do not own stores here in the hood. Even the stores that sell black women's hair products are owned by Asians. Chain store sandwich shops maintain the same hiring practices. Even though their clientele is 85 percent black, no blacks are employed in any of them. What message is being transmitted to children who will enter these establishments a thousand times before they reach the age of 18?

And all of this has its impact on my hood and yours. According to Monique W. Morris,

- 23 percent of all children in the United States live in poverty, while 39 percent of black children live in poverty.

- Although black (including multi-racial black) people make up just 14 percent of the U.S. population, 37 percent of people who are homeless are black.

- African-Americans account for 50 percent of the people enrolled in programs that address chronic homelessness.[2]

The Price of a Felony

Have you ever looked at a close friend or a family member through the 6-inch-thick glass at the local jail? Sometimes funerals are easier to take than to see a loved one buried alive. I have an uncle who died in prison some years back. In the black community, most of us have someone close that has been snared by the penal system. I feel tears welling up in my soul as I write these words because I've lost so many to the beast with teeth made of iron bars.

After being drawn into the underground trades and experiencing arrest, so many of our neighbors and friends are systemically barred from societal benefits like public housing. Even after the terms of incarceration are completed, the debt to society is never paid. Many employers will not hire them if they are honest on a job application, even 20 or 30 years after the incident. Voting rights are rescinded, making one, in effect, a non-citizen.

David Simon, creator of *The Wire,* my favorite TV series of all time, said, "The fact is that these really are the excess people in America, we – our economy – don't need them. We don't need 10 or 15 percent of our population! And certainly the ones that are undereducated, that have been ill-served by the inner city school system, that have been unprepared for the technocracy of the modern economy – we pretend to need them. We pretend to educate the kids. We pretend that we're actually including them in the American ideal, but we're not. And they're not foolish. They get it."[3]

Without an education that can allow them to be competitive in the workplace, many of the young people turn to the streets. Simon goes on to say, "… . the most destructive form of welfare that we've established … is the illegal drug trade in these neighborhoods. It's basically like opening up a Bethlehem Steel in the middle of the South Bronx or in West Baltimore and saying, 'And you guys are all steel workers.' To just say no? That's our answer to that?" I have been cursed out only three times in my years as a minister in the hood. Trust me; that's a miracle. Some folks get cussed out every day. It's just one of those things you're going to face when you interact with people trapped in a pressure cooker.

One night, a young man who was extremely discouraged because of his inability to find work called me. In my attempts to encourage him, I corrected his language. I said, "No, my brother, you are a *formerly* incarcerated person." He blew up! "Rev, there's no such thing as 'formerly.' I hate when people say that s——" (to paraphrase for tender ears)! He said that even after you have been released, you still live with the stigma of having once been incarcerated. It can prove stifling and frustrating. Like I said, I can't say it like he said it, but you get the point. In a song called, "The Man Above," rapper Rakim says, "You spend your childhood in a wild hood/You're in debt for life."[4]

Life after arrests is a series of random intrusive body searches, probation visits, parole, ankle monitors, restitution payments, and child support demands. A misstep over any one of those potholes can land you right back in a jail cell.

According to Monique Morris, black people make up 14 percent of the United States population but account for 38 percent of all inmates in local jails. The average time black Americans serve in state prison for all offenses is 32 months (2.7 years), compared with an average of 26 months (2.2 years) served by white Americans in state prisons. Black people account for 49 percent of prisoners under the sentence of death in the United States. More than 80 percent of people convicted of crack cocaine charges are black. One in every 13 African-Americans of voting age is disenfranchised because of a felony convic-

tion, a rate more than four times the rate for the rest of
the U.S. population.[5]

Incarceration has such an intense hold on the people
of the inner city that we must visit the subject in greater
detail later in this book.

Unfathered

Although the cover on this book says my name is Harry
Louis Williams II, my birth certificate says I'm a "Jr." I
didn't fully appreciate what that meant until I started talking with young men who had never shaken hands with
their father and girls who told me their mothers didn't
even know who had fathered them.

There are many reasons for this tragedy. As an anger
management facilitator in the inner city, I met men who
were willing to jump through any court-mandated hoop
for the opportunity to be in their children's lives. And I
saw first-hand that there are scores of men, good men,
who are hindered by the court system from bonding effectively with their children. This is not to mention the
fathers who will tell you that they laid on prison bunks
crying into their pillows at night because steel bars hinder
them from providing for and protecting their children.
And yet the truth remains, as painful as it is to write it:
The absence of fathers from the home is an issue that cannot be glossed over. It is hurting us.

What I'm saying here is politically incorrect, and a lot
of my activist brothers are probably shaking their fists at
me right now, but I know I'm right. They want to talk
about something they read in a sociology book written by
someone who has never walked down a block like mine.
I'm going to tell you what I've seen with these two brown
eyes. Many, many men are like bees. They impregnate a
woman in one place, but before the pregnancy comes to
term, they are off and at it again in some other woman's

bedroom. The vanished father is one of the greatest problems facing the hood.

The Homies

In the absence of strong family bonds (e.g., a strong, loving father in the home), spiritual community, and societal connection, the friends that one comes of age with take on an extremely powerful role in one's life. They are actually more than friends and sometimes closer than kin. I once asked a very intelligent young man why he was out on a street corner risking his life in the dope game. He told me clearly, gesturing at the group of young men behind him, "These are my homies. We came up together." And that was the end of that particular conversation. I had heard him loud and clear.

Homies define the "hood" or "turf" as a portion of real estate where their family members and close friends have lived, sometimes for generations. They will fight and die for that place because it symbolizes their identity and the reason for their existence, even if it's a crumbling ghetto where not a single person they know actually owns their own home.

The homies are the people who come from your block or your hood. If you're at a party and a fight breaks out, instinct dictates that you stand with them even if the odds against you are tremendous. They are from your block. They are members of your crew, your clique, your team, your set, your gang, your mob, your squad, your street family ... or whatever you choose to call it. And loyalty is the most highly desired quality in your world. If you should fall in battle, know that the homies will avenge your slaughter or die trying.

Gangs are romanticized in movies, but for the most part, they start out as just neighborhood kids. Large gangs, like the Crips and Bloods with formal admission

processes and blood-in, blood-out oaths, do not domi-
nate black hoods in the San Francisco Bay Area where I
live. Here, blacks bang by blocks, hoods, and turfs. In
any Bay Area black community, something is understood: If we grew up in the same housing project, we are
street family.

In the Bay Area there are Latino gangs that do adhere
to a blood-in, blood-out oath. Blood has to be shed for
you to join the gang, and blood is going to be shed if you
choose to leave it. That means that a group of members
may choose to beat you up as an initiation. They may
require you to hurt or kill a rival to gain membership.
Usually, those initiated are very young. They make a lifetime commitment, often before they reach their teen years.

You can have a measure of affiliation with the local
gang, even if you are not a full-fledged member, but know
that your street address or the friends you choose to be
identified with can get you killed. If a car pulls up to you
in the dark and someone hollers out, "Where you from
homie?" riders may shoot you even after you holler back,
"I don't bang."

O.G.s

I once met a Crip from L.A. way up here in the Bay Area,
a good 6-hour car ride away. He was perhaps 30 years old.
Back home his life was on the line. The boundaries in his
neighborhood had shifted. His long-time Blood enemies
had captured a piece of territory that bordered dangerously
close to his front door. He'd been shot at several times, but
so far they'd missed. One morning he looked out the window of his home to find some of his enemies trotting,
heads down across his front yard. A case manager from a
local community organization put him on the next thing
smoking to San Francisco in an attempt to save him. Our
paths crossed at a community event one day.

"I had a fantastic mom but a woman can't teach a man how to be a man," he told me. "So, when I got to be a teenager, I went out to the block looking for male role models. My O.G. homies put on the shoes my father should have worn."

As I looked into his eyes, I saw deep, dark pools of regret. "I have a daughter," he told me. "One day, she pointed at the store down the block and said, 'Daddy, take me there so I can get an ice cream.' I would have liked to do nothing more, but I had to tell her, 'Baby, Daddy can't go to that store. That's in my enemy's hood.'" He takes the blame for the choices he made in his life. Still he says, "It took some people I trusted to show me the way. That would be my big homies."

I never saw him again. I wonder if he's still alive.

The O.G. (i.e., original gangster) has put in his work. He's done his dirt. This individual has aged out of active status. He is no longer expected to perform drive-by killings and jewelry store licks (robberies). A lifetime of violence, gang involvement, and incarceration is his or her resume. Triple O.G.s are just what you might guess. In the streets it is said that they were "seriously with the s—," in the center of the mayhem. Today, they might be law-abiding citizens, but their reputation still gives them power.

O.G.s are often street-level community leaders who can use their influence in a positive way. For instance, when violence-interrupters want to stop a feud, they can go to the O.G.s and ask them to use their status to defuse a situation. Conversely, an O.G. can be a negative influence by persuading impressionable youths to do negative things – including acts of violence – to prove their loyalty.

Respect

"SALUTE ME OR SHOOT ME." That was a tattoo I recently saw scrawled across someone's chest. For some people I've met, that says it all. Respect has a high price tag in a world where people lack access to material things so common in the nearby suburbs. In the streets, disrespecting the wrong person can get you killed.

A few weeks ago, I was walking through the mall when sounds of chaos started attacking my ears. Two young women, who resembled Malibu Barbie Dolls, quickly walked past me. They were hollering at someone behind me while showing him the one-finger salute. The object of their fury was also headed in my direction, talking to himself, shuddering with rage, and muttering under his breath what he was going to do them. It wasn't pretty. Clearly, he objected to the sight of their middle fingers.

As he came alongside me, I glanced at this poster boy for anger management and said, "Say, Bruh, don't do that."

He didn't even look in my direction; his eyes remained fixed on the two girls as he hurried on, growling at me, through gritted teeth. "I'll knock you, Bruh!"

He quickly caught up to the girls. Drawing to within the distance of a nose-length away, he said to the brunette, "Say something else." One of the young women declared that he had called her the "b" word because she had ignored his howling and vulgar catcalls.

Eventually, the angry man walked away scowling. I told the young women, "You should have just walked away. That guy could have hurt you badly."

What fueled his anger? His paper-thin sense of manhood had been challenged by their refusal to acknowledge his lustful calls for attention. When they answered his profanity with their own, he felt disrespected. People view disrespect as the wrong hand sign, the wrong thing said to a girlfriend, trespassing on an enemy's hood, writing the wrong thing in graffiti on the wall, gossiping about the wrong individual, stepping on the wrong person's shoe, glaring at the wrong person with an eye-to-eye stare, calling the wrong person the "b" word, and half a million other things. In the hood, people kill and die over disrespect all of the time.

Who is easier to work with, someone in the correction system or your average church member? You might be surprised to hear me say "the former." People who are incarcerated or who have been incarcerated put a high premium on manners and respect. Whereas, I have met some lifelong church members who will speak to you any way they feel like. Please remember though, good manners go a long way on the block.

Desensitized to Violence

I remember the first time I ever saw a man dead in the streets. It was back in the 1980s in Harlem at the height of the crack epidemic. One night, as I was walking home from work, I saw policemen milling around a young black man who lay splayed out on the sidewalk.

I heard whispers and grumblings from the growing crowd as I stood there with my breath turning to steam in the frigid New York City winter night. Witnesses were saying that the newly deceased had been walking down the street as some young men walked toward him from the opposite direction. He held his ground, refusing to clear the sidewalk to let them pass unimpeded. For no other apparent reason, one of the young bucks pulled out a pistol and let loose on him. Rather than simply walk around him, pride caused them to shoot him down in the street like an old stray dog.

I watched the scene for awhile and then walked toward home. Two young men walked in front of me. One of them gave his benediction to the scene. With a slight shrug of his shoulders, he said, nonchalantly, "Oh, well. That's just the type of thing that niggas up here have to handle."

I was mortified, more by his words than by the sight of the dead body lying on the cold sidewalk. The fellow was so used to the chaos around him that death and murder had lost their meaning. He felt no more empathy for the young murder victim than he would have for a dead rooster or a turtle.

Post Traumatic Stress Disorder

I've sat across the coffee table from people who've seen horrendous things I hope you never have to see. Imagine yourself in this situation. You're seven years old, home from school, and ready to play. With your favorite toy in hand, you open the door and start to walk down the concrete steps from your duplex. There, lying in a pool of blood at your feet, is your next-door neighbor, Mr. Reynolds. As you lift your gaze from the body, you see a tan Ford speeding away. Staring at you from the car window is a girl you recognize because she hangs out in front of the Dollar Store; you've often seen her on your way home from school. Your eyes meet.

You run inside in search of your aunt, who is raising you while Mom is away. At this point you're screaming, near hysteria. You holler your aunt's name over and over. Tears are streaming down your face. As Auntie comes down the stairs, you blurt out what you've just witnessed. You grab her blouse sleeve and tug on it, begging her to come outside so she can attest to the reality of what your eyes have seen but your brain refuses to believe.

Auntie's eyes grow wide with fright. She yanks her sleeve from your grip and slaps you across the face. Hard. The shock causes you to stop crying. Your mouth drops open in wonder. Auntie stoops over you like a tree bent by a stiff wind. She shakes her finger in your face. "Child, you must never tell another living soul what you have just seen. You can't tell your brother. You can't tell your teacher at school. You can't even tell your mother. Only you and I will know about this thing, and we will keep this inside and never mention it again, not even to each other. If you don't listen to me, we are all in danger. Just like they hurt Mr. Reynolds next door, they'll hurt us." Auntie shakes you by the shoulders. "Do you understand?" she demands. And then you notice there are tears in her eyes, too. The secret will live – and die – between the two of you. But something else has died; alongside the body of Mr. Reynolds lays your childhood and your innocence.

Chapter 7

It's a Hard Knock Life

 I wouldn't be surprised if statistics are available indicating how many inner city people, from 1965 to the present, have died as a direct or indirect (e.g., overdose, fatality from long-term addiction, murders, suicides) result of illegal drugs. I'm sure it would be enough to populate a country.

Illicit narcotics have been in the hood forever. However, it's said in the streets that not long after Rosa Parks made her stand in Montgomery, Alabama, hoods all over America became flooded with deadly, addictive drugs. Fertile minds were deadened, futures crushed, and wars waged. Drug dealing and gunplay are twins. You don't have one without the other.

Why do people walk into a game where the cards are so heavily stacked against them? Many will tell you, "I'm just trying to eat." Translated: "I'm just trying to survive."

The Underground Economy

Mr. House was my barber back in the '80s when I lived in Harlem. He was a round, light-skinned guy with straight hair. He looked like a pecan-colored Jackie Gleason. Normally, no subject is off limits in a barbershop, so that means there's lots of interesting conversation, and Mr. House's shop was full of fascinating dialogue. But one day, when I brought news of an upcoming revival at a local church, Mr. House said, "Hold it right there, young blood. Not in here."

That puzzled me so deeply that I just couldn't just let it drop.

"Mr. House," I asked, "what's up with that?"

Mr. House's clippers dropped to his side. That was the signal that school was now in session. "When horse [heroin] came to Harlem," Mr. House began, "it could have been stopped. Back then these big preachers had the respect of the entire community. They could have gotten out in these streets and sounded the alarm. They didn't. I think they got bought off. I think they got new Cadillacs in exchange for their silence."

He had me there. I had no rejoinder. Following a long silence, I offered something profound like, "How about those Knicks?"

The heroin epidemic of the 1960s devastated Harlem. Crime spiked. Harlem was never the same. Did the mob pay off those preachers? Did some of the big preachers find pistols pointed at their foreheads followed by an offer they couldn't refuse? Or were they were just too lazy, comfortable, and apathetic to fight the monster called "horse"? Damn shame. A lot of good people died.

In the movie *The Godfather*, members of the crime families have a conference. One of the dons says, "I don't want heroin sold to children! That's an *infamia*. In my city, we would keep the traffic in the dark people, the coloreds. They're animals anyway, so let them lose their souls." The movie, of course, is fiction, but that's not to say it didn't accurately capture attitudes and practices of the time.

In the 1950s, Harlem was a relatively safe village where the poor had found a haven. When I lived there in the '80s, the poor still lived there, but the village had changed – a lot! Village elders told me of a Harlem from the past where you could leave your front door open and never have to worry about intruders. Some of the residents didn't even own door keys. But when the white horse came charging through the streets in the '60s, everything changed, the elders said. Young people sat in doorways nodding and scratching. Robberies and petty crime became a way of life as addicts sought the dollars that would beat away the monstrous withdrawal symptoms.

The Second Middle Passage

By the time I found my seat in Mr. House's barber chair in 1986, the heroin epidemic had dissipated, but a new monster had crossed 110th Street. It was called "crack," and Ricky Ross was largely responsible for that.

I met Ross many years later when his speaking tour brought him to the main branch of the San Francisco library. I got there early that day so I could have a cup of hot tea and enjoy a new book. I looked across the room and there he was – a bearded, brown-skin black man chatting away on a cell phone. When he had finished his conversation, I walked over and introduced myself. What a mass of contradictions! Ricky couldn't read when he dropped out of high school, and yet he had the marketing genius to devise a plan that would spread crack cocaine across the nation. He made millions.

When you speak with him, you're looking into the eyes of a mellow guy who, in conversation, comes across as a loyal man of his word. On the other side of that, however, history will remember him as the man who spawned genocide so evil that they call it the "second middle passage" (the first middle passage being the voyage that brought blacks from Africa to the shores of the Americas to be slaves).

Of course, "Freeway" Ricky Ross didn't do this entirely on his own. At the height of the Contra/Sandinista war in Nicaragua, a Contra operative landed in Los Angeles. He connected with a poor kid from Los Angeles and told him how he could make a fortune. He gave him huge amounts of highly potent cocaine on credit and then taught him how to transform the powder into something called "ready rock." The new product produced immediate demand in the streets. Eventually it took on the name "crack," either because it looked like cracked off pieces of soap or because of the crackling sound it made when smoked in a pipe. No one is sure. Freeway Ricky Ross used Crips and Bloods as couriers and entrepreneurs to carry his merchandise from one city to another.

I've met people who became addicted to crack by just inhaling it once. The saying went: "One hit is never enough and a thousand is not too many." I was living in Harlem the summer crack first hit like a nuclear bomb. I saw it destroy people I knew quite well. Crack transformed them from every day working people to fiends who would lie, cheat, and steal from their own mothers.

In those early days of the epidemic, I had a good friend, an office worker, who ended up on whore stroll; another friend became a fugitive from heavy hitters he had robbed at gunpoint during a three-day smoking binge.

In 1986, I remember walking on sidewalks littered with empty plastic capsules. The next day, someone would sweep them up, but by the next morning, it would look as though capsules had rained down from above during the night.

Crack made overnight-millionaires of young men and women barely out of their teens. Fur coats, diamond rings, and European luxury cars dazzled impressionable inner city youth. Predictably, the new money brought in high-power firearms at numbers no one could have imagined. Drug lords needed Uzis and AR-15s to hold off rivals, but with the money that poured in from the new generation of addicts, money for guns was no issue. Murder rates climbed to astronomical levels in hoods across the nation.

There had never been a drug like crack. A strung-out mother might leave her infant with a neighbor while she went down to the corner store for a "pack of cigarettes" and not return for two weeks. Pregnant women gave birth to addicted children who were saddled with the title "crack baby." Children were raised by the streets while their parents were off chasing that blast. Growing up without love or direction in a war zone, where death was anything but a foreigner, created child soldiers, youngsters without consciences, who could leave your brains leaking on the sidewalk for the price of a pizza slice and a Coke.

In his book, *My Name Is Curtis Snow And I'm AG*, independent film star and Atlanta, Georgia, hood legend Curtis Snow states: "I use to serve dope to my own mama, I use to be like, 'F—- that, I already know Mama gon' get the s—- from somewhere.'"[1]

Scarface as God

In 1983, Brian DePalma released *Scarface*, a film starring Al Pacino. *Scarface* was the story of a Cuban refugee with a sketchy past who becomes muscle for a mid-level coke dealer. Eventually ambition takes him to the top of the game. One of the most memorable scenes in the film shows a dozen of his men, one by one, toting duffel bags filled with coke money into a bank.

Unfortunately, *Scarface* became the blueprint from which many urban youths created an underground career. The theme of the film is that when society locked this man out of a legitimate path to success, he created his own way. Many real people died or found themselves in prison for life chasing the Scarface legend.

The New Truman Show

When I talk to kids in the hood, one of my first questions is, "What do you want to do as a career?" The top two answers? Basketball player and rapper. My next question is: Do you play basketball for your school team? Often, the answer is no. I ask, do you have any hip-hop videos released on the Internet. Again, most times, no.

In the back of my mind I'm thinking about how, in March of every year, the NCAA has its college basketball tournament. It starts with 64 teams; then the 32 winning teams play. The teams that go on in the tournament are called the "Sweet 16." Then it's the "Elite 8," and that's followed by the "Final 4." Ultimately, only the National Champion stands undefeated. The most highly skilled and gifted athletes in the sport of basketball compete in this tourney, yet only a slender handful will go on to be selected to play professionally at the next level. Now, you want to tell me that you don't even play for your high school but you expect to out shoot, out maneuver, and out run those well-conditioned college athletes for that spot on a professional team? And to become a hip-hop artist who will make a sustained living from the music would even be a harder task. Despite all that, each day thousands of young people wake up with that same dream. If what I am saying is true, why would these kids limit themselves to such farfetched goals? Let me tell you what I believe.

One of my favorite movies is *The Truman Show*. The character Jim Carrey portrays starts out as a baby born on the set of a television show. The world tunes in as he comes of age. His whole world is staged, and each day millions watch him as he goes about the business of life. Everyone – except Truman – knows he is starring on a television program! Unbeknownst to him, his friends, and later his wife, are paid actors.

Because of the nature of the show, Truman can never go on vacation. He is never allowed any knowledge of the world outside the village where he lives. Everyone he knows lives in that quaint little slice of suburbia. Here's my point: When you think about it, that's sort of like the hood. Your entire life is informed by the people living within the boundaries of your world. In the hood you aren't going to meet many engineers, lawyers, accountants, or theologians, but chances are great you'll meet plenty of gang bangers, drug dealers, and chronic alcoholics.

If you're a child of generational poverty, sitting in a room with your elders, you may learn how to get public housing and additional welfare benefits by having children you may not even want. If that's what you see and hear, chances are you'll be influenced by the poison. The old saying goes, "You cannot be what you do not see." In the hood, sometimes your dreams begin and stop at the end of your street.

One of the ways Master kept slaves in bondage was to limit their travel and deny them knowledge of the outside world. If a slave was found with a book (or, God forbid, a map) he or she might have a hand chopped off or be sold to another plantation. The master understood that education would destroy his ability to keep his slaves on the plantation. Knowledge is freedom, and so lack of knowledge keeps you on the ghetto plantation.

Code Switching

Other things will keep you chained to the economic prison. When I was a little boy, my mother would send me to the barbershop. On any given Saturday morning, men who held responsible positions as bus drivers, lawyers, city workers, and business owners would hang out and enjoy each other's company. Even brothers who weren't there to get a haircut would just hang out and chill. At times, conversation got raucous. Often women were the focal point of the discussion. I still remember conversations about everyone from James Brown to Muhammad Ali. The barber was the neighborhood philosopher, using the clippers as his pointer. These brothers cussed. They threw around the N-word like it was nothing. And they told an endless stream of mostly clean jokes that made me double over with laughter – when I could understand them.

However, if you were to see these same men in church the next day, they'd be wearing black suits and shined shoes. On Monday they would adopt perfect English and impeccable manners when they walked through the door of their job. In fact, if you ran into one of these men at a job interview, you might barely recognize him as the same person you saw in the barbershop.

We learned early on that "code switching" was a survival tactic. In Richard Wright's classic novel, *Native Son*, Bigger Thomas is the prototype hood figure. He lives in a rat-infested apartment with his mother, brother, and sister. He spends his free time (which is all the time) in the pool hall. He talks trash and carries a knife.

Eventually, the day comes when Bigger has to square up and get a real job. As a chauffeur, a paid employee, he doesn't use profanity. He speaks when spoken to. He recognizes all the rules of cordiality and civility. Bigger knows how to code switch. He can effectively (if not smoothly) navigate between two worlds.

Many young people don't know the fundamentals of code switching. When an individual walks into a job interview, a judgment is made about them before they are seated. The style of their hair, gold caps on their teeth, their grammar, their dress, their tattoos, even their handshake and greeting send a firm message to the potential employer before they open their mouth to answer the first question. I once counseled a young man who was fired from his job for lighting up a marijuana blunt in the warehouse on his 15-minute break. He was surprised when the supervisor not so pleasantly invited him to get out and never come back.

When I was young, the brothers in the barbershop had a strong understanding that they were living in two worlds. Maybe that knowledge came from a father or some invested uncle. Perhaps it was passed down from the O.G.s in the neighborhood. Maybe they had traveled out of the neighborhood enough to realize that different codes of speech and behavior were considered normative in different settings. Today, many young people have been framed by the limitations of the ghetto. They can't take off the street armor to function in that other world. They don't know how.

Seeking Work

When I was young and unemployed, I would pick up the Sunday newspaper and turn to the classified section. Next, with a red pen I would circle labor positions located in traveling distance of my home. If there was nothing there, I made calls or went to visit friends with the question, "Where are they hiring?"

Factories that once paid a living wage to unskilled laborers are dead now, rotting hulks, taunting reminders of the days when a man could sign an application and end up with a job that would feed his family and might even pay a mortgage. These abandoned buildings are memorials to a bygone era, a time before the factories relocated to the suburbs and then left the country, period, and for good. The day when unskilled American laborers were in high demand is over. Yet the double-digit dropout rate at some inner city high schools guarantees there will be an army of people on the streets at any one time looking for stable employment that no longer exists.

You see, looking for a job nowadays is a process that requires a skill set of its own. Mastering the job search is not something usually taught in high school (even though it ought to be). Great numbers of people don't know how to create a resume or a mistake-free cover letter, let alone post them online or respond to an ad via the Internet. A lot of us have 20th century skills in the 21st century. Add to this brown skin and a criminal record and you are facing some large obstacles. I've seen many people leap over those obstacles, but it always seems to take a heroic effort on their part.

Years ago, I accompanied a group of formerly incarcerated people to a job fair. One very friendly young man, who had spent his entire youth in the penitentiary, arrived neatly turned out in a black pinstripe suit and shiny Florsheim shoes. He looked as though he was ready to make a great impression! But when we arrived at the site, he turned to me with a look of what I can only describe as terror and said, "Can you help me Mr. Williams? I've never applied for a job before." In seconds he had devolved from a wide-strutting model of confidence to an old man in a near fetal position. He was terrified. I did my best to help him, though I couldn't deny that his sudden transformation shocked me.

Education or Eradication?

An education today is not a luxury. It's a survival mechanism. The San Francisco Bay is now the center of the tech industry. Corporations like Google, Yahoo, Twitter, and Facebook are all here. These massive employers compensate their workers with profit sharing, stock options, and hefty wages. This is not the job market of the future; it's the job market of "the now"! I've seen statistics showing that some 60 percent of Silicon Valley's workforce is white; 30 percent is Asian; 8 percent is other. Purportedly, only 2 percent of the people working in the Bay Area tech industry are black.

The techies are going to want to live near their jobs; who can blame them? With a dearth of available housing in the Bay Area to start with, where do you think the techies will live? If you get guessed that the poor will be uprooted so that the techies will have a place to live, I'd have to give you a gold star. There is no more cotton to pick. The factories are closed. Without an education that matches the times, many Americans have become obsolete citizenry. Where will they go?

The View From Inside the Classroom

My friend Leena Bakshi recently received her doctorate degree in education from the University of Southern California. Speaking of the challenges of inner city youth in the classroom, she said, "In the 21st century there is a huge demand for STEM: Science, Technology, Engineering, and Mathematics. Those also happen to be the fields where one will find the lowest representation of black Americans. It is really difficult to cope with that reality.

"We have forgotten to teach our students how to think critically. They are so programmed to pick A,B,C,D, that they don't know what to do when asked to think critically. In science it's not always only about getting the right answer but grappling with the process and trying to revolutionize your thoughts. In the real world, you don't take a bunch of multiple choice tests.

"I don't know where this will leave people in the hood. We are going to have increased poverty levels and increased homelessness. If we don't find a way to change this the poor will be left even further behind."

Separate and Unequal

Leena goes on to say, "If we don't change, the inequity will continue. I have to repeat this; it's not about race. It's about culture. If you grow up in a culture where education is treasured, you will succeed. People are put together in communities of poverty. The country operates on academic capitalism. The rich get richer. The disadvantaged become even more disadvantaged.

"There is an overrepresentation of minority males in Special Education in the United States. School officials reason that he has issues with focus and concentration; therefore, let's medicate him and throw him in Special Ed. There is a dearth of those same students in the gifted classes.

"The higher income schools have an entire community and village raising that child. There's a culture of scientists, doctors, mathematicians, in the community. It's not, 'Am I going college?' but 'Which college am I going to?' There's a parent/teacher association that will be able to raise vast sums of money for computers, extra-curricular programs, and cross-country education-enhancing trips. In a high-income community, the school might have microscopes. In an economically deprived inner-city school, the kids may be using magnifying glasses."

The Crip King and the Disciple

Just from this cursory view, you can see that that many of the hood's deepest problems stem from neglect. Nothing spells it out clearer than a scene that appears in Tookie Williams' autobiography.

The night the Crips were born, Raymond Washington and Stanley "Tookie" Williams brought the factions they commanded jointly for a meeting to the bleachers at a high school football stadium. Washington later wrote, "It would have been a police photographer's Kodak moment to have captured all of us on film that day. Standing and sitting around on the bleachers was the largest body of Black pariahs ever assembled.... . Throughout this state and country, we embodied only a small division within a multitude of reckless, energetic, fearless, and explosive young Black warriors. Though we were often seen as social dynamite, I believe we were the perfect entity to be indoctrinated in cultural awareness and trained as disciplined soldiers for the Black struggle. Nevertheless, this opportunity to mold us as a valuable resource was never seen in its true potential by society, schools, churches, community programs, Civil Rights movements, or other organizations.... For me, the thin line between nihilism and being a warrior was so blurred, that I rushed headlong toward self-immolation."

Why was no pastor able to see the potential in the young men who eventually became the worldwide Crip army? Why didn't some church form an outreach to the troubled youth of that community? Why didn't some church leader, stopped at a red light on a Sunday morning, park his car, get out of his vehicle, and talk with the souls wandering around aimlessly near the front of the liquor store? Why didn't some church devise programs that could provide assistance and respite to the parents? By sheer neglect or hesitancy to act (i.e., fear), we Christians are implicated in the creation of a situation that has cost the futures and lives of generations of people.

But nothing under the sun is new. After God struck down Paul on the road to Damascus, he spoke to a disciple named Ananias. He told Ananias that Saul was also seeing a vision and that this vision was of a man named Ananias who was coming to lay hands on him so that he could regain his sight. Nothing in the story leads us to believe that Ananias doubted he was hearing from God. And yet, he began, like Moses, to make excuses. As they say in the streets, Saul was "gangsta wid it." Ananias concretizes Saul's interactions with the early Christians into one word: "fear."

The beginning of the next sentence is powerful. Almighty God commands Ananias to "Go," adding that Saul is His "chosen instrument."

Imagine being called "God's chosen instrument." Who wouldn't want to be known by that name? And yet God didn't lead Ananias to the front gates of the local seminary or to the ministers-in-training meeting. God led him to the house of the most feared and notorious outlaw Christ's followers could think of.

Let me ask you a question. Do you think God has changed? After all, that was almost 2,000 years ago. No? Well, if He hasn't changed, what is God thinking when a group of brothers walk past Him wearing red or blue bandanas, sipping high-alcohol-content malt liquor, and swearing incessantly? More than likely, God's thinking the same thing God thought when God shook up Ananias by telling him to go find Saul. Imagine how many Sauls never became Pauls because we have been either too chicken or too condescending in our attitudes to go out into the world after them?

Chapter 8

Immigrants in Real Trouble

 So far, the focus of this book has been the African-American community in the hood. However, my home, East Oakland, is populated by people of color from all over the globe. Many of our neighbors came here from Latin America. Some of the issues we face are similar; others are unique to our cultural contexts.

Born Again, Brown, and Undocumented

I was sitting in the back of a coffee shop in East Oakland one day when my friend Jose walked in. Ironically, his car had broken down in front of the building, and until help arrived he had taken refuge in the coffee shop I call "my office." I saw his arrival as divine providence. I asked, "Yo man, can I interview you for this book I'm writing?"

That wasn't a simple question. You see, people in Jose's shoes don't talk about their immigration status out loud, let alone into a recording device. I'm thankful for his trust. He felt that his story needed to be told. So rather than simply telling it to you, I'm going to let him share it in his own words.

"I was born in Managua, Nicaragua, in 1985. Ten years later my parents got divorced; it was a very rough time.

My mom came here first, in 1999; three years later, in 2002, she brought me here. I was 17 at the time and had recently converted to Christianity. I was on fire with my faith. I wanted to study, go into seminary, and become a priest. So I got a job, never realizing that education as an immigrant would be so expensive. I worked and studied part time over 6 years.

"Along the way, while living in Concord, California, I got involved with *Comunidad Sandimas,* a volunteer prison ministry. One day, I was reading a magazine in Spanish. It had a one-page ad for training that qualified you to do volunteer ministry with kids in Juvenile Hall. I called. I qualified. I went through the training. Now, I have to admit, I was kind of afraid. I even had nightmares about being caught in a war between gangs.

"My first time in Juvenile Hall, I was nervous. I didn't know what to expect from these hardened prison inmates! Then they came out. Wait... . They looked just like normal young kids. Within a few minutes the nervousness was gone. Ahh, they're young people. You listen to them. You connect with them. There is no fear. Even though I was from a different background, I was happy to be there. I usually proclaimed the word on Sundays. The kids called me 'preacher.'

"After awhile I realized I still wanted to pursue full-time ministry, so I entered a religious order, the Augustinians in San Francisco. I was a candidate for a few years, taking courses in philosophy and then theology. I loved my studies, but at some point I realized that I didn't feel at home. I felt a calling in a different direction. I felt lonely. I didn't feel the call to celibacy. With that, I left the order.

"Looking in a new direction, I decided to join Inter-Change Ministry. (InterChange is a Christian outreach to people caught up in urban street situations.) I was really attracted to that.

"When I first came to the U.S., I entered with a tourist visa. My plan was to come here for a little while, return home, and then re-enter, so my visa wouldn't expire. Unfortunately, when the time came to re-enter I didn't have the money, so I asked for an extension from the United States government. I received one response. The letter said they had received my application and that it would be processed. So I waited. A couple of months went by. My time expired. I had overstayed. I had no choice but to wait. The response never came, so I went to speak to a lawyer. He said, 'If you go out, they'll ban you from coming back to the country.'

Life in the Shadows

"At the beginning you can accept it and go with it, but after awhile it begins to weigh on you, heavier, heavier, and heavier. There's no way to get an ID. You dread the question – 'Can I see your I.D.?' – when you go to the store. Friends would invite me for a drink; I couldn't go. I didn't have an I.D.

"I started feeling dirty and sinful. You feel like God is angry with you. I remember in the beginning going to bed and just crying because I felt like a criminal, and I just felt like I was in this sin and I couldn't do anything to get out of it. Going back to Nicaragua was not an option. It would mean leaving my family, my ministry, and the life I had built.

To Walk in Fear

"I have seen undocumented workers being taken advantage of. They have their work hours cut. They are asked to work overtime without pay. Sometimes they are abused and threatened at work. On occasion they are paid less than minimum wage. If they complain they are told, 'Oh, if you don't like it, I'll call Immigration.'

"We are afraid of the police. You entrust information to the wrong person and you might get in trouble. It happens to lots of people. I have a very close friend from the ministry. I met him in Juvenile Hall. When he got out he got baptized and, later, married. He changed his life. A couple years after getting married, he got into an argument with his wife. In anger, he knocked over the TV set. The neighbors heard the commotion and called the police. My friend was sent to prison, and after that, he was deported.

"Eventually, my friend came back to reunite with his wife. He called and said, 'Oh, I'm in Arizona now.' You have to understand that even though he is Latino he looks white. He told me that once there was an immigration raid, but he wasn't asked about his status because he looks like a white man. The agents didn't ask to see his papers because they didn't know there are white Latinos.

Message to the Christian Opposition

"Lots of people have died of dehydration trying to cross the Arizona desert. Very sad news. What a horrible way to die, dying of thirst because you want to be with your family. We should value family ties over laws.

"A lot of the conservative Christians come against us. People told me I shouldn't be here, that I am a criminal. They say that they don't want my presence because I am an illegal. The strongest voices come from the Christian right. People I consider to be my brothers and sisters are treating me this way. I still feel hurt and ashamed.

"The church's response should be trying to understand the needs of people, not only people in the U.S. People come here not because they're lacking in character and criminals. The reality is that if you are poor in Latin America, it is impossible to come here legally.

"When you read the Acts of the Apostles, you see a community united in meeting the needs of the poor. Instead of pointing fingers at the poor, look at people who are abandoned, poor, and most in need. Church should be a place where the poor and the marginalized should be welcomed. There is nothing more Christian than welcoming the oppressed.

"A lot of times U.S. laws and policies have affected us negatively. For example, the United States supported dictatorships in Central America and in places like Nicaragua, El Salvador, and Guatemala. Those things impacted the economy of people who wanted a better life. If you are asking them not to look for better opportunities, you are asking them not to be human.

What You Can Do to Help

"If you are a believer who has sympathy for our plight, we need you to be the voice of the voiceless. We need you to take our voices and make them heard. Our voices can be silenced by our status. We're afraid to come out of the shadows. Once you are labeled a criminal, your voice loses moral authority.

"If you are somebody who is opposed to our immigration, I will pray that you will get to know us on a personal level, get to know our stories so you can understand why we came here. Once you know our stories, then should you still oppose allowing us to enter, then you can at least be opposed with more integrity."

Thus far, I have taken you on a journey through the streets of the hood. It's never a pleasant trip, because while we travel we're faced with the realities of multiple failures: education, housing, and employment among them. The failure of individuals in and out of the community, government, and business, and sadly, the absence of the church as a strong presence in a world where everything has come apart bedevils inner cities across America. Worse yet, these failures – our failures – have cost thousands upon thousands of lives, most of them young. Lives of great value and worth. Lives of the children of God Almighty!

Part 2 will take us deeper into the life and death struggles going on in our cities right now. Fires – figuratively speaking – are raging like flames in high, dry grass. New issues have blown up in the 21st century. Many of you will find yourself surprised by the pervasiveness of some of these crimes against humanity in a world right across town from where you live.

In upcoming pages, you'll hear from folks who have been shot, stabbed, and prostituted. You'll hear from those who have had their loved ones laid down by gunfire. You'll also hear from those who have previously been at the helm of the havoc, both in the streets and in prison. And you'll hear from those that God sends out into the streets every day to stop the madness.

Hear the voices of those who live in the hood. Learn from them. Some of what they say may very well be answers, or lead you to answers, that you'll need to understand – perhaps even heal – the streets. Most important, I want you to see the church through the lenses of those who live in the nether world of the hood.

Pick up your highlighter. Are you ready? Let's ride.

Chapter 9

Gang Banging 101

 I remember going to see the film *Colors* for the first time back in 1988. Gangs and the gang culture had existed in New York City in one form or another for more than a hundred years. However, *Colors* exposed a whole generation to the world of L.A.'s Crips and Bloods by depicting the hood gangsta style with a West Coast twist. Movies and media made gang banging look cool. And what young person doesn't want to be cool?

The Roots of a Terrible Tree

Soon, gang banging was springing up all over the world. Gang members from L.A. migrated to other parts of the United States, bringing their gang culture with them. Today, gang culture exists not only in America's big-city hoods, but you can find it in the suburbs and even rural areas. If you're a pastor, you may have gang members in your Sunday school classes, even if they're just wannabes. Remember: Gang members recruit children. In fact, before long, one of the church's toughest challenges will be in redirecting its evangelistic energies toward gang-impacted youth.

Full disclosure! I've never been a gang member, though I've met plenty of them. I've ministered to them, but I've never been jumped in (initiated). I've never hung an AK-47 out a car window and started squeezing off shots at my enemies. So, it would be disingenuous of me to write about something I know of only as an outsider. With that in mind, I reached out to one of the most famous hood figures in America, someone with platinum street cred. Let's see what he has to say about the matter.

From the Mouth of the Shot Caller

"You can call me Jiwe," he says when I refer to him by the name on his birth certificate: Dashaun Morris. Jiwe means "stone" in Swahili, and the name was given to him by his godfather, perhaps the most famous Blood of them all, L.A's. T. Rogers.

Jiwe is a shot caller, a founding member of an infamous Bloods street gang set in Newark, New Jersey. He's tall with long dreadlocks and multiple facial tattoos. His athletic abilities once landed him a college scholarship to a renowned historically black university. Pro scouts quickly took notice of his speed and agility. Unfortunately, his gang lifestyle followed him to Delaware State University. He was arrested and incarcerated following a violent incident. Interested parties representing the NFL turned cold when notified of his gang affiliation.

While behind bars, Jiwe began writing his life story. A major publisher took interest, and *War of the Bloods in My Veins* became a bestseller. Jiwe played a major part in *Brick City*, a hit documentary TV series (2009) produced by Forrest Whittaker for the Sundance network. In 2013, Jiwe produced and starred in a full-length motion picture called *Death Coast*. Jiwe is real, his street cred unquestioned. He has been called to speak to troubled youth in faraway places like Sierra Leone and Mexico City. He is one of the most widely recognized hood figures in the world.

Jiwe is in his early 30s. I'm thankful I hadn't met him earlier in life, for he says, "When I was 19, I would have robbed you, slapped you in the face with my gun, and told

you to run. It's one thing when you do it to gang members
– they sign up for that – but when you do it to civilians,
it's ugly. I'm sick when I think about it."

We get right to the point. "Why do people join gangs?"

"I've talked to people from both sides of the fence –
the suburbs and the inner city. I've found that the basic
need is to be accepted. Whether you come from the best
or the worse, you want to be accepted. They want attention. They want to feel valued. In the hood, kids lack love,
but rich kids can wrestle with the same thing. When you
remove those elements from people, they are open to the
lure of gang life.

Influence That Leads to Involvement

"I got involved in 1990. I was 9 years old," says Jiwe.
"Today you have people who have been exposed to gang
life through social media and cell phones, those type of
things. People get involved through computers today. We
didn't have any of that. We saw violence and drugs in our
neighborhood, and they had an impact. But today you
have kids, even those with parents and the stability they
bring, who try to emulate the styles they see in entertainment media.

"That music has an impact. I deal with depression and
anxiety. When I'm in one of those foul moods, I won't listen to Tupac. It would feed my misery. If hip-hop can
impact *me*, a 33-year-old, picture these youngsters. Flip
that situation with a 14- or 15-year-old kid. That music
makes you think that being a trap boy [drug dealer] or a
d-boy [dope boy] is cool.

"When you get in that position, it's more than 'I'm putting out music.' You have a moral obligation. You're not
physically forcing anyone to do anything, but when your
influence is that big, it's more than music. You are programming a young person to follow a certain way of life.

These rappers don't see it though. They see they checks. They think money."

Child Soldiers

In *Death Coast*, a film that Jiwe both produced and directed, there is a chilling scene where a young child is invited by adults to get into a car. He's given a paper bag filled with glue and told to inhale. Next he's handed a bandana. He wraps it around the bottom part of his face. The final part of the ritual is the awarding of the weapon, in this case, a handgun. His mission is to shoot one of the gang's rivals in a drive-by.

When I asked about this, Jiwe said, "That's a snippet of what actually happened to me. I got officially put on the neighborhood when I was 11."

His book tells the full story. As evening approaches, a 9-year-old Jiwe climbs onto the passenger seat of a '64 Pontiac *Catalina*. The car is full of Bloods. As they drive through the neighborhood, someone passes him marijuana. Before long they enter Crip gang territory. Jiwe is handed a silver pistol with black electrical tape around the handle. They crawl down on a corner at 5 miles per hour.

Jiwe recalls the rest, "Pop … Pop … Pop … Pop … Pop … Pop … click, click… . Pulling the trigger gives me a hypnotizing power that surges through my extended arm, up my shoulder, and down my back. My ears ring as my gun pukes its contents… . Crip bodies crumble after each shot. I feel a connection that no other can replace, jubilation at its purest and ripest form. It's the utmost penalty man can physically give and receive, and I'm behind it. I now have the power."[1]

I ask him, how and why gangs recruit such young children.

"See, this is what you have to be mindful of. In foreign countries they have child soldiers. I moved to Arizona at age 9. I moved from poverty. I moved into a neighborhood where I had no knowledge of gangs, the strategy of an organization, the way you talk and put your words together. I was a young, scared child moving into a situation organized and running for years. How could I know that violence, drugs, alcohol, sex, and prostitution were not a way of life everywhere? I had never been anywhere to measure up against where I was actually living. I knew nothing of a world beyond. If you have nothing to measure up against, the world around you becomes natural. You live in it long enough, it's natural.

"Kids 9 years old, this is bred into them. They're forced to grow up faster. They're not your typical 9-year-old. Age-wise he's a kid, but the life he's forced to live has made him grow up faster. When you're given a pistol and told to stay in a certain section of a park, when you're taught to identify rivals and enemies and taught who might bring you harm, when part of your education includes what neighborhoods we did not get along with and those we are cool with, you're an adult.

The Need for New Legs

"Now to get to the question of how adults can recruit kids into gangs, you have to deal with the gang mentality. Those kids are the future. You're going to be on the earth till you get murdered. It's like building an empire or a football team. You're in constant need of young legs. You're in search of kids who are loud, rowdy, and wild. They're keeping the neighborhood alive.

"They're looking at kids 9 or 10. The gang is all they have, and recruiting children is how they ensure their legacy will live on beyond them. By the time I was 9 or 10, I was toting a pistol. I did what people told me. I was led by individuals who wanted to strengthen the neighborhood and keep it."

What Keeps it Going?

Jiwe doesn't see an eventual collapse of gang life. He said, "There is always going to be violence, crimes, and drugs. As long as these things exist, there will be gangs. The hood is filled with drugs and crack-addicted parents who can't take care of kids. Like I said earlier, these children want to be loved and embraced. Now you have a child who has no one to take care of him. When the parents can't or won't, the homies will."

Additional factors continue to fuel gang life. "It's all about economics and the job market," Jiwe says. "You see, you have this felon coming home from prison. He's an ex-con. He needs a job. I'm not talking fast food. He needs a job that will allow him to provide for a family. Drugs is like the market for us to survive. You don't have no job interview. Anybody can do it and make money. If you want to attack the gang issue, you're going to need to attack the issue of economics."

Gang warfare has spread like wildfire. Years ago, the Crips and the Bloods existed in a small swath of territory in Los Angeles. Now they thrive in places like London and Liberia. Can this be stopped?

"If anything, gang warfare is becoming *more* vicious," Jiwe argues. "As the menace of gang warfare has grown and transitioned from generation to generation and even country to country, it's lost some of its meaning. Everybody killing everybody, no structure, no brotherhood theory. We're trying to restore some of that. Our identities have been stripped. I've gotten more and more in tune with our black history. The average 16-year-old in the hood will not know much about our history. They'll know Malcolm X; Paul Robeson, yes. They'll know a lot more about their neighborhood and the O.G.s who are taking care of them right now. They could care less about what King and X were talking about."

I live in a gang-impacted neighborhood. When I speak with someone with as much first-hand knowledge of gang life as Jiwe has, I want to ask him how I might make a difference.

Joining the Solution

"It's a touchy situation when you talk to people who have not been involved in the madness [about how to stop it]. Be a part of the solution other than just complaining. If you want to change it, remember there is strength in numbers. I'm not saying Mr. Walker at 50 years old can't get kids to stop shooting. But if Mr. Walker, Mr. Green, and Mr. Smith join forces, they have a better chance.

"Don't attack and fight the community. You don't surrender to the sickness and the madness," Jiwe says. "Open up the lines of communication. Get to know the gang members. Talk to them. Ask how you can bring about the resolutions? You can organize neighborhood watches, but sometimes they'll continue to fight and shoot, and you'll be trapped in that world. I see it all the time. You're dealing with these wild, crazy youth. They want violence and controversy. They're going to say, 'We gonna sell our drugs and our weed.'

"Some communities have ties to the gangs. They have set rules that the neighborhood respects. I've never been a part of it, but I've heard that it exists. The elders say, 'This is *our* section. This is what can be done and this won't be done.'"

A Pastor to be Emulated

In the first season of *Brick City*, the documentary follows Jiwe as he fights some serious criminal charges that could put him behind bars for many years. His family is offering emotional support, of course; however, an unlikely character is in his corner. I'll let Jiwe tell you about him.

"Pastor Ron Christian of Newark, New Jersey, is one of the first pastors I ever met. From 2007 I had been traveling and speaking about my organization, Full Throttle, made up of guys from my neighborhood, 18 and under, with personal, life, and family issues. This preacher had heard about what I was doing and felt I had a powerful presence and could redirect the streets, so he put the word out that he wanted to have a meeting.

"At the time, I was home on bail, having been arrested in 2009 for attempted murder, and was trying to fight my case from the streets. The pastor jumped in feet first with my case. He got resources. He got to the bottom of what had happened. He was present at every court date. He made sure I was presentable. All the attempts and efforts that could made, he made. He was always right there.

"There are different types of pastors. Pastor Ron's style of delivering sermons will go beyond the average pastor. I'm not religious at all. I got tattoos all over my face and body. Pastor Christian's ministry is for those who are sick, lost in the darkness, don't know whether they should go right or left. Those are the people he's assigned to help.

"He's out meeting gang leaders, not to support their garbage but to help. Most pastors interact with those who are safe," Jiwe observed. "His purpose is to get to the sickest people out there. He's well respected. He won't break no laws or violate nothing. I respect him. [On October 30th, 2015, Pastor Ron Christian passed away. He was 51-years old.]

If You Really Want to Help ...

"A lot of people involved in gang life deal with low self-esteem and low regard for themselves. They want to fit in, so they adopt behaviors they see around them. Too many develop a streak of violence to the point where it becomes fun for them. Shooting someone should never be something that feels good. It's learned behavior. Think of it this way. If you put the average 9 to 5 person in front of a TV to watch UCF fighting, they love it, but people who have been in shootouts in the hood see it from a different perspective. They feel for the person that's getting beat up. You grow up in a neighborhood and are taught to be violent, you see it differently. We're forced to be in it."

There are no easy answers, but Jiwe muses, "I have a motto: 'Remain strong even when you feel weak.'

Race Against Time

"We have to find things that give us strength. Sometimes in life there's nothing you can do. There's no magic pill. You must take the road, take the journey. Instant gratification is not real. What do I tell a mom who has two sons, 13 and 15 years old? She's got no job. She can't move. I can't give her a job. What can we do?

I tell her it's not enough to put a bowl of cereal down in front of your son. Parent, what else are you doing? You can't be running down to Atlantic City, out in the casino doing this, that, and the third, and think it's all going to work out for your child. You better pour everything you can into your son's life before he gets that 25-to-life (sentence) or before he gets a bullet in his head. It's a race against time. Find out what the kid's skills are. Find out what he likes to do. Connect him to resources. Get him into after-school programs."

And to preachers and community activists who may be getting weary, Jiwe leaves us with one thought. It comes from his late friend Malcolm Shabazz III, Malcolm X's grandson who was murdered in a Mexico. He said: "My homeboy Malcolm said, 'It takes one person to say something that can change your life. One speaker comes in to speak to a youth. No effect. He hears the message five times. The sixth time he hears the same message from a different person, he might get up from his chair with a twinkle in his eye and say, 'I got that!'"

Chapter 10

Healing the Homies

 It's summertime in East Oakland. The heat and haze of daylight are quickly being swept away by the cool Pacific breezes. We're deep in the hood now. I take the bus here from another part of the East, but I'm determined to find a ride home later because it's not going to be safe wandering around this hood in the dark looking for a bus stop.

To Empower Inner City Youth

Cesar lives in a tough hood. Dozens of kids, most of them gang members, are crowded in his backyard. Barbecue smoke floats up from the grill. Plenty of gangstas are here, but everyone is on his best behavior. There is no gangsta rap being played here tonight, only positive rappers like Talib Kweli and Dead Prez are blasting through the stereo.

A private bus pulls up to the front of the wood frame home, and out steps Immortal Technique, a New York rapper appearing on the "Rock The Bells" super star hip-hop tour. Tech was a knockout artist, a street cat who once went to jail for breaking somebody's jaw, who has become one of the most significant conscious rappers in the hip-hop game. He's taken time out of his schedule to make this detour, at Cesar's request, to share dinner with the young people and drop knowledge.

So, welcome to Cesar's home. Where else are you going to find a world famous rapper in the middle of the hood talking Hegelian philosophy and Egyptian theology with gang-impacted high-school-age kids? Cesar Cruz is the founder of Homies Empowerment, a warrior for peace in a violent place. Cesar grew up in the hard times that characterized the lives of so many of the young people around him. He came of age an undocumented person (his mother was twice deported) who learned how to walk in a cloak of invisibility. At just the right time, a schoolteacher took special interest in Cesar, showing him that there was life beyond the hood. Cesar ended up studying at the University of California-Berkeley, arguably the most prestigious public school of higher learning in America.

After graduation he landed a job as the academic dean at Arise High School in East Oakland. He also founded Homies Empowerment, an organization offering mentorship and hope to gang-impacted kids in Oakland. Cesar could have taken that Berkeley degree and fled to corporate America, but he didn't. He's gone to the lost and forgotten and told them there is a place for them in this world. Cesar places a strong emphasis on learning one's history and culture. A great number of people who were headed for the cell block or the "hood block" are now headed for college because of this committed, innovative educator. He is greatly loved here.

But this is the last hurrah – at least for now. Cesar and his family are packing up. DVDs, CDs, and other knick-knacks are for sale. Cesar has enrolled at Harvard University in Cambridge, Massachusetts, where he will study for his doctorate in education. He hopes to return. He dreams of creating a home for his brainchild, Homies Empowerment, where young people can heal from PTSD, learn history and culture, and develop leadership skills.

Touching Hardcore Kids

"How does one approach young people who appear, well, unapproachable?" I ask Cesar. I paint the picture of a young man with sagging pants, a wife-beater T-shirt, and dreadlocks.

He replies, "When people see a kid walking down the street with his pants sagging, his hat backwards, and a blunt hanging out of his month, they see O-Dog, America's worst nightmare. [The 1993 film, *Menace To Society*, featured an irredeemable thug murderer known as 'O-Dog'.] They see Malcolm Little [pre-conversion Malcolm X]. I see a human being. You've just described an exterior – some clothes and a blunt – but we don't know what's on the inside. The exterior leads you to make assumptions about this person. I'm wondering if it's God manifest, and if he is, how do I interact with a child of God? I don't want to make the assumption that this young man does not have the capacity to be a scholar or a revolutionary.

"If you were to open the door to my apartment, you'd see a picture of Malcolm Little getting arrested as a young man. This was years before he became a student of black history, years before he would debate some of the greatest intellectual minds on national television. That picture is the image of a young pimp, dope dealer, hustler, and burglar. Next to the picture of Malcolm Little is the man that he became, the man known to the world as Malcolm X, the older, mature Malcolm; the Malcolm who spoke at Harvard and Oxford Universities. The frame above the picture says, 'Never give up on our children.'

"If you had gone to a young pimp named Malcolm Little and tried to give him some counsel about choices concerning his future, he might have looked at you with his eyes glazed over, helluva high and just tell you to f—— off. That's why I can't let someone who has just cussed me out move me. I can see past the alcohol and the weed. He might be wearing the armor of society and not the armor of honor. What you look at as thug gear, he might wear as the new body armor for survival. If I were to talk to this young person, I'd be trying to give off as much positive energy as I can. It's not my place to judge his clothes or the fact that he's smoking weed. I'm not even looking at that.

"The young man you're talking about may have had a father who was killed. His mother might have post traumatic stress disorder but been diagnosed as 'crazy.' No one will hire this kid, so he may have turned to the underground economy."

How Do We Stop the Bullets?

When asked how violence in the hood might be stopped, Cesar gave me an answer I wasn't expecting. "It's going to be hard to stop violence in the hood. There's a lot of money in killing. Cemeteries are making money. Rosary shops are making a bundle. The shirt store at the mall that makes R.I.P. shirts is adding up dollars. Pastors make large amounts for delivering eulogies over dead bodies. Dead bodies equal screen time on TV news. It seems that everyone loves a dead body."

He also points out another complexity involving the drug trade that has saturated America's inner cities. Cesar says, "Understand the reality of things. Don't just blame the drug dealers. The major drug dealers don't own planes. They don't own airports. Somebody is bringing it here. Now think; do you honestly believe that we can send people to the moon but we can't stop the importation of heroin? Please! Drugs make money! So, are we going after the heroin addict or the system that allows the importation of heroin? Next question."

Missed Opportunities

Other than the liquor store, the only building you're going to find on every other block in the hood is the church. Therefore, I have to ask the hood legend to explain why pastors drive past poor people in the hood without struggling to find a way to reach them?

Cesar answered, "I'm not at liberty to judge the pastor, but I will say that sometimes faith is *smaller* than a mustard seed. Some pastor had to have given up on Malcolm when he was a young man walking the streets of Boston. The church gave up on him. In prison, however, there was someone who didn't see him as dirt and invited him to join the Nation Of Islam. He took *that* invitation."

A few years ago, Cesar saw a path to hold a gang summit in Oakland. He went to the spiritual leader of a Christian congregation and asked if he could use his sanctuary. He guaranteed the safety of the participants. Cesar gave his solemn word that the building would in no way be damaged and that there would be no violence. And Cesar's word is platinum in the hood. The preacher said, "No way." The gang summit did not happen. Cesar was greatly disappointed; however, philosopher that he is, he drew some conclusions.

"Jesus asked us to love our neighbors as ourselves. Have we ever made a mistake? Have we ever sinned? My sin might not be drugs. It might be pornography or thinking badly about my neighbor. Instead of demonizing the people in the hood, we have to look at people who were given little who still went on to change history."

To Heal

When the subject turns to healing the psychic scars of the ghetto's wounded comes up, Cesar begins speaking in spiritual terms. He carefully measures words like "redemption," "restoration," "reparations," and "forgiveness." And I'm listening carefully, because these concepts do not come up in normal conversation in the land of an eye for an eye and a tooth for a tooth.

Cesar goes on: "If I continue to have hatred for my oppressors, I cannot heal. So, I started out with that forgiveness, not for them initially but for my own heart. Healing is a slow process. There is no 12-step program for this. These kids are doing unhealthy things in an unhealthy situation. As far as counseling, you don't need someone with a Ph.D. to diagnose your reality. You are a Ph.D. in your own reality. Your survival dictates that you are going to have a strong measure of resiliency. We need to empower kids with real counseling that happens without the clinical 'something is wrong with you' perspective. In reality, kids are always a mirror. They are manifesting what they see. They are surviving in an alternative reality. If the church is going to weigh in on this modern-day struggle, we first have to ask, 'What is the plan the church has for these kids on an every day basis?'"

Is Cesar is correct? If the way of forgiveness and restoration must be taught to warring armies embroiled in blood feuds that go back generations, whose responsibility is it to teach that way of forgiveness and pardon? Seems to me that falls upon pastors, church leaders, Christian neighbors. Do we have a plan for these kids day to day? If so, can we look past the smell of marijuana, the sagging of the pants, and the sound of profanity in a desperate attempt to reach a human soul and to rescue untapped potential? Will we?

The Proof is in the Pudding

I struck up a conversation with a kid in a burrito shop one summer afternoon as I was waiting for my steak burrito with extra onions. I asked him about his plans for the fall, and he started testifying like a minister in training. "I used to be a gang banger. I used to carry a Glock to hold down my block," he said.

"What happened?" I asked.

"Now, I'm a revolutionary," he asserted. "I'm headed back to my sophomore year in college."

A smile broke out on my face. A big one. I love a good success story. "So what happened to lead you toward that change?" I asked.

He nodded and grinned. "Cesar Cruz and Homies Empowerment."

Chapter 11

Street Cred in the Aftermath of Bullets and Gun Smoke

 He was a proud, young black man – a hood soldier. His dreadlocks hung down on his shoulders like thick black ropes, but there wasn't a single hair on his chin. When he tilted forward to speak to me, he whispered as though each word was part of secret code decipherable only by my ears. "Harry, I'm not going to be around for a while," he said.

"Why? What's up?"

"I caught a gun possession case, and I've got to do 8 months."

I shook my head back and forth. I give a lot of one-on-one sermons, and sometimes it feels like I'm preaching to a brick wall.

Before I could start in on Point Number 6 of my ongoing sermon, the young fellow blurted out, "I have two brothers who died from gun violence."

I exploded. "You mean to tell me, you've seen two of your brothers laid down out here and you're still playing around in these streets?"

I thought of his mother. What must it have been like to have to bury two of her children? That poor woman.

But that wasn't the end of her sorrows. Nine months following our conversation, this 19-year-old man was shot to death on a cold street corner, right in his own hood. Everybody saw it and nobody saw it. His life was just another number in the newspaper, except for people like me (and now hopefully, you) who knew him. His mother lost three children to gun violence. Can you imagine that?

Lots of guns are busting and bullets flying in these streets. And the aftermath of a direct hit does not blow away like the wind after the funeral is over and the shrine of Hennessy bottles, teddy bears, and balloons has been dismantled. Each homicide leaves the deceased's family members trapped in a cocoon of depression, despair, and devastation.

What makes it worse is that often the family members know the killer. Long after the funeral clothes have been hung up in the closet, family members will come face to face with the murderer. They'll see that individual in the produce aisle at the local supermarket pushing his daughter in a cart. They'll walk past the killer when they leave their building to go to work. He will be standing in front of the building smoking a Newport cigarette and discussing the basketball game with his homies. He might even give his victim's mom a wicked glance and then start snickering. Of course, Mama will melt with fury, but what else can she do? In the streets there's a saying: "It's not what you know; it's what you can prove."

I have held them in my arms, the walking wounded. I have listened to the stories that never lose the fire of immediacy, the tales of the phone call that summoned the grim reaper into their lives, the shaky voice that said: "Your child is never coming home again." I've met people who 10 years later still remain frozen in that single minute. Tears cascading down their cheeks, they're unable to move beyond the question: "Why, God?"

Why do I bring them up in this book? Because if you say that you love God and that you're called to do urban ministry, then their problem is now also your problem. How do you comfort them? What can bring any measure of relief from their sorrow? You'd better start thinking about those questions, because these folks are everywhere, and their pain is ever present.

The Mother Who Chose to Fight Back

I step gingerly onto the front porch of a small house tucked on a cul-de-sac deep in the heart of East Oakland. The floorboards creak beneath my feet. This is where Brenda Grisham's only son, 17-year old Christopher LaVell Jones, fell in a hail of bullets. That was back on December 31, 2010.

The sun is beating down through the clouds on this calm Saturday afternoon. The San Francisco Bay weather is changeable, and so the balmy, California sunshine brings the neighbors out into the streets to enjoy the combination of a warm sun and a cool Pacific Ocean breeze. A huge jumper on the front yard is filled with neighborhood kids. The music of the Temptations; Earth, Wind and Fire; and Blue Magic serenades the block. A family friend flips hamburgers and hot dogs on the grill. Dominoes get slammed down and senior citizens at the folding table grin, each believing they've been dealt the winning hand in a game of tonk.

Brenda Grisham hosts these events periodically to promote the idea of peace in a neighborhood that can at times resemble the Syria/Iraq border. She opens the door for me and points to a fluffy couch in the middle of the living room. "Have a seat. Let me make sure everything is straight outside, and then I'll be back."

My gaze drifts around the living room but comes to a screeching halt at the montage of newspaper clippings above the fireplace mantle. One headline reads "Teen Slain, Sister Hurt In Oakland Shooting." Next to it is the 2010 Oakland Homicide Victim photo collection. It's a grisly piece of journalism that immortalizes Oakland's deceased and marks them in the order they were murdered that year.

Community residents often forego referring to their lost loved ones by name. When speaking of the lost, they quote the year and the person's number on the list. Next to the clippings is the grinning photo of a brown-skinned young man with shoulder-length dreadlocks. Adjacent to his high school diploma is a teddy bear with a note: "R.I.P. Chris Jones." He's just a boy.

Gone

By all accounts Christopher Lavell Jones was a good kid. He was born deaf. But even without hearing, the child was drawn to music. He would feel the tops of musical instruments to sense the vibrations. Through the gift of modern science, he was eventually given the ability to hear as a toddler. He took to the drums. Young Christopher developed a love for gospel music and would use his gifts to accompany the church choir.

One evening, the church keyboardist didn't show up for a rehearsal. Christopher told his mother he would take his place. Brenda had never heard him play the piano before. Bemused, she gave him the nod. At the end of that rehearsal, the church keyboardist was out of a job. Christopher was the new church musician.

On December 31st, Christopher LaVell Jones had been tapped to spend New Year's Eve playing music at a local church. He would never make it there. That evening, the

17-year-old asked his mother to drive him four blocks to the neighborhood Burger King. His mom willingly obliged.

Hitters on the Block

As Brenda Grisham approached the car, she saw an ominous sight – one that will remain locked in her memory until her final day. Three young men were standing behind another car. They clutched heavy automatic weapons, locked, loaded, and aimed in the direction of her family. Ms. Grisham's only thought was to get her children to safety. She ordered her daughter and son to run for the house. Bullets began exploding all around them.

Christopher's sister was the first one to be shot. Hearing her scream, 17-year-old Christopher turned around. Instead of running through the front door, he turned around and rushed back toward his family. Without warning, his body dropped on the porch. Brenda Grisham dove forward, landing on Christopher's back, more than willing to give her own life in an effort to shield her son from the assault rifle bullets.

Christopher had taken a head shot. Bullets had penetrated his face and jaw. His mother credits him for saving her life. She says, "If he hadn't stopped, I wouldn't be here."

As it turned out, the gang members were targeting another youth in the neighborhood. Ms. Grisham says, "They didn't see Christopher that night. They were just shooting. They thought the target was in our house, and they were shooting away at the house."

Half of all people who get shot in Oakland are innocent. They have nothing at all to do with what is going on in the streets.

Turning Tragedy into Ministry

The next day, New Year's Day 2011, a vigil was held in front of Brenda Grisham's house to commemorate the passing of her son, young Christopher. She addressed the gathered. That was the genesis of her role as a community activist.

Brenda realized that many of her son's beloved high school friends would be traumatized by the news of his grisly demise. She made arrangements to visit the school and to connect with staff and students. She recalls: "That day at Christopher's high school many young people expressed how they felt about him. One young lady was going to flunk her art class because she couldn't draw, so Christopher took her assignment home. The next day he told her to open her desk. The completed picture was inside. Christopher was an excellent artist. He had done the assignment for her.

"Another young lady told me she had come to school without her uniform shirt. Christopher took the shirt off his back, handed it to her, and then went to the office to get a loaner shirt. The stories came one after another; kids who had borrowed lunch money from Christopher or received encouraging words in a time of crisis all spoke up. I was handed a four-inch-thick binder filled with letters of condolence and remembrances from kids who had not even been in his class.

"After Christopher's passing, people just started asking me to come and speak [at community gatherings]. One person asked me to speak, then another, and another, and it went on from there. They wanted to meet with me. They wanted me to speak about the plight of families who have lost loved ones to gun violence."

On to City Hall

In August of 2014, the idea was raised to confront Oakland city officials about the huge number of unsolved murders. Ms. Grisham recalls, "I said I'm not coming by myself. I wanted to bring 15 representatives of families who had experienced the unsolved murder of a loved one. My phone kept ringing. I got 15 people. Together, we discussed what we expected to happen when we got to City Hall. We were calling for a unified relationship between the Mayor and the Chief of Police. We wanted public policy established that would eradicate the trafficking of guns in Oakland. Thirdly, we wanted them to publish a grid that would display the most dangerous neighborhoods in Oakland, complete with the AC Transit bus routes that run through them.

"I broke the group into three separate subgroups," she said. These groups formed to tackle other demands like a call for a monthly town hall meeting with Oakland's city officials and murder-victim family members, as well as a public posting of guidelines that must be followed for law enforcement to prosecute a murder case.

There was also a call for the District Attorney's office to stop plea bargaining murder charges. Brenda Grisham remarks: "The victims didn't get a chance to plea bargain! One young lady was cunning enough to set up a young man to be killed. She's just out of her teens. When she gets out of prison, she'll still be a young woman, while his life is gone forever.

Pressing for Change in Police Community Relations

"Many of the families of murder victims have been treated with disrespect by the police," Brenda said. "We expect the police to be more cooperative with the families of murder victims. Sometimes they have been downright rude. A detective told one lady in our group, 'We don't have to tell you anything. You're only the grandmother.' A mother left with four sons told me that her husband was murdered in their family automobile. The car was impounded as evidence. When the investigation was finished, she was told that she would have to pay $800.00 in storage fees to get her car back. There was no waiver. She lost the car.

"We are asking for the authorities to create an oversight board for the families of murder victims so that they can receive accurate and up-to-date information. I spoke to one mother whose son was killed in 2003. She hasn't heard from anybody about the progress of her child's murder investigation." And she's not alone. Brenda Grisham and the family members of victims are at the forefront of a movement.

Blue on Black, Black on Black

Brenda Grisham is also upset about the attention that police murders, known as blue on black murders, receive as opposed to the much more frequent black on black homicides. The death of a young black man at the hands of one of his peers will rarely draw a crowd, where as alleged police murders draw crusade-level responses, even rioting.

When asked about the role of the clergy in the blood storm around her, she says that "fear" and "a lack of resources for young people" are reasons she's been given for the inactivity of many local faith leaders. This seems to cause her no small degree of angst.

Brenda Grisham also decries the demonization of police in her community. She notes that criminals are often better armed than the police. She acknowledges that they have a hard job, stating, "Everyone wants to go home to their family at night."

Meanwhile, she continues her mission of challenging young men to put down their weapons and pressing the community members to become more involved in the lives of their youth. "Plenty of parents know what their kids are doing out in the streets. If your child has taken somebody's life, turn them in!" Brenda cries.

Blessed Peacemakers

A few years ago, some community partners and I wanted to organize a Stop the Gunfire gathering in a dangerous park in Oakland. This public space was in the center of gang territory. It would have been unwise to simply go into the community and host the event. We needed to reach out beforehand to the shot callers and people connected with the gang that makes things happen in that hood. We needed an intermediary.

After someone has been fatally injured people call the police; *before* that bullet gets fired they call Community Youth Outreach or Men of Influence. People call these organizations when unconventional means are needed to get things done in the hood. Glenn Upshaw works for both organizations. Community Youth Outreach and Men of Influence are city-funded violence interrupters who broker peace between rival gangs and talk people out of retaliation. They are not the police; neither do they gather information for the police. On the contrary, most of them have a background deeply enough rooted in the streets that people trust them enough to call their numbers when the storm starts brewing.

Glenn's team reached out to the right people before our gathering and got a green light for us. Due to the pre-event intervention efforts of Community Youth Outreach, no one so much as broke a fingernail that afternoon.

Peace in the Mean Streets

Glenn Upshaw reminded me that nobody likes war. "Nobody likes to be in a situation where they could pull up to a red light with their children and have somebody start dumping bullets into their car." That's why they ring his phone when the street rhetoric turns up.

Why do they feel comfortable turning to Glenn? I'm reminded of a line from the movie, *Training Day*. A corrupt cop named Alonzo, portrayed by Denzel Washington, says, "Sometimes in this business you got to have a little dirt on you for people to trust you."

Glenn has "a little dirt" on him. "I did some time back in '82. I had an armed robbery where my "crimee" was killed by an undercover officer. I did time on an assault charge. I'm a reputable guy in the streets. People don't have to second-guess me."

And that works down here. Let's face it. Nobody from the Mormon Tabernacle Choir is going to be able to walk up to some of the notorious figures in the city and say, "We need to figure out what can be done to stop y'all from tearing up the neighborhood."

Violence interrupters are hired precisely because they have that type of street cred. Only people who are known and respected in the streets can get a hearing that can stop a bullet.

"There are feuds," Glenn notes, "that began in the '70s and are still going on. It's really difficult getting in those feuds because they have lost so many loved ones. It sounds a little harsh, but we tell them to swallow their losses and move on before we lose more. It's a little difficult for some of them to understand because they've lost someone so close to them. Some of the housing projects don't know why they're feuding. They're from one place, and the people shooting at them are from another.

How it Works

"With most mediations," Glenn explained, "I get the call from the person who is in the midst of the problem. When I get that call, I get permission to speak to the other party they're feuding with. If I don't know them, I'll reach out to someone who does know them to get me in the door. So when I take it to that other party and ask them if it's okay if I speak to them, most times both parties are open to resolving these situations without violence. In the mediation, I must have both sides, of course, to figure out how we can reach a common ground. In most cases it takes a little bit from both parties to give a little something. "You'll hear things like, 'I'm sorry. I didn't know it was like that' or 'I won't come out that way no more. I'll stay out of your way.' It's pretty easy to resolve when I have both parties participating.

"Sometimes I'll have one party wanting to participate and the other not wanting to. That's when I have to dig a little further and really get someone they respect to tell them they really need to get this resolved, because a lot of times the violence causes problems for everybody in the community. People don't want the problems. They don't want the police hanging around.

"Sometimes I deal with hustlers, and they certainly don't want the police around. I also deal with people who no longer hustle, but they don't want that drama around their parents' homes. It all comes down to being able to reach the person with the influence. They might not want to intervene in the middle of a feud, but they welcome me doing it.

"There was a shooting in West Oakland a few months back, and I was called in on it. I calmed it down. I don't think it's totally resolved, but I fixed it for now. Those are the things that keep people confident in my work. Even if I can't get it handled, I'm going to put my best foot forward."

A family once reached out to Glenn after their home had been burglarized. They knew the individual who had done the crime. Apparently they didn't go after him directly; they were concerned that if they did so, they might not get back some priceless family heirlooms. It turned out that the objects had already been sold off, so when they found that out, the mediation was over. The family wanted the thief's head. Glenn and his co-workers had to work quickly to get him out of town.

He recalls, "To that point I had been so successful that I started thinking I was some kind of superhero. Before long I'd be on my way to the Middle East to resolve those things in a flash," Glenn declared with a laugh. "I never saw the curveball coming. That curveball knocked me down bad. But it woke me up. It reminded me that I'm human and that humans have flaws. I felt bad because, despite my best efforts, I knew they were going to do something to him. I felt like quitting. It was that bad. But, in the end, I stayed in the fight, and it worked out for the young thief to live another day."

The Seriousness of the Work

Obviously, Glenn takes his work seriously. "I don't look at it like a job. I look at it like a responsibility in the community. I'm a resident of Oakland, and even if I weren't, it seems to be my calling. I don't look at it like a job, because people call me all through the night, morning, all different times. I feel rewarded when the results are positive. I'm glad when I can put a smile on people's faces.

"When I go into mediation, I don't go in with the thought that there's going to be a violent act. I go in thinking, 'How am I going to resolve this?'

The Peacemaker and the People of God

"A minister told me – and I respect this minister – but what he said turned me off: 'We ain't never gon' stop this violence.' I expect to hear that from people in the streets, but not from a minister. It's almost like he had given up. I could understand his point, but I don't think that's the right attitude to have, especially being a minister. You're supposed to be working toward peace wherever you can. It was like he was saying, 'It ain't no hope for them guys.' And that's how people outside of the community see us already. It didn't sit well in my stomach.

"I started Men of Influence because I grew tired of people saying there's no hope when you need to put your two cents in and help. There *is* hope. It's a hard fight. Believe me it's a hard fight, but there is hope. Back in slavery, I'm sure some slave said, 'We might as well get used to slavery because we're always going to be slaves.' Back during the time of the holocaust, it must have been difficult for some Jewish people to see that a better day would come, but it did.

Suggestions for the Church

"Churches need a contact person – a minister or church member who has a connection with people at street level in the community. That way," Glenn says, "when something kicks off, the church already has a connection in the hood. This person builds a bridge with the people who are leaders in that hood.

"People respect the church. There's a respect level there that other individuals don't get. Everybody knows the minister when they see him. If they're gambling, they get up off their knees and salute. They won't sell no dope in front of the minister. Preachers could use that respect for the good of the community. They could just walk by every so often and ask, 'Is everything O.K.?' This is the way you build a bridge of communication."

Thinking Outside the Box

At the conclusion of our Stop the Gunfire peace rally, I looked around for hands that would help me put things back in order. It's amazing how people tend to scatter at the end of an event. Now, if you were there, you would know that the hot dogs have to be put away, the chairs have to be folded, and a dozen or more other details need to be taken care of before calling it a day.

One of the few people who stayed behind this time was principal organizer Jennifer Argueta Nieves. She and I stacked folding chairs and tables into the back of her pickup truck and then drove them to the location where they would need to be left. I don't recall whether or not Jennifer made a speech that day, but I do remember her flipping burgers and talking with community residents. Jennifer is a true community activist. She does whatever is needed to get the job done. And I know this to be true because I've rung her cell like it was the Bat Phone. Whether I need her to sit down with me over lunch to share with some youth who needs guidance or to organize a peace event, Jennifer Argueta Nieves will have only two questions: "Where?" and "What time?"

Jennifer works for an organization known as Oakland Unite Messengers 4 Peace. Whenever I have an idea that might interrupt violence, she's there beside me before I can hang up the phone. Community building is more than a job to her. She was born and raised in Oakland, and the people of the city seem to be in her heart.

I met Sister Jennifer (as I call her) at a gun buy-back she was hosting in Oakland. Three children had been murdered in separate incidents, one of them the youngest homicide victim in the history of Oakland. She was putting her ideas and energy together with community members to see what could be done to stop the bloodletting.

Watching Sister Jennifer has taught me that the people who do the most real work in the community often get the least recognition. On the day of the gun buy-back, the photo-op was usurped by people who had not been involved in the planning or implementation of the event at all. Although Jennifer had raised the money and done all of the networking to make the event a success, the faces of community ministers who had not thrown in so much as a bobby pin, were on the front cover of the newspaper the next day.

Jennifer seemed unfazed by the lack of personal recognition. The event had done what it was planned to do. It brought awareness of the blight of gun violence to the people. It had also taken some firearms off the streets.

One thing that *has* frustrated her, however, has been her inability to enlist churches in the struggle for peace. She said: "When I first started here, my job was to engage clergy members. That didn't work out very well. I knocked on church doors. I spoke to pastors. Half of them said (or inferred), 'If you don't have any money, then I don't care what you have to say.' Others were very welcoming. We have more than 200 churches in Oakland with about 250 clergy members; I have a working relationship with about 5 of the pastors."

Rebuilding Community/ Police Relations

Sister Jennifer came back from an urban workers conference a few years ago with a powerful idea. She said, "This is what they're doing in L.A. Why don't we try it here in Oakland?"

She started a 10-week program designed to keep kids off the streets. The program had her working with families and community members alarmed by the specter of increasing gun violence in East Oakland. She spoke with teenagers and young adults about violence and how it impacts them. And she encouraged open dialogue between community members, politicians, and police that had previously been closed. According to Jennifer, outside of arrests, police rarely interacted with youth.

She added, "When you say, 'OPD' to a youth, they say, 'F—- that.' Not all officers go out there with the intention of arresting young men. In reality, most of the officers want to help, but because they have such a bad rep in the community, it's really hard for them to jump over that hurdle. Hopefully, one day we'll be able to say, 'It used to be that way; now it's this way.'"

Today, Jennifer Argueta Nieves is doing her part to make that change happen. Church leader, what could *you* do to rebuild the connection between the community and local police?

Chapter 12

Fight the Power: Facing the American (In)justice System

 "These are what you call straight ribs," he said, never once looking up from the stove. He was a magician in that kitchen as he went through the varieties of ribs and how they were to be prepared. The only thing I know about cooking is where the knife and fork go after the meat is put down on my plate. Yet, I nodded and passed the occasional, "Oh, I see." It was a beautiful day for a barbecue in Oakland. Guests were in the backyard of the small house enjoying the sunshine. But I sat right there in the kitchen chatting with the chef.

I put my fingertips down on the kitchen table. I looked around at the other chairs and I marveled, for this was no ordinary kitchen and no ordinary house. The Black Panther Party for Self Defense was formed right here. The Black Panthers' 10-Point Program was drawn up right at the table where I was seated.

Prophets of Rage

When I was a little boy I was taught that the chef preparing the ribs was someone to be feared, like the boogie man. Posters of Bobby Seale's piercing stare glared at me from posters and from the cover of the Black Panther newspaper. His black jacket and black beret made him look like a commando ready to wage war. But on that day back in 2008, as he labored back and forth in a red, white, and green apron, he seemed more like he could be a beloved uncle rather than the dangerous figure the press had once made him out to be. In the 1960s, he woke up in dangerous times, and he and some of my other neighbors in Oakland rose to face the threat.

Police brutality has been a problem in Oakland since anybody I know can remember. In the '60s, blacks were followed and stopped without probable cause. They were harassed, threatened, beaten, and shot by officers. African-Americans who had fled Southern racism were appalled. Bobby Seale, who studied the writings of Malcolm X, sought a way to apply Malcolm's belief, that blacks should defend themselves, to the situation where he lived in Oakland. Sometime after Malcolm's assassination, Bobby met a student leader named Huey P. Newton, who had also been touched by the teachings of Malcolm X. The two formed the Black Panther Party for Self Defense.

In his autobiography, *A Lonely Rage*, Bobby Seale describes a 1966 Panther encounter with the Oakland Police Department. He and Huey P. Newton arrived at a party carrying guns. The police were not far behind. One of the officers looked at Mr. Seale and said, "Let me see your gun... ."

Supreme Servant of The People, Huey P. Newton, jumped in and said, "Say, look swine! You think you can come on with this petty illegal search. Well, I'm not going for it because you have no reasonable cause to."

The officer issued a veiled threat. "You boys are going to get it, sooner or later."

Huey P. Newton spoke in a tone the officer was unaccustomed to hearing from a black man. He said, "And we're going to catch you wrong, with your brutalizing asses. So I'm letting you know we'll defend ourselves. Now go tell that to your swine chief and your swine mayor, and if you don't like it... ."

That event was the beginning of the famous Panther patrols. Bobby Seale said, "From then on, almost every night for a month Huey and I patrolled the police in my car, hoping to see an arrest going on – so we could get out and observe and ensure with our guns and law book there would be no police brutality."[1]

The Black Panther Party for Self Defense took the most extreme stand of any revolutionary group born and bred on American soil. Chapters were formed all over the United States. Their black leather jackets and black berets made them icons. Many died or were imprisoned in the fight for human rights.

However, their efforts were not enough to stop police brutality in Oakland, let alone America. By 2003, a band of rogue cops nicknamed the "Oakland Riders" were on the witness stand for beating innocent people and planting drugs on suspects. The city of Oakland was forced to pay out millions in lawsuit money. In fact, by 2012 the federal government was threatening a takeover of the Oakland Police Department because of systematic complaints of corruption and brutality.

Murdered by the System

Jack Bryson is one of my partners in activism. He is an SEIU union leader and community activist in Oakland. If I have an idea for an action, I will likely call him or vice versa. One Saturday morning last year I asked Jack to meet me at my favorite breakfast spot on MacArthur Boulevard. We began to talk about the incident that launched him into activism.

The series of events remains as fresh in Jack's mind as though it had happened yesterday. He was on a Hayward, California, street corner with his two teenage sons when a car pulled up. A young man, apparently an acquaintance of his sons, jumped out and said some things in a manner that Jack didn't care for. Words flew back and forth between them. At that point, Jack's two sons and the driver jumped into the car and sped off. Jack learned later that, as they drove off, the driver looked in the back seat and asked Jack's sons, "Who was that? Your brother?" One of the sons said, "No, that's our father."

The next time Jack and the driver met, the young man apologized for his harsh words. He introduced himself. He said, "My name is Oscar. Oscar Grant."

Jack goes on to say, "I remember December 31, 2009. I worked a half day since it was New Year's Eve. My son Jackie called me and said he was coming by with a few of his friends. The conversation turned to what everyone was doing that night. I told them, "Whatever you do, don't go to San Francisco.

"They told me it was cool. Nothing was going to happen. Later that night, my girl and I got a room at the Hilton in Pleasanton. All evening I was blowing up my sons' phones asking where they were. The response always came back, 'We're good. We're good.' As a parent you worry about where your kids are going and what they're doing.

"My last phone call was at about 1:30 or 1:45. I dozed off for awhile, waking up around 2:30 in the morning. I called my son's phone. No one answered. Where is this kid? About 5:30 a.m., my phone rang. A friend's voice said, 'Did you see your son on the news?' Then my son's mother called, 'One of the kids has been shot.' There was chaos in the background. All of the boys' mothers had begun calling each other. This was a nightmare. In the mayhem of voices I heard, 'Oscar's been shot.' I turned on

the television in time to see my son, along with the rest of
the young men he'd gone out with that night, being
escorted by the police down a Bay Area Rapid Transit
(BART) escalator. His mother called the BART police, but
they wouldn't give her any information."

It turned out that the police officers had ordered the
young black men off the train, stating that there were calls
of a disturbance. Oscar Grant was placed face down on his
stomach. There seemed no way that he could pose a threat
to the officers from that position. Apparently, one Johannes
Mehserle thought different. He put a bullet though Oscar's
back, and then the young man was handcuffed. Oscar had
been executed in front of hundreds of witnesses, several of
whom had filmed the incident and uploaded it to the Internet. Soon, the Oscar Grant killing had gone viral.

Jack Bryson went to the offices of John Burris, a highly
regarded civil rights attorney from Oakland. The incident
was on the TV in the lawyer's office when Jack arrived.
Burris's whole office seemed startled by what they had
witnessed on television. "How are you tied to this?" the
attorney asked Jack when he asked for help. "I said,
'Those are my sons on that train platform right there next
to Oscar!'"

Burris looked Jack in the eye and said, "You have to
organize around this. Be careful of the police as well as
the people you clique with. Some of them won't have good
intentions. It won't be about Oscar Grant. It'll be about
their own selves."

An Activist is Born

Burris was right. Jack Bryson found the activist community laced with glory seekers and dollar bill hounds. Some
of the community "leaders" were actually left wing figures
whose interests seemed to be the exact opposite of what
the community was asking for. He later mused, "The cats

on the block are the real revolutionaries. If you could mobilize them, you could turn around many of the community's problems."

Rioting shook the streets of Oakland, California. Anarchists broke out store windows in the city's shopping district in the wake of the shooting. Marching throngs cried out, "No Justice, No Peace!" The eyes of the world turned to Oakland.

Church Leadership in the Wake of Tragedy

As a man who'd come of age in a world where the black church was the most stable institution in the community, Bryson looked to God's house for hope. It was a hope that failed. He recalled, "To see the clergy do what they did was disappointing. They didn't reach out to the parents of the people impacted by the tragedy. It wasn't about Oscar Grant. It was about that other Grant, the one whose image appears on that piece of green paper in your wallet, and it was about yet another Grant. They were hearing voices, 'Boy, you best be quiet about this or you won't get that grant you've applied for.'

"I always wanted to be a man of God. I read in the Bible something like, 'Be careful of misleading leaders.' The same system that killed Oscar Grant and Sean Bell is the same system that killed Jesus. He was falsely arrested, found guilty by the court system, and then murdered. And you say, 'I'm fighting for Jesus,' but what happened to Jesus is happening to people every day around the world. The same system that killed Jesus, killed Medgar Evers, Martin Luther King, and Steve Biko. We've been saying, 'No more murders!' Well, it should have been, 'No more murders after Jesus.'

Law Enforcement in the Age of Gentrification

United Playaz of San Francisco has a slogan: "It Takes The Hood To Save The Hood." Misha works for United Playaz. She is a community activist in San Francisco, where a broad scale displacement of families is under way to make space for high-income employees of tech firms that have located in Northern California. She believes the police force is part of a systematic plan to quicken the gentrification of San Francisco's historically Latino Mission District.

Misha said, "I became a site coordinator for the Excelsior community center. It had always been a hub for young people in that neighborhood. Unfortunately, during the time I was there some incidents took place with the police department as a result of a new community policing model they were trying to roll out. The program was new for everybody, and the groups were already experiencing feelings of anger, mistrust, and hurt.

"Because that rift was already there, and there was no way for us to have the time to address those issues in a really heartfelt way, the conflict – the us and them – became really evident. The young people felt harassed by the police and were just really scared, so they didn't want to be at the center anymore. It wasn't that the neighborhood was so bad, but now instead of a place for young people, it's become more of a senior center. I felt really discouraged and not taken care of as a community member, so I had to leave the work for awhile.

"There has been a lot of media coverage about Valencia Gardens, a housing project at Valencia and 15th Street. It has been 'redeveloped' to make it 'more aesthetically fitting' for the neighborhood. But what about the old residents who have lived there their entire lives and are still living there? That's where they belong; that's where their home is. And now they have new people moving in, but instead of families, the developers want the single-occupancy person who is making big money at a tech company or a trust-fund kid who wants to live in San Francisco. There is a systematic push."

Misha recounts the horrendous beating that a Valencia Garden resident named D. Paris Williams took at the hands of four undercover policemen. They took issue with him for riding his bicycle on the sidewalk. Friends who came out to try to stop the thrashing were themselves set upon by police.

"There's an invisible plan that says, 'It's fine for you guys to leave because we have a vision that you are not included in, even though this is your space.' Part of what we are seeing feels like bullying by law enforcement."

The War on Drugs

Is God tugging on your heart to reach out to the people of inner city America? I don't care if you're going to the projects or the trailer park, perhaps the most deadly virus that you'll have to help people combat is the poisonous stench of mass incarceration. One of the biggest crises facing the people you feel called to minister to is the explosion of the American prison system.

Mass incarceration is spreading through the hood like the fictional movie monster, "the Blob." Few people that you'll meet will have been untouched by the prison industrial complex. "Why?" you ask. The answer is simple. There are billion of dollars connected to incarceration.

The truth is, the crime rate in America has been decreasing significantly for about a decade, but the rate of people being incarcerated continues to rise. The United States represents less than 5 percent of the world's population yet incarcerates about 25 percent of the world's prisoners. America locks up people at a rate far higher than Russia, Iran, or South Korea. In fact, America incarcerates people at a rate higher than any other nation on the face of God's earth. A great number of the prisoners are poor people with brown skin.

The New Cotton –
Prisons are a Cash Crop

Let me break it down for you. Every time a black or brown man is arrested the cash register starts singing. The police make overtime pay. The prosecutor is guaranteed a phenomenal salary. Cities are built up in the middle of the desert where the state will build prisons at a cost of millions.

Some American ghettos have what sociologists call "million dollar blocks," so named because the amount of people under the supervision of the criminal justice system brings in one million dollars annually per city block.

Consider this, California built 22 prisons in the time it took to build one university. Each one of the prisons needs scores of employees. The prisoners are stuffed into these concrete slave ships like sardines in fetid water. However, before you finish this sentence, somewhere in California the police will have scooped up another poor person to feed to the beast. The punishment industry is so profitable that privately owned prison stock is traded on Wall Street.

Guilt or innocence is of little consequence when you come in contact with the criminal justice system. I once accompanied a neighborhood mom to her son's arraignment. His last cry as they dragged him shackled toward the dungeons was, "Mama, get me a pay lawyer!" For you see, everything that happens to you from this point on depends on the expertise of your attorney.

Justice for All?

About a year ago I got a call from a friend back in New Jersey. The police had busted into her garage. They found her teenage son sitting with 12 friends in a cloud of marijuana smoke. They called him a racial epithet and then dragged him out in handcuffs in front of the neighbors.

Oh, did I mention that the other kids in the garage were white and that he was the only black one? The police did not even ask for the white kids' names. They looked around that room of 13 people and saw one black teen. They had their suspect. No need to arrest anyone else. No need to ask for names and addresses. The rest of the kids were simply shooed off.

My friend, who has probably never had a parking ticket in her life, just about lost her mind. Neither she nor her husband, two middle-class, suburban homeowners, knew anything about how the criminal justice system works for black people. They raised the bail money and got the teenager, who had never been arrested before, out on bond. Soon she was calling me and asking, "What do I do now?"

I knew his situation was serious. He was caught with a miniscule quantity of contraband in a room full of suburban, white young people. Still, everything I've seen in my life told me that this could spell prison time, first offense or not. I prayed with his mom over the phone and then said, "Hold tight, Sister. I'll get back with you."

You Need a Shark Who Can Fight a Drug Case

I was in California; she was in New Jersey. The first thing I did was make a call to someone I knew back home in Jersey who lived close to the streets. It was a short conversation. "I need the name of a lawyer who can beat a drug case." The answer came back the next day via text message. It was only one word long – a last name. I found the lawyer's website, read his battle record, and then called the kid's mother back. "Write down this number," I said.

Before they walked into the courthouse, the attorney looked at my friend and said, "Don't worry about a thing." This man was a shark, and he had come there to earn the hefty price tag he had attached to the kid's freedom. The lawyer acted out in the courtroom. He scoffed, rolled his eyes, and flipped his hand in disgust at the D.A.'s charges. He glanced at his watch and yawned. He picked at his fingernails. When it was his time to go work, he ripped the D.A.'s argument to shreds. They hadn't read the young man his rights. They had referred to him by a racial expletive in a room full of witnesses. No one else had been arrested. Why, not? And that was just for openers.

Needless to say, my friend's son walked out of the court that day a free man, and that lawyer walked out with her family's life savings.

Slaves in the Courtroom

Later, she reflected on the experience. What shook my friend the most was the gallery full of young black men who sat at in the courtroom, dour-faced, in matching uniforms like captured field slaves. I explained to my friend that without that top-notch lawyer on her team, odds were great that her son would have been just another one of those slaves.

My friend is a staunch political conservative, and she had a hard time accepting all of this, even though she had seen it with her own eyes. But the truth is the truth. In America, it's not a question of guilt or innocence; it's "How much justice can you afford?" America's prisons are chock full of people whose only crime was poverty. They were accused, shackled, and thrown away, many as innocent of the crimes of which they have been accused as Jesus was, and yet they had no money with which to mount an adequate legal defense.

Prison is for Poor People

There's no such thing as a "fair shake" in the court system. Justice (if that's what you want to call it) costs money. Lots of it. If your family can't put that money together, if you are dark and poor, prepare yourself, because to hell on earth you will surely go.

Prison is the ghetto afterlife, where the weak get chewed up and spit out by predators who have made the system their home since childhood. Same-sex serial rapists roam the dank halls, hunting terrified victims. Convicts are fed substandard food and then caged in close quarters with far too many people or even solitary confinement boxes. There is something unnatural about a world where heterosexual men are never allowed contact with women. The place smells, and cage life wreaks mental havoc on even the strongest.

The Game Behind the Game

"Innocent until proven guilty" is another flagrant falsehood. An unsubstantiated charge is all it takes to leave you languishing behind bars. The police have arrested you. They have charged you with a crime. You haven't been to court, but you can't make the bail bond fee. You're "innocent until proven guilty," and yet they have you locked away from your family, church, and community. They toss peanut butter sandwiches and jelly packets at you at meal time and have you walking around in a jail uniform. And yet, you're – theoretically – innocent!

Eventually, the district attorney may offer you a deal. Plead to a lesser charge, guilty or not, and we'll let you out. You say, "I didn't do this thing. I'm completely innocent." Let's assume you truly *are* innocent. Like I said, it really makes no difference, but for argument's sake, I'll go there with you. The D.A. may well say, "Take the deal. If you fight us in a courtroom and you lose, instead of doing a year, I'll bury you for 20 years!"

They've got you by the whatchamacallits. A jury trial might be your right, but it's an expensive, time-consuming right. If all prisoners insisted on it, the system would overload and collapse. Therefore, it's greatly discouraged. If you lose, they're going to bury you alive so the next victim will think twice about exercising that right.

The D.A. builds his or her career and reputation on a powerful conviction rate. Guilty or innocent, once they've got you pinned down, it's not in their best interest to let you see daylight again. They become experts in convincing a poor brown or black person that the fate of the multitudes has now befallen them, and it's in everyone's best interests if they plead to a lesser charge that's being offered.

How Did We Get Here?

Nothing has contributed to the systematic mass incarceration of people of color more than the so-called "War on Drugs." Most people in state prisons have no history of violence or record of selling large quantities of drugs. Michelle Alexander, author of the *New Jim Crow*, says, "Drug offenses are the single most important cause of the explosion in incarceration. They account for two-thirds of the federal prisoners and half of those in state prison. More than 31 million people have been arrested for drug offenses since the drug war began."[2]

On October 14, 1982, President Ronald Reagan declared drugs to be a threat to the security of the United States. Later, when Nancy Reagan was visiting a school here in Oakland, a fourth-grader asked what she should do if offered drugs. Here, Mrs. Reagan coined the famous phrase, "Just say, 'no.'" Later the Bill Clinton administration instituted draconian drug sentencing measures which caused the American prisons to burst at the seams with black and brown people.

Consider this. Cocaine and heroin enter the United States by the metric ton from locales as diverse as Afghanistan, Columbia, and Mexico. They come over this country's borders by way of planes and ships. Few people in the hood own tankers, and yet we have borne the weight and focus of the nation's war on drugs. The majority of those incarcerated are people addicted to drugs who were caught with small quantities. The system focuses on punishment, not recovery. There is no help for addicts trapped in the system. Eventually, they are set free to reoffend and ultimately reenter the lucrative punishment industry.

Rapper Melle Mel once said, "... the war on drugs is really war on soul brothers."[3] And that seems so. When the War on Drugs began, 350,000 people were in U.S. prisons. Twenty-five years later that number had grown to 2.3 million. There are no statistics to prove that blacks are more likely to be guilty of drug crimes than any other racial group. Michelle Alexander states, " If there are significant differences in the surveys to be found, studies frequently suggest that whites, particularly white youth, are more likely to be involved in illegal drug dealing than people of color.[4]

The War on Drugs has had a staggering impact on the black community. The think tank Sentencing Project tells us that, according to statistics, and if current trends continue, two out of every three black males can expect to serve prison time, and one in six Latino males are headed for the same fate.[5]

Once you've been convicted of a felony, in many states you lose your right to vote. You are no longer eligible to live in public housing or receive public benefits. You must now check "yes" when a job application asks if you've ever been arrested. Your ability to feed your family is greatly impacted. You are often treated as a non-person, with a stigma that is going to be difficult to fight long after you've paid your debt to society.

An Ex-Probation Officer
Takes Us Inside the System

Debra Mendoza knows the system from the inside out. She worked in it for years. Here she shares her first-hand experiences and insights.

"I am for anyone who stands up for a cause whether it be big or small. I support people who are willing to go out on a limb and do some radical change for the better. I say more power to them. It was hard to operate in that way as a probation officer. It was definitely a challenge. But I think I'm authentically genuine with people. I care about people. I want to see them do better and improve. People can feel that. I understood my role, and I would make that clear. I would work within that to whatever degree I could. But I really did have some moments where I felt that the things I had to do came against my core values.

"It was 2001 when I started. I did supervision. There wasn't really a rhyme or a reason to things. I just remember that I got a caseload of 150 kids from East Oakland dumped on me. I went to see them all once a month. And then if they violated their probation, I had to deal with the situation.

"I remember this one mom putting pressure on me to revoke this kid's probation, and I ended up going to his school to arrest him. That's so counter-productive. Why are you going to go to the school and arrest the kid when he's doing right? Maybe he doesn't go to school all the time. Maybe he stole a computer from his mom. Arresting him is not the solution. And there are other things I feel really bad about – things I haven't really come to terms with – like to be a good employee, I just went along with stuff. And that's people's lives!

"I had to testify at one young man's hearing; they were trying to send him to adult court as a juvenile. He *had* done some crazy things as a juvenile, and so I jumped on the bandwagon to get him remanded to adult court. But that's so much against what I believe now. I don't think children should be sent to adult court. That's why we have juvenile court, and that's why we have adult court. Their minds are not fully developed. They're not thinking as an adult would. They don't have the capacity. So, I feel guilty about that. I still do."

Chances for Rehabilitation

According to Ms. Mendoza, positive family relationships, opportunities, and structure are all key to a young person's successful efforts at rehabilitation after having been incarcerated. She notes that having a strong family structure and a supportive community are also important. That being said, she notes that the recidivism rate is high. She estimates that some 80 percent of those released from incarceration reoffend. She blames this dilemma on "brainwashing."

Said Ms. Mendoza: "The system is oppressive. The more involved you are in the system, the stronger the dependency that's created. It's like programming. That's why people have such a hard time being released from incarceration; they've been programmed. When you're told when to get up, what to wear, when to eat, when to sit down, and when to go to sleep, you're so limited.

"Plus, there is no physical contact. Humans thrive on touch, on human connection, and that's not part of the program there.

The Ultimate Life Disruption

"Imagine, you're living your life," Ms. Mendoza says, "you're doing your thing. Then, all of a sudden, you're removed from that. You're dehumanized. So you don't really have an identity other than being a criminal, a prisoner, detainee, or offender. We're dehumanizing people. And that's what makes it easier for people in supervisory positions to treat people the way they do, because when you can't see people as your image, you're going treat them like s——."

How the Prosecution Works

Regarding quality representation Mendoza says, "The district attorney totally manipulates and re-victimizes wounded people by their representation of them. I don't think there's any real type of justice for victims. They are used as pawns by the district attorney for their own advantage. I've seen it with my own eyes. It's evil. They don't get healing. Surviving family members don't get closure. They are manipulated, and they are not given opportunity for real healing.

"I got to know hundreds of these stories over 10 years. I started to see things: disposable people, inordinate sentences, greater value placed on certain kinds of people than others. You're at the mercy of a system that doesn't care about you or see you as an individual. Your case is just running through the mill of a factory.

"It's better to be a guilty rich man than an innocent poor man. People make deals all the time because they're desperate to get out of jail. Public defenders are overwhelmed with high caseloads. The D.A. has about twice the resources of the public defenders in terms of attorneys, investigators, caseloads. So the money is going to the D.A., the sheriff, and the probation officers; a little bit goes to the public defender. So no, the poor don't get good representation; not at all."

The Devil is Busy

When I discussed this whole issue with my senior citizen mentor, Ms. Irma, she said, "When I was little girl, my father had a book full of illustrations from the Bible. There was one picture that showed two roads. One road was filled with big crowds of people on the way to hell. The other road was narrow. Those people were headed toward heaven.

"The criminal justice system is something like that," she said. "You have these two roads, and one group is headed for hell, in this case jail. It's full of people – black and brown people, poor people. The other road is narrow, and it's pointing toward freedom. The way they do poor people is an abomination. You can picture the devil smiling and grinning when people do things like that. He runs the world. So you have to careful and alert because he's doing a lot of devouring."

I'm Walking Out

Pastor, if you don't have a message that deals with the reality of the hell on earth that people in your parish face, you can count on me to walk out in mid-sentence. Pray for me or curse me; it makes no difference. The people you shepherd are looking to you for some real answers about things they are going to face when they walk out the front door. If you doubt that the criminal justice system has sunk its razor-sharp claws into your congregation, Pastor, try an experiment. Next Sunday, ask everyone who has an incarcerated loved one to meet you at the altar. Next, ask everyone who has a recently released loved one who is having troubling finding work to stand behind those already at the altar. My e-mail address will be at end of this book. Write me and tell me what happens.

Preacher, please come up with something that will help them connect with local programs that assist the formerly incarcerated. Start some program that can help the formerly incarcerated with their job searches. Help prisoner families reconnect with their loved ones on visiting days. Contact the elected officials you put into office and hold them accountable for this mass incarceration madness. Finally, pull the shade off the monster. Call on your ministry leaders and members to read *The New Jim Crow*, by Michelle Alexander. Have a discussion about it.

If you don't do your best to understand how the prison industrial complex beast is devouring your community, you have no street cred at all in my book. God is looking right at you, Pastor. Get it cracking!

Chapter 13

Human Trafficking in the Hood

 When my novel *Straight Outta East Oakland* was released in 2008, my community held a celebration at a large bookstore in Oakland. Dr. Alvin McLean and the praise team from Allen Temple Baptist Church provided the music. The bookstore provided delicious soul food. When my time had come, I stood up in front of the audience and began to read from the book. When I finished, I asked if there were any questions.

A beautiful, young woman in the back of the room stood up. She didn't have a question but a plea for help. She said, "I'm trapped in prostitution. I need help." God works when God works. It doesn't matter if it's at an altar call or during the Q & A segment at a book event. Our challenge is simply to catch the cues and then get busy.

Church members surrounded Sister. They embraced her. They laid hands on her and prayed for her. And the blessings didn't stop there. She is in our lives to this very day.

The Ultimate Evil – Looking the Devil in the Face

The commercial sale of human beings for sexual purposes is one of the greatest evils to hit the planet. I put it up there with the atom bomb and the killer diseases. It's more than just exchanging money for sex. Someone's self-esteem and basic humanity are part of that bargain.

"Having sex with a prostitute is like renting an organ for half an hour." So said a john in an interview about his pastime. His detachment from the basic humanity of the individual with whom he is engaging in this most intimate act is alarming. For this man, she is not a human being with a beating heart, thoughts, feelings, emotions, dreams, and family. She has been reduced to an organ provided for his pleasure.

Prostitution is called the "victimless crime." Proponents for its legalization are heard to say, "Whatever two people consent to in the privacy of their bedroom is nobody's business."

Is prostitution harmless? Hardly. I don't say that because I read a position paper or once attended a symposium. I say it because as a minister of the gospel, I have met many women (and men) who have been forced into human trafficking. The sex trade rarely exists where the elements of coercion and exploitation do not breed simultaneously like mold spores.

The Misunderstood Menace

In Oakland, the trafficking of human beings often takes place in front of church buildings. Scantily dressed young women walk up and down the street, often with cell phones pinned to their ears. They range in age from 12 to 60. Who are they? Well, I can tell you I've met plenty of them. Most of them came from poverty-stricken homes. A great percentage of them were the victims of sexual abuse from the cradle to junior high school. Some are kidnap victims. Many stand under the hawk's eye gaze of a pimp. He's in the car that casually cruises by every 15 minutes. They'll barely make eye contact. A glance is all that's needed. Her "daddy" (pimp) can't be associated with her when she's working. Pimping is a crime punishable with heavy penalties. Nevertheless, the exploiter is there, working his (or her) dark magic.

The Mack

Oakland has a problem with human trafficking dating back generations. In fact, the first time I ever heard of Oakland as a child growing up on the East Coast was in conjunction with the flesh trade. The blaxploitation film, *The Mack*, released in 1973, was an underground classic. It centered on a car thief released from prison who arrives back home in Oakland via Greyhound bus. He is destitute, and with little in the way of job prospects, he runs into a childhood friend, a young prostitute. She teaches him the pimping trade.

Goldie is a fast learner. And he has one of the most useful tools that any pimp can possess – a heart of ice. In the dead of night, the young woman who taught him the game runs up to his pimped-out luxury ride in near hysterics. She claims that a client has just assaulted her. "He tried to kill me, Goldie. He took all my money... ," she manages to squeeze out through a veil of tears.

Goldie's response to her near-death experience? "Let me tell you something now, and you listen to me, and you listen closely. I don't give a s—- what happened to you. Now get yourself together and get back in there and get me my money. I don't care how long it takes you; you get out there and get it. NOW GET!" [1]

Exploited Children

My friend, Nola Brantley, is a deeply committed soldier in the war to stop the commercial sexual exploitation of children. I call her the "Harriet Tubman of Oakland." For just as Harriet Tubman freed the slaves, Nola is an engineer for the 21st century version of the underground railroad. She has seen the horror and hell of it all, and the stories are almost too much to bear. She starts with the tale of a teenage girl who returned to a pimp she'd run away from before she was arrested. According to the rules of the game, the soulless bottom dweller had to deal with her for breaking the rules. He tied her to a bed and then went into the kitchen. He heated the bottom of a cast-iron skillet until it was white hot. Then he carefully lifted it up by the handle and took it into the bedroom. I can only imagine the child's screams as the pimp slowly lowered the smoking, glowing pan down on the baby-soft flesh of her belly. That is obscene depravity at its worst.

The New Wave Dope Game

Crack cocaine was extremely lucrative in the late 1980s. Somewhere along the line, police finally found a way to slow down the crack game. They used state of the art technology to do surveillance. They flipped big time players and turned them into informants. In the beginning, crack dealers would hide the drugs near them but not on their person. If rousted, they would say, "That's not mine!" Eventually, the rules changed; if the cops found a rock near you, it was your rock. The pool of consumers also dried up. Once people figured out how lethal crack was, they knew better than to take that first hit. That's not to say there is no longer money in crack; there is, but not as much. I once met a crack dealer who was rolling so hard back in the '80s that he kept a black Hefty bag full of bills in his apartment. Rarely will you find people doing it that big in the 21st century.

Hustlers had to find a new way to make money. So many of them started trafficking young girls. The product is reusable. The risk is low. The pimp can make thousands a week while feeding the girl McDonald's Happy Meals and housing her in a roach-ridden motel on a back street in the hood.

It may surprise you to know that not all pimps are men. Some are women. And some are other family members. Older siblings pimp younger ones. Even mothers have been known to put their daughters out on the track (the area where johns cruise for "dates"). I have even heard of a man living near the track who told his young daughter, "You're always out here anyway. You might as well make me some money."

Daddy's Little Girls

Pimps hang around foster group homes like vultures circle around an animal carcass. The younger the child, the easier it is to brainwash her, to persuade her to use her body to prove her love. Besides, if a foster child disappears, the search for her probably won't be the same as it would be for a young child from an affluent, two-parent home in the suburbs.

Nola told me: "Foster kids between the ages of 12 and 17 are the most vulnerable to traffickers. They have no control over their lives. All of the control in their lives has been given to foster parents, social workers, and judges. None of these people really know these children, who they are, their desires and dreams.

"Why do the girls stay in a situation where they are sexually exploited? Obviously, the situation they were in previously must have been worse. Children who are part of the foster care system have already been removed from their families because of neglect or abuse. This vulnerability makes them highly targeted by traffickers.

"Many young people in the foster care system, particularly teens, have not made meaningful relationships with adult caregivers. Many of the caregivers see the children as a way to raise extra money, to heighten their income.

The children feel that. They feel that sense of 'I'm just here for money.' So they feel that 'If I'm going to be here for money for the foster parent, I might as well be with the pimp for money. At least the pimp gives me what I think is love or affection.' Even though the pimp is also using and manipulating them, that's how the young people rationalize it. In the foster care system kids will say, 'People have been making money off me all of my life, so how is this so different?'"

Friend and Enemies

Veronica serves foster youth and girls in danger of being trafficked. She says, "Foster kids have faced so much instability. Many have severe reactive attachment disorder. They are either completely withdrawn or indiscriminant as to whom they bring close. A lot of young people really haven't had a security base. They don't know what it means to be safe. They learn a disjointed way of what it's like to be in a relationship. They let people come way too close, or they're too terrified to let anyone in.

"Some of these kids have trouble identifying safe boundaries. They don't know when they are safe and when they are not. As a result, they are looking for love in all the wrong places. They are looking for a way to relieve the pain. They find partners who are not safe.

"I also believe that men who prey on these girls have a lot of damage and injury, too. Predators can smell prey. They hunt out the vulnerable and the weak. They say to themselves, 'I'm going to take advantage.'

"Pimps have lost touch with the life inside. When you've had so many bad things happen, you lose touch with your life. Often they are abused men who are angry and afraid. Men who strike out and hit are afraid of losing their place. Real powerful leaders are not violent. You only jockey for power and control if you are absolutely terrified inside.

"How the child exits from the life is important. Either she continues down that path or becomes a damaged woman who becomes a predator herself. If she doesn't get healing, she can be on the metaphorical track of the mind, one terrible relationship for another."

The Life

Young women who are trapped in the game often become victims of the "Stockholm Syndrome." They come to develop a deep affinity for the trafficker who mercilessly exploits them. One young man told me, "You have to get inside of a bitch's head like a neurologist." The pimp does this by making the victim dependent on him for everything and impressing on this person that they are nothing without him or her. I heard the story of one pimp who rationed out toilet paper squares to his "teammates."

I once met a young woman who had been yanked out of her mother's car by a guerilla pimp when she was 14 or 15 years old. He took her across state lines, changed her name and forced her out on the track. The next time her mother saw her, she was a grown woman. Imagine what it would be like to try to rebuild your life after such trauma!

It's Not at all Like *Pretty Woman*

Melissa Farley, Ph.D., is one of the world's leading experts on the subject of human trafficking. She is the Executive Director of Prostitution Research. She once did a nine-country survey among human trafficking victims and concluded that exploited women have the same symptoms and severity of Post Traumatic Stress Disorder (PTSD) as combat veterans from Iraq. "Two-thirds of these women," she told me, "emerging from sexual slavery have the highest level of PTSD that psychology has ever found."

According to Melissa, films like *Pretty Woman*, starring Julia Roberts, paint a picture of sex for sale as a preferable, alternative lifestyle. She says that the rise of the porn industry has dehumanized women and served to spread the curse of human trafficking. According to Dr. Farley, pornography is human trafficking on the screen. She says, "Most women getting out of prostitution have criminal records. They are not going to get away from prostitution without dealing with their petty theft, prostitution, and other felony arrests. No landlord will rent to them. No employer will hire them. They need extensive legal services. They also need high-quality job training that will propel them to employment with a wage that will sustain life.

"Many of the kids have serious mental illness," Dr. Farley notes. "It erodes your personality or sense of self. Some are bipolar. Some suffer from depression. Some have poly-substance abuse problems with six or eight substances. Authority issues in jobs are unbelievable. Multiply any problems you or I might have by 50! These kids need sophisticated rehabilitation."

The View From the Therapist's Couch

Dr. Janet Hazen, Ph.D., was driving down a street where women have been trafficked in Oakland for generations. She noticed something. Most of the mature women were gone, replaced by teenagers. One day, my friend Nola Brantley came to speak at the center where she was working. Soon, Dr. Hazen found herself counseling children caught up in the life.

Dr. Hazen notes: "It starts with the girl and her self worth and her sense of worth. Does she have an internal sense of herself and resources? How was she raised? What is her history? If she has the right configuration of weaknesses, frailties, and difficulties and she falls prey to a man who can exploit her, half the job is done. If he gets her in there initially, there is brainwashing. He lowers her self-esteem and self-worth. He creates a powerful sense of dependency. Multiple factors work simultaneously. It's not difficult once the process has begun.

"There are other girls in the pimp's stable or 'family.' This is the culture. This is what the girls do. Imagine that a young girl has had no father, no role model. That creates a huge vacuum. She melts under the control of the perpetrator. She submits.

"The children develop a warped sense of family from the exploiter. They may be runaways, or they may have been snatched from their home. They almost always have a severe mistrust of other women. They mistrust any systems."

Can I Trust You With a Life-And-Death Secret?

According to Dr. Hazen, "Pimps have no empathy. They are sociopaths. They lack the capacity to care for another human being. Someone who will go to any length to use another human being for their own benefit or finds himself dependent on women is detached from their own humanity. Often there is no connection to a mother figure. This is someone without the creativity or ability to take care of themselves. This is someone with absolutely no internal resources who is extremely clever, very power hungry, greedy, desperate for control, and both empty and vapid inside.

"If a young person caught up in human trafficking chooses to trust their secrets to you," says Dr. Hazen, "they are literally placing their life in your hands. If the pimp finds out that the victim he is exploiting is talking to you about his machinations, he could have them brutally beaten, injured, or tortured. You might also be putting yourself in danger.

"People are mesmerized by the sensationalism of the life. However, it's imperative to hold people's stories sacred. It's their life in your hands. If you can't keep stuff to yourself, don't do direct service. Pastor, don't use people's names or identifying information in your sermons. The ability to keep confidence is a ministry within itself."

Where Was God When I Was Kidnapped and Turned Out?

According to Dr. Hazen, many of the young women believe God has failed them. "They face a spiritual crisis," she explains. "So many young black girls are being exploited! Generally, most black families have some spiritual practice. So many of the girls are raised in homes where there is faith. So they ask, 'How did God let this happen? Where was God when I was being trafficked over state lines or raped in a hotel room over 14 days? Where was God when I was molested and then thrown out of a moving car?'

"Once they have been rescued from the life, these spiritual questions are very, very painful. They might also ask, 'Where were all these people who said they were Christians? Why did they look at me like that? Why didn't they come out and talk to me? Why didn't they help me? Didn't they see me when they were leaving Bible study at night? How did they just walk by me?'" Those are excellent, relevant questions.

To Seek and Save the Lost

Vanessa Scott has the most engaging laugh. Her giggle is infectious, and when she grins she is all pearl-white teeth. Just by looking at her, you wouldn't know she's a soldier who goes out to the track with a Bible and armed body-guards to rescue commercially sexually exploited children. She didn't come from the streets. It's evident when you listen to the King's English roll off her tongue. In fact, she has a very secure job in corporate America. In her spare time, she teaches dance.

A few years ago, one of her dance students disappeared. She went on a search for her and found that she had become ensnared in human trafficking. Vanessa knew nothing about that world at all, but she was a quick study. She found that she needed $40,000 to help the girl escape the streets and get into to a facility where she would be safely housed for a year.

Over dinner at my favorite Chinese restaurant, Vanessa told me, "My pastor allowed me to get in front of the church one Wednesday. We took an offering for $25,000. The response was an eye-opener. God showed me that He would provide if I stepped out. As it turned out, I found a place that would provide free services and housing to the young woman. I gave all the money back to the generous givers."

Time to Serve

With the help of her pastor, she formed Love Never Fails. Eighty amazing volunteers signed up to help. Vanessa stated, "If each individual would take responsibility for what they can do, we could turn this thing around!"

Vanessa believes that everyone can do something to help. She points to the single mom of four children who is afraid to go out to the streets. Instead, the woman stays home and makes burritos, which the Love Never Fails street team hands out to young women being trafficked on the street.

Love Never Fails has a board member who is in a wheelchair. She loved to do outreach, but occasionally her wheelchair would get caught in the cracks in the broken sidewalks. So she shifted roles and now serves as the organization's accountant.

Vanessa notes that "A large percent of sex buyers come from affluent families in the suburbs. Human trafficking affects that community as well as the inner city. A portion of the suburban community is plagued with the issue and, so, has a responsibility to help crush commercial sexual exploitation. The Great Commission knows no social or economic boundaries. God says, 'Go.' Prepare yourself to do just that. Google the city where you live, and put the word 'Escorts' next to the city name. See what comes back. I guarantee there will be thousands of ads where people are being sold in your very neighborhood."

Is There Anything You Can Do to Help?

The final words on this topic are reserved for Nola Brantley. She says, "Connect kids to adequate resources and networks of support, so that when they age out of foster care they still have support they can rely on in the form of individual relationships with people, agencies, and organizations. They need to know how to build their own families. Out in the world there are do-gooders with resources who will essentially adopt you and do things for you if they understand the importance of investing in those kinds of relationships.

"I definitely see the faith-based community being able to be involved in that kind of care through mentorship and opportunities for housing. It's going to take the faith-based community meeting these young people where they are at and not expecting them to be where you are. Instead of trying to lead by demanding their participation, we need to lead through example. Young people want to be inspired to be of that faith or seek out God because of the example they have been shown, not because you say, 'If you want to be in my house, you have to attend church every Sunday.' After the child sees the Christian caregiver responding through love or patience on a consistent basis, they'll say, 'What is this person about? Because whatever it is, I want to be about it, too!'

"A lot of times we think we can help them; in exchange we demand that they participate in the faith and that will lead them to God. That's just not sustainable. It will lead them to God – until they don't need the help anymore.

The Church's Greatest Challenge?

"I found getting the Christian community to join the fight on behalf of CSEC to be a challenge," said Ms. Brantley. "I find that first and foremost, just as a person who has experienced different types of trauma, I went to many faith-based communities desperate just for someone to be friendly. I'd pray, 'God if this is where I'm supposed to be, reveal that by letting someone show me kindness and welcome.' And it's not revealed. I come in and I go out. Sometimes I'll go somewhere for three or four weeks just to see if someone will notice me and my children and try to offer support to us. It doesn't happen. I could be someone walking in there who was suicidal, but no one would ever try to reach out to me beyond saying, 'Hi, Sister. Welcome to the church.' That's not enough. You have to invite people into your homes, to your groups. Anyone can show up in your faith-based community and be turned away because people are not genuinely reaching out to them.

"You go to church to hear the word of God. But your main objective should not be to socialize with your friends; it should to look for someone you might serve as a bridge. I don't see that happening at church. I see everyone excited about going to church and seeing people that they already know.

"The church talks about God's love, and they talk about God's work, but talking about it and doing it are two different things. If someone comes into the church dressed like a bum, how do the church people treat them? Is that God's example? Is that Jesus's example? That's not every church, because there are some churches that are more social-justice oriented. Some churches are social-justice focused in making sure that their members are educated on social justice, and then there are churches that have members who are social-justice, action-oriented because that all connects into the Bible.

"Praising God and lifting up His name are important, but a little less of that and a little more praise through your deeds in the community to the poor and struggling is what we need. Everything I know about God and everything I feel about Him intuitively would tell me that He would desire us to be out in the community helping people who are struggling. Amen?"

Get Involved!

Nola says, "Human trafficking exists in every state. That's part of what it means to be engaged. Look around and find out what you can do. There are other issues like childhood abuse, sexual abuse, and what's happening to children in the juvenile justice system. When you see drug dealers or robbers, or anyone who does something that we look down on in society, more than likely they had a bad childhood. They've experienced abuse, trauma, and pain."

At any point when you see a young person headed in the wrong direction, you should intervene. It might mean the difference between that person being a loving, productive member of society or a pimp or human trafficker. When it's an older person, you might be relieving pain when you intervene. When you help a young person, you might be preventing it.

Getting Ready for That Conversation at God's Throne

"We are all interrelated as human beings," acknowledges Ms. Brantley, "but a certain amount of finances can keep you in a bubble. If you are able to live in that inflated bubble and not be touched by some of the terrible pain of the world, then you're lucky. And you can live in that world – unless you come into that one-in-a-million chance that someone with a lot of pain tries to rob you and blows your brains out.

"The best thing is to understand that we are all interrelated, and you should step out of that insulated bubble and realize that you might have been raised on a bed of ease. But understand that there are people in this world who have had the exact opposite experience. They were born into suffering, pain, and hunger, and if you care to help them, then you can. But if you don't care to help, then you don't have to, I guess. Some of us who have come from that pain and poverty and who live closer to it and see it everyday might feel more compelled to do something.

"When people from the other world become engaged, sometimes it feels more meaningful to me because they don't have to. We are going to be standing on Judgment Day in front of the Maker of our souls and we will have to be accountable. It's about choices. So do what you may, for your life is not eternal, but your soul is definitely everlasting."

Not a very pretty picture is it? In fact, you're probably deeply disturbed, maybe even mortified. Generations of people have lived lives marred by the aftermath of slavery, social injustice, incarceration, genocide, and oppression. If you've read closely, at some point you've no doubt wondered if there is any way out of this darkness. As a minister of the gospel, I shout in the affirmative: Yes! I believe that when the supernatural anointing that falls from Heaven meets the elbow grease that comes from humankind, miracles happen. And that is what we need isn't it? A miracle?

So do not despair. God is the answer. He has a plan. Part 3 will delve into the theology that undergirds our belief that God is at work in the hood and bids us join in.

Chapter 14

Blessed Are They
Who Thirst

 One of my favorite Public Enemy tracks is a little-known song from the *I Got Game* soundtrack called, "What You Need Is Jesus." The Jesus mentioned in the song is actually a basketball player. The Jesus I'm talking about is, of course, the Son of God. And the question I want to ask is this: Is Jesus Christ concerned about the children forced to live in mayhem and squalor? Can Jesus even relate to their suffering?

Where is Christ in All of This?

Where is the Messiah in the land where infants must inhale the putrid aromas of dried blood and gun smoke? In the back of my mind, I can almost hear him whispering His words recorded in John 12:26a, "If any man serve Me, let him follow Me; and where I am, there shall also My servant be." You may be asking, "Where *are* you, God?" But because your mouth is open and your ears aren't, perhaps you can't hear God when He asks, "Where are *you*, Child?" You see, you are God's hands and feet. And if anything is going to change, in the way that you'd like to see it change, it's going to take you. The term "body of Christ" is more than a theological expression. It's anthropomorphic.

Let me explain it like this. Years back I attended a health-and-wellness event, called Homeless Connect, in San Francisco's Billy Graham Auditorium. The city and its private sector partners sponsored an open house designed to offer resources to those who were without homes and finances. Doctors volunteered for this event. Social workers were there. Even animal care professionals were there to provide veterinary services for the pets brought in by the homeless. However, there was one group of people whose compassion startled me. There were the massage experts who were there to wash and rub the feet of the homeless.

Washing the Feet of the Poor

Homeless people spend a lot of time on their feet, drifting from one locale to another. Sometimes police officers use their night sticks to smack the bottom of the feet of the homeless folks they find sleeping in a public area. If you look closely at a person who has been homeless for a long time, you may notice that they're limping or walking slowly. Bad shoes, wet socks, and endless walking have punished their feet. People who have mental health or severe drug issues may not change their socks or footwear for months.

Imagine yourself sitting down in front of that homeless person like a shoe salesperson would. Now, visualize yourself stripping off their socks, first one and then the other. Can you see the dirt caked around their ankles and against their cuticles? Can you smell the stench? Now, slide that small pan of warm water over between you and the brother or sister you're serving. Good job. Now, scrub their feet clean. Almost instantly the water in the bowl turns jet black.

Once this is done, it's time to massage aching toes, sore arches, and tired insteps. Hear the groans of relief! Welcome to the gospel. This is what it means to be the hands (and knees) of Christ. What? You thought you were joining some kind of social club? No buddy, this is real, and it takes a high level of commitment, humility, sacrifice, and love. Jesus did it. Do you think he expects any less of you?

Woman at the Well

I shall be eternally thankful for the Sunday school teachers who taught me the scriptures in my formative years. They were excellent storytellers who brought the great tales of the Bible to life in vivid Technicolor. Today, one of my favorite stories recalls the chance encounter Jesus had with a woman of questionable reputation at a well. Her background was so well known that she had to draw her water at a different time of day from the other women of the village lest her moral shortcomings prove contagious.

As they say in the hood, Jesus wasn't tripping. He crosses three cultural lines here. First, a rabbi wouldn't have been caught alone conversing with *any* woman in that society about *anything*. Second, she is a Samaritan, a member of a group that most Jewish people roundly despised. And third, she is a woman who lives in open adultery and fornication.

There are so many points that can be raised from this timeless story; however, I'll pick just one. Jesus would never have met this woman had he limited his ministry to the traditional house of worship. When their paths converged, Jesus was outside, in a place where everyday people met.

In Luke 19:10, Jesus said, "For the Son of Man is come to seek and to save that which was lost." The image the scriptures portray of Jesus is of the shepherd who is in the villages, traveling the muddy roads and sitting down at the dinner table with people who today would be gun-runners, drug dealers, pimps, and con artists. He didn't wait in the synagogue for the lost to come and find him. He went out to find the lost sheep. He got intentionally close.

Awhile back, I flew into the Oakland Airport. From a thousand feet in the air, I could make out bridges and some of the taller buildings. Compare that view to the one a person might have from the passenger seat of a moving car. From here street signs are visible and faces are discernible. But there is a third view. Consider what you might encounter should you get out of that car and walk through the neighborhood. On foot you could walk past domino games, vendors selling sweet corn and onion rings, children at play, and cars idling at red lights blasting hip-hop music. On foot, you can blend into the community. Like Jesus at the well, sooner or later you're going to actually have a conversation with someone. As you become a living, breathing part of the social organism, you make yourself vulnerable to be known. That is the root of the evangelistic enterprise. Jesus didn't throw gospel tracts at the woman he met at the well. He didn't start out by preaching. The truth is that Jesus and the woman were two travelers who happened to meet at a well in the course of day-to-day life. God took it from there.

In the 21st century, the church's paradigm has shifted. The preacher closes the church service with the phrase, "The doors of the church are open ..." as he or she extends the call for those without Christ to meet them in the altar. However, the model Jesus Christ demonstrated – the servant out in the streets, seeking to save the lost – has largely disintegrated. Evangelism is often a niche ministry, not the driving mission, or central purpose of the body.

Jesus' personal mission was full of vitality. Because he was constantly interacting with the people he was sent to save, there were always interesting stories and encounters. When the church loses its desire to go out beyond its walls, it loses the vitality that creates the great and timeless stories of God's intervention in human affairs. You get to see that only when you're obedient to God's commands.

Blessed are They Who Thirst

One of the first things I realized as I walked the lonely streets of East Oakland was that many of the people in the hood truly desired a relationship with a Savior whose transforming love could meet them right where they were. I met people, young and old, who had a thirst to meet God.

Take Shelly, a young lady trapped in the world of prostitution. We met as I was waiting for the bus at the corner of East 85th Avenue near International Boulevard. She was waiting as well, but not for the bus. I struck up a conversation about the weather, which soon drifted over to the goodness of God. She loved God. She recited verse after verse from the Bible. She'd grown up in a Christian home, but somewhere along the way, someone or something had lured her out here into this netherworld.

I asked her if she had a prayer request that I could lift up before the Lord for her. Her answer filled one word: "deliverance." Just then an elderly gentleman in a lime green knock-off Polo shirt pulled up in a Jaguar and rolled down his window. After 30 seconds of conversation, Shelly hopped in. Her prayer request hung in the air. "Deliverance." She was thirsty for it.

I remember watching two children crouching in the weeds in front of young evangelists in a glass-strewn field in the middle of a ghetto. Between them was a worn Bible-story book that someone might well have thrown out. The kids sat open-mouthed as the evangelists taught the story of Jesus' life from the tattered picture book. The young kids were thirsty.

The Thirst

In these streets when they say that someone is thirsty, it means that person has a desperate craving. Most often the phrase is connected with an addiction to drugs. However, I've met people caught up in the darkest things who still have a thirst for God. I've met known drug dealers who spend all Saturday evening selling their product and then close up in time to make the 11:00 a.m. service at a local church.

I asked two of them why they would shut down business to go to church on Sunday morning, which is seemingly in direct contradiction to the way they live their lives. Neither knew the other, and yet they both gave the same answer: "Rev, everybody wanna hear what God got to say."

God is at work in the hood. Look closely. You'll hear him speak through the mouth of a child at a taco stand. God has spoken to me through a homeless man with an alcohol addiction who sits on the corner of East 84th and International Boulevard in East Oakland.

Introducing Ghetto Storm

In the hood, nicknames, handles, aliases, street names, and monikers are most often bestowed upon an individual by peers or some revered elder, and they usually highlight some unique characteristic or behavior. Many on the street are known only by their handle. There are a number of reasons for this; foremost might be that monikers give us the opportunity to reinvent ourselves.

Street names also make it easier for one involved in shady dealings to slip into the landscape without detection. If the police ask questions, the only name snitches know you by is "82nd Avenue Shorty," "AK," "True," or "Bullet."

Take for instance a thug I'll call "Ghetto Storm." *"Thug!* How dare you, Reverend?" I can hear you shouting from the back of the choir loft. Not to worry. The designation "thug" is not an insult here in the heart of East Oakland. To the contrary, some wear that badge with pride.

However, to hang the title "snitch," "informer," or "cooperative witness" on someone down here in the killing fields is another story. But thug? Even if Ghetto Storm knew that I was referring to him as such, it wouldn't upset him. And he won't know. You see, he goes by another nickname, one that would be instantly recognizable both in the badlands and in the penitentiaries. It's so recognizable; in fact, that I've decided not to use it here.

I remember the first time I became aware of this brother's presence in the streets. I was working as a case manager for a program that assisted recently released prisoners in their efforts to reintegrate into society. One day during my lunch break a co-worker asked to walk with me to my favorite soul-food spot.

If you spend enough time in the hood, you can feel trouble approaching. It's like the drops of mist that wet your brow moments before the monsoon. Sure enough, a few feet away from the restaurant's front door, I saw two young men hollering and pointing at each other. A tall, wiry fellow who looked like he could have been a small forward for an NBA team bent down to nose level with a muscular fireplug of a man. Three or four other men stood on the periphery goading them on. And then I saw it. The shorter man dipped his shoulder. It was a move that you've seen a thousand times on ESPN sports highlights during a face-off between a couple boxers in a ring. That man's shoulder dip was followed by a mighty left hook. The taller man went flying. He lay sprawled out on the cold pavement like a dead fish.

The shorter fellow stood over the prone body and raised his arms in victory. His ecstatic well-wishers pounded him on the back. "Yeah! You showed that nigga whass up!" they roared. You could hear someone rapping along with old school hip-hop artist Big Daddy, "Got beef? You better save it for the m.f.'ing meat market... ."

My co-worker looked on, mortified. We never did get our fried catfish and French fries that day. Ghetto Storm and his war party were blocking the restaurant entrance. Plus, we'd have had to step over the loser's horizontal frame to get inside. It just didn't seem worth it.

Not long after this event, Ghetto Storm and I met for the first time. He confronted me on a street corner not a block away from the church I attend. As good fortune would have it, Ghetto Storm has a profound and genuine respect for preachers. I don't know if he's ever said the prayer of faith. However, he believes deeply in Jesus Christ. If that were not enough to blow your mind, Ghetto Storm can recite long passages of the Bible verbatim. The Storm and I became instant friends. His face would light up when he saw me. This made walking through the hood in a traditional preacher's suit much less dangerous. Ghetto Storm told brothers who frequented local corners scoping for prey that I was his uncle. I can't tell you how far that went in the lawless streets where people fear and respect so precious little.

One day, Ghetto Storm followed me into a local grocery store. As soon as he set the toe of his Air Jordan sneaker down inside the front door, the owner picked up the phone and started hollering for the police. I found that strange. Ghetto Storm hadn't said, "Stick 'em up," "Break yo'self, fool!" "Reach for the sky!" or even "Hello." His eyes had not even met the owner's, and yet the proprietor's eyes grew wide with terror as he begged the police to hurry. I coaxed Ghetto Storm into leaving that day, but that gave me some idea as to who he was in the streets.

Searching for Jesus

"Ghetto Storm, why don't you come to my church on Sunday?" I asked him one sunny day.

"I do come to your church, Rev."

That shocked me. And I knew it was true, because he was not the type to lie about something like that.

"I've never see you there."

"I stand up way in the back. I just stand there for awhile. I listen, and then I walk out."

And then one day he was gone. Ghetto Storm simply disappeared for three years. In Oakland, the second most dangerous city in the entire country, when someone vanishes without a trace, they have usually ended up in one of two places – the graveyard or the penitentiary. For the Storm, it was the latter.

Ghetto Storm Re-emerges

Awhile back, I got into a quarrel with someone at church. Don't get me wrong. I'm not a troublemaker. The thing is, I never seem to fit in. I don't like wearing a suit. I never get the lingo and the handshake right. I like hip-hop way more than traditional gospel music. And I tend to ask too many questions – questions that can make people feel uncomfortable. Questions that might start or end with the phrase: "What's the point of this?"

I had royally angered someone at church on that hot summer's morning. It sort of put a cloud over the entire morning for me. After service, I left the church building headed for the fish and chips spot down the boulevard. On the way there, I waved at lost men and women who sat on milk crates watching the endless flow of traffic drift by. In less than ten minutes from the time I had walked away from the church, I reached my destination. I ordered the chicken wing and catfish combo, and then I sat down with my back to the door – a serious no-no, as I said earlier. It didn't take long for my order to come up. I swallowed the fish, and I was breaking apart a chicken wing when a voice behind me forced me to quickly turn my head toward the door. Someone had come through the door half begging, half intimidating people for money.

It had been at least three years. His face had grown rounder. He was missing a few of his bottom front teeth on the left side. I called out his name. He squinted. He's nearsighted, I observed. "Rev!" he called. He crossed the room in two steps. I stood up. He squeezed me so hard my ribs hurt. When I stepped back, he said, "I love you, Rev!"

Instantly, my mind went back to the encounter I'd had at church earlier that day. I had been all but cussed out by a saint. But here, in the heart of the ghetto, a freshly released ex-convict was wrapping his arms around me in front of a room full of people, saying that he loved me.

As a dining room full of perfumed, suited, and booted churchgoers looked on horrified and mystified, I said, "Tell me a scripture, Ghetto Storm." Jaws dropped all around as he quoted flawlessly from the book of Proverbs.

A Preacher Should Never Be Without a Sermon

I still run into Ghetto Storm every once in awhile, though never in a church building. Over the years, he developed a ritual. When he appears, usually out of nowhere, he says, "Reverend, what's the word for the day?" That's my cue to start preaching right there on the sidewalk. Early in our relationship, I was startled by that question one afternoon. I honestly couldn't think of anything to say. I'll never forget that day. It was the only time I've ever seen him angry (at me). He turned on his heel and muttered, "A preacher should always have a word."

You might be thinking that people in the hood are not interested in the words of Jesus. If you've arrived at that conclusion, you're as wrong as two left shoes. There's a thirst for the words of Jesus. There is hunger for hope, from the cradle to the senior citizens' home.

If you feel a calling to reach out to people who are thirsty, you need answer only two questions: first, are you willing to put the truth into forms that people can understand (see the parables of Jesus); and second, are you willing to take your faith to the places where people need it most? Dangerous places. Places where people are thirsty for the living water.

Chapter 15

Toward a Reasoned Faith

 Do you want to make a difference in the hood? You're going to need Jesus, point blank and hands down. You're going to need a direct line to the Son of God who walked on the stormy waters and puffed the breath of resurrection into dead lungs.

Jesus and Hood Religion

There was no antiseptic or baby powder in the stall where He was birthed. When they smacked His bottom, the first thing He inhaled was the scent of cow droppings. Jesus' parents were too poor to offer the traditional temple birth offering of a lamb. Instead, they had to settle for the sacrifice of the poor: two pigeons. The Son of God was another brown baby born into the lap of crippling poverty.

Mary and Joseph were not alone in their economic struggles. Ancient Israel was a place of rampant poverty. Jesus' neighbors and friends worked like dogs to pay Rome's soul-crushing tax burden. Eventually, personal debt would grow so large that farms that had been in the family for generations would be confiscated, leaving the former owners landless and destitute.

Needless to say, anger brewed in the streets and alleys of ancient Israel as rootless men without work collected in the shadows unable to feed their families. Terrorists with long daggers concealed under their cloaks would follow to the great temple rich people who cooperated with the Romans. They would inch their way through the crowds, sidle up to the mogul, and in an instant run him through with the weapon before melting back into the crowd unnoticed. Revolutionaries gave speeches that called for insurrection and the overthrow of Rome. Coming of age in a hood called "Lower Galilee," Jesus would more than likely have known of these figures personally and perhaps even heard their speeches.

You see, Jesus grew up on the wrong side of the tracks. Many of the people that came up with Him more than likely became bandits and gangsters who did what they felt they had to do to survive. When Phillip marveled that he had found the Christ, his friend Nathaniel smirked, "What good thing can come out of Nazareth?" That was not said lightly. Jesus was from the hood. Jesus would have recognized any of the scenarios painted for you previously in this book.

Blessed are the Poor ...

Among His most quoted teachings is the phrase, "Blessed are the poor, for theirs is the kingdom of God." Jesus would later say of Himself, "Foxes have holes. Birds of the air have nests, but the Son of Man hath nowhere to lay His head." This is the textbook definition of homelessness.

It was prophesied of Him, "He was despised and rejected – a man of sorrows, acquainted with deepest grief. We turned our backs on Him and looked the other way." At the end of His earthly journey, Jesus was laid down in a borrowed tomb. He lived and died a poor man.

Jesus' teachings expressed God's special concern for the poor. In Luke 16, Jesus tells the story of a man who lived a life of conspicuous consumption. He was known far and wide for his great wealth. His banquets were a thing to behold. At these extravaganzas, the chef carved up fine meats for members of the in crowd.

In the ancient world, bread scraps were used like napkins. The revelers would wipe the grease and food particles from their lips and beards with pieces of bread. Servants would fill baskets with these bread scraps and then take them out to the beggars at the gate.

Poor Lazarus. Life hadn't treated him as well as the rich landowner. His ravaged skeletal frame was bent over and covered with festering sores. His greatest treat in life was to receive the bread scraps that fell from the rich man's table. The only relief from his misery happened when stray dogs wandered by to lick the pus from his bumpy, knotted flesh infected with leprosy.

One day they died, the rich man and Lazarus. There is no mention as to what creed they adhered to or where they worshiped on earth. It simply says that the rich man lifted up his eyes from the flaming pit of Hades, while Lazarus was comforted in the bosom of Abraham, the most favored place a person of the Jewish faith could imagine.

Why hadn't the rich man tried to bridge the gap between himself and the poor man during life on earth? That is one of the mysteries of all time. Jesus doesn't spend time in the scripture trying to unravel it. He simply gives them their eternal room assignments. Apparently, the fact that someone with great means and wealth walked by a man who was impoverished on a daily basis was enough to condemn him to the great fire that is never quenched.

In America, the poor don't have to sit down at our doorsteps. Internet and cable television can beam them right into our living rooms. We might not hear them crying or see them cringing in dark corners, shivering from the cold night winds, but we know they're out there. We see them every time we touch the TV clicker. We see them on the 6 o'clock news. Their stories are made into TV dramas, documentaries, even reality shows. Even when we can't see them, we sense them out there, somewhere in the dark, struggling for life as we wrap up in our favorite quilt and wait for our Earl Grey Lavender tea to simmer in the pot. In some ways we are even worse than the rich man in the story. God help us.

Jesus and the Marginalized

Biblical scholars argue about what these preachments about God's concern for the poor mean. Some say they don't refer to people in material poverty but those who are impoverished in some strictly spiritual sense. It's hard for these Biblical contortionists to convince us that they mean other than what Jesus stated. There are just too many of them.

In Matthew 25, Jesus gives a powerful picture of the great day of judgment. Those who will inherit are separated into camps by the angels and labeled the sheep and the goats. He refers to the ones who attend to the needs of the poor as the righteous. Theirs is the Kingdom of Heaven.

And then there is mention of those who failed to attend to the needs of the impoverished. Christ says, "Then He will say to those on His left, 'Depart from me, you who are cursed, into the eternal fire prepared for the devil and his angels. For I was hungry and you gave me nothing to eat, I was thirsty and you gave me nothing to drink, I was a stranger and you did not invite me in. I needed clothes and you did not clothe me, I was sick and in prison and you did not look after me.'

"They also will answer, 'Lord, when did we see you hungry or thirsty or a stranger or needing clothes or sick or in prison, and did not help you?'

"He will reply, 'Truly I tell you, whatever you did not do for one of the least of these, you did not do for Me.'

"Then they will go away to eternal punishment, but the righteous to eternal life."

Jesus' meaning is clear. Real religion consists of meeting the physical needs of people who have little. It consists of putting clothes on the back of people who are struggling. For Jesus, relationship with God causes a believer to create connection with people who are incarcerated. Jesus sees Himself and feels the very essence of who He is while staring into the tattooed face of the gang member or the tears of the homeless.

Does Jesus say, "When you did it to one of these, it was *like* you did it to Me?" No, the phrase is much more personal. To shower kindness on the abandoned is to do the kindness to Jesus. To ignore them (or worse) is actually to ignore the Messiah's suffering.

The Friend Of Sinners

Jesus received some of his most virulent criticism over the company He kept. In fact, He was called the "friend of sinners." Jesus' choice of company was such that it caused His religious contemporaries to marvel at His sheer nerve. Jesus befriended tax collectors who were widely viewed as notorious cheats, extortionists, and Jewish traitors. Today, Jesus' friends and the object of His missionary efforts would be crystal meth chemists and back alley gamblers.

To share a meal with someone in the ancient world was a sacred thing. Some referred to the meal table as an altar. The scriptures tell us that Jesus sat down to eat with people like Zaccheus and Matthew, which would have been a serious breach of rabbinical law. Hebrews did not sit down to eat with common criminals or people they did not respect. Because of the sacred nature of the sit down (or rather reclining) dinner in that time, one can easily understand what people would say if they saw Jesus passing the fried chicken and collard greens to known hood figures and ex-felons.

Christian friends I have a question for you. If the Jesus you serve went out of His way to reach people who were caught up in all types of hood life, why don't you? If Jesus didn't think He was too good to sit down at a prostitute's dinner table, why aren't these same people sitting down in the fellowship hall at your church? If Jesus went out of His way to share the good news with thugs and gangsters, why do you cross the street when you see them and then talk about how bad they are from your pulpit, Christian? If you identify that closely with the Jesus in the scriptures that you read, it looks like you might come out of that suit, lace up some sneakers, and go shake hands with those boys with the bandanas hanging out of their back pockets. Take some fat sandwiches and sodas with you when you do it. They'll appreciate that. And you don't necessarily have to preach. Just the fact that you introduced yourself and showed up with some goodies will be enough for now. You've created a bridge between your fort and the occupied territory. Keep working at it. It'll change them, and equally important, it'll change you.

Touching the Untouchable

Mark 1:40-45 recounts the story of an encounter Jesus had with a man afflicted with leprosy. Leprosy, as we know it, was rare or non-existent in Jesus' time. More than likely, the man had something like psoriasis. However, this disease made the man ritually unclean. He could not enter the sacred temple. The leper was forbidden from making flesh-to-flesh contact with adherents of the Jewish faith. He was cut off from his wife and children. His condition, through no fault of his own, made him an outcast.

One day, the poor man, probably in rags, falls down in Jesus' path. He looks up from his knees and proclaims, "If you are willing, you can make me clean." Jesus looks down at the man, so overcome with compassion, that He reaches out to touch him. "I am willing," Jesus said. "Be clean." To touch him was to share his fate as an outsider, an outcast, a rejected one, but Jesus, the Creator, knew that the need for human touch is powerful. Who knows how long the leper had been forced to live without it?

After Jesus touches the man, He sends him out with a stern warning. "See that you don't tell this to anyone," He said. "But go, show yourself to the priest and offer the sacrifices that Moses commanded for your cleansing, as a testimony to them."

The ecstatic man did not follow this command. The scriptures say: "Instead, he went out and began to talk freely, spreading the news. As a result, Jesus could no longer enter a town openly but stayed outside in lonely places." By touching that outsider, the perception of uncleanliness now passed on to Jesus. However, it did not slow His ministry one bit. The passage goes on to say, "Yet the people still came to Him from everywhere."

The Touch That Heals Outsiders

Once you start touching gang members, women trapped in human trafficking, homeless people, and the addicted, people will start avoiding you, too. You see, they'll start looking at you as one of them.

Years ago, I served as a minister to the homeless in a church in New Jersey. A crew of homeless people frequented the downtown area. Most of them have since passed away, but back in the late '90s, they became like family to me. One day, I ran into one of the crew on my way to breakfast. Thank God there was enough money in the wallet to feed both of us that morning.

As we started into McDonald's I saw a group of my fellow church members marching in my direction, suited and booted. You could smell the expensive perfume wafting across the morning air. "Good morning, family!" I shouted. They didn't turn around. It was if they hadn't heard me. But how could that have been? I was only a few feet away. I tried again, but still they ignored me, marching past as if I were invisible. I was puzzled. And then I looked at my friend. His hair was matted. His clothes were caked with dirt, and he was unshaven. He had terrible body odor.

Later that morning I had an epiphany. After I'd parted company with my friend (for some reason, he didn't want to come to church with me), I saw the same clique. They hugged me like I was a long, lost relative. I was hardly as friendly. I took the attitude, if you don't want my friends, then you don't want me. Maybe that's what Jesus was saying in Matthew 25.

The Kingdom of God

Jesus went to a people who were living beneath the boot heel of Roman oppression and preached that, with His coming, the Kingdom of Heaven had broken into human history. When Peter expressed his belief that Jesus was the long awaited Messiah whom it was prophesied would usher in the Kingdom, Jesus said, "Flesh and blood hath not revealed this to thee but My Father who is in heaven."

The scripture says that Jesus went to Nazareth, where He had been brought up, and on the Sabbath day he went into the synagogue, as was His custom. He stood up to read, and the scroll of the prophet Isaiah was handed to Him. Unrolling it, He found the place where it is written:

"The Spirit of the Lord is on me,
    because he has anointed me
    to proclaim good news to the poor.

> He has sent me to proclaim freedom for the prisoners
> and recovery of sight for the blind,
> to set the oppressed free,
> to proclaim the year of the Lord's favor."

Jesus' message, which harkened back to Isaiah, was revolutionary indeed. First, Jesus is sent to proclaim good news to the poor. What is that good news? Is it that the day is coming when the playing field between the very rich and the very poor will be made smooth? Is it that a kingdom is coming where there will be no more hunger, no more homelessness?

Jesus proclaims a day where slaves would be liberated and the sick made well. Jesus is proclaiming a time when the oppressed will be set free. Finally, He makes a reference to the year of Jubilee, a time when debts are forgiven, slaves are emancipated, and the title deeds handed back to families who had lost them.

A Revolutionary's Death

Death by crucifixion is one of the most brutal measures ever imposed upon a human being. But there Jesus hung, writhing on the cross between two known criminals. Historian E.P. Sanders notes: "[They might have been] robbers, bandits, or highwaymen, interested only in their own profit, but who also may have been insurgents, whose banditry had a political aim."[1]

The man in the middle had not been accused of any such charge. The sign above his head said simply, "King of the Jews." Jesus did not bear a crown of thorns nor have a Roman spear thrust through his side because of his theological beliefs. The designation "King of the Jews" was a political one. He was executed as a criminal of the state.

The Jewish nation was a vassal state subject to the massive and mighty Roman Empire. The Jews did not bear the yoke easily. The nationalist gatherings were often cauldrons of discontent that caused the Romans to look on with a wary eye. Sanders writes: "The Roman prefect and additional troops came to Jerusalem during the major festivals to ensure that the huge crowds did not get out hand. Public assemblies were, on the whole, carefully watched in the ancient world, and the festivals in Jerusalem were known to be hazardous. During the 150 or so years before Jesus' death, we know of at least four substantial upheavals that began during a festival – this despite the fact that both Jewish and Roman rulers were prepared for trouble and had forces nearby."

Into this highly volatile atmosphere enters one Galilean prophet who cannot be silenced or bought, a religious figure operating outside the control and influence of the state-sanctioned priesthood whose primary message concerns His coming kingdom. When this prophet proclaims that the temple will one day be brought down to cinders, when He overturns the tables of the moneychangers in the courtyards, His days are numbered.

Sanders writes: "The range of legal disputes between Jesus and others was well within the parameters of normal debate, and there is no reason at all to think that they were in conflict…. Conceivably Jesus opposed Pharisaic views about what produce was foodstuff and should be tithed (Matt 23:23), but such criticisms were not matters of life and death…. Caiphas had Jesus arrested because of his responsibility to put down trouble-makers, especially during festivals – this corresponds perfectly with all the evidence."[2]

Jesus claimed to be the Alpha and the Omega, the very Son of God. However, that was not why the Roman government executed Him. Jesus was crucified as a political dissident.

What Does This Mean For Us?

Jesus was born an outsider, a poor man. He preached a message of a kingdom where equity and fairness would be restored, where debts would be forgiven, where peace would reign, and where food and justice would exist in abundance for all. Jesus associated with the abandoned and the forgotten, and He cared deeply about the incarcerated. In the Lord's Prayer Jesus is quoted as saying, "Thy kingdom come. Thy will be done on earth as it is in heaven." This meant that the Kingdom of God had broken into human history through His coming, and if justice was the normative in heaven, then we had to fight for it on earth. Jesus told stories of people who faced eternal damnation because they ignored the suffering of people on earth.

Jesus talked across to people, not down at them. He never had to say, "I love you." Love was coming out of the pores of His skin. Anybody who was around Him for any appreciable amount of time felt it. He also partnered with the very people He came to minister to. It was never "us and them." Everyone was treated with dignity, whether they were naked and poor or possessed great wealth like the rich young ruler.

Often, when we serve the poor, we act as though we're doing them a favor. And it's not hard to figure out when someone doesn't see you as an equal but as a beggar, a "less than," or a street urchin who is lucky that they've become the beneficiary of your largesse.

Years ago, I was assigned as the minister to my home church's ministry to the homeless. I arrived that first day with my 20-pound King James Version, ready to do work. I walked up to Deacon Brenda Woods, the lady in charge, and asked, "Are you ready for me to deliver the Word?" She was so gracious. So humble. She said, "Brother Harry, we really don't need that right now. I'll tell you what. Why don't you just go over there and sit down with the folks? Go sit down with them, and I'll bring you some food. Talk to them. Get to know them. You eat with them."

I'll never forget that day. It changed my life. For you see, I was no longer the messenger of God charged with an assignment to deliver a message to sinners. I saw myself as one of those sinners, albeit saved by grace. There was no difference between them and me. After that first meal together, when I walked down the street those people hollered at me because they knew my name.

I believe that the Bible is the inspired word of God. Jesus' personal example shows a God who touched people, who fed people, who healed the sick, who embraced children. He never said, "Don't worry about all that because when you get to Heaven, all of those things will be taken care of." That's slave religion. No, Jesus never went there. He met the needs of the suffering and the abandoned in the present.

Meet The Needs ... All Of The Needs

The truth is if you don't follow Jesus' example, you'll never have any street cred. People in the hood might even scorn you. First, you have to talk to people like they're human (like you). That's rule number one. And if a member of your team isn't following rule number one, grab them by the arm, pull them in a back room somewhere, and say "(excuse my hood vernacular), we ain't doin' it this way potna. If you can't talk to these people the way you'd want someone to talk to you, pack it up and go home. I'll catch you on Sunday." Sure, they'll be mad as hell. But I'd rather endure their anger than God's wrath.

Once you start addressing the issues that confront the hood, like mass incarceration and child hunger, on a consistent basis and without an agenda, you'll have everybody's attention. You can't divorce life in the hereafter from life in the here and now. You can't separate eternal life from hood life. It's not Biblical, and it's unrealistic.

Undeniable Love

Once folks can feel genuine love and mercy pouring out of the pores of your flesh like sweat, they'll listen. I don't care if you have purple skin and orange eyes; once people figure out that you're real in those areas, you're pretty much guaranteed a good listen.

And real love can't be faked. One day, I was dressed in jeans and a T-shirt, serving food in a soup kitchen when a homeless gentleman said, "Say, you're a minister aren't you?" I was startled. I said, "Why yes, how did you know?" He said, "I can always tell the difference between religion and bull s——." And that pretty much sums it up, doesn't it?

The Whole Counsel of Scripture in Relevant Religion

Whenever I'm scheduled to be interviewed for a radio show, I like to be huddled up inside in a quiet place like the sanctuary of my bedroom. It's like the radio host is the pitcher and the stands are filled with thousands of unseen people rooting for me to hit or strike out. In these moments, I'm a batter trying to hit curve balls out of the park. So, I can't abide distractions.

Not long ago, I was scheduled to be interviewed, but I couldn't get home in time. So I pulled up to a bench in San Francisco's Yerba Buena Park and called the station at the pre-appointed time. The producer greeted me, and then I was put on hold. The radio show played through my iPhone. I could tell immediately that the talk show host was a conservative. Even the commercials seemed to follow the party line.

Finally, my host introduced me. I was on the air. Her first few questions gave me an insight into her view of the African-American community. I heard the usual code words: "violent," "lazy," and "ignorant." Her remedy was something like, "They just need to read the gospels."

I sat back on a concrete bench, took a breath, and looked straight ahead. It happened that I was seated across from a huge manmade waterfall. Religious symbols are few and far between in San Francisco, but the creation of the waterfall that flows night and day on Mission Street was inspired by the words of God, as spoken through the prophet Amos. "But let justice roll down like waters / And righteousness like an ever-flowing stream."

For the news commentator, true faith centered solely on the Ten Commandments, soul salvation, and the after-life. Her theology did not offer legitimate answers to some questions. For instance, what did the Bible have to say to the black man living in the Oakland hood who will live 20 years less on average than a wealthy Asian man living in the city's most posh Zip Code? What does the Bible say to the mother with the tears running down her face as she dresses her children to attend schools with ill-prepared teachers and defaced textbooks?

The Answer in That Waterfall

Amos was a shepherd, not a theologian, when he felt the call of God upon his life. He took a walk around an afflu-ent Israel and found himself appalled. The words of Almighty God burned in his chest and eventually came pouring out of his mouth. Apparently, God was incensed at the great disparity between the rich and the poor. He used the prophet to rail against the rich who used and exploited people without power and means. Amos said that if justice didn't begin to fall like a waterfall, God's wrath was going to pour through the street.

For Amos, there was no line of demarcation between the otherworldly aspects of religion and daily societal life. Amos, the prophet, quotes God as saying, "For I know how many are your offenses and how great your sins. There are those who oppress the innocent and take bribes and deprive the poor of justice in the courts."

In his book, *Amos Among The Prophets*, author Robert B. Cootes says, "The elite own not only the land but also the peasants, in varying degrees of serfdom and slavery. Even when peasants own the land they work, they often find it difficult to maintain their independence or to survive.... To this ruling class Amos announces: God will answer your war against the peasantry with war against you and turn your festivity into lamentation."[3]

God was so incensed by the unequal distribution of wealth and corruption in the court system that he promised the nation that it would fall to invaders if change did not come. What's interesting to note is that God doesn't point out individuals. God is angry about a sin that has been allowed to fester in Israel's system of economics and governance. Because Israel has allowed the rich to get fat and the poor to be cheated and hungry, the whole nation will be judged, according to Amos.

If God is angry at the disparity of wealth and its distribution in America, God is not just looking at the top 1 percent; God's rage will be poured out on America, period. It might start at the church because we have the Bible – we know how things are supposed to go but we choose to systemically ignore the things that burn God up.

Sin is in the Machine

If you ask Christians to define "sin," most would define it using a laundry list of transgressions. A child walks into a candy store and slips a Snickers bar into his pocket. A driver breaks the speed limit because he's late for work. A grandfather mutters a cuss word when the pitcher is behind in the count in the bottom of the ninth.

Ron Sider, author of *One-Sided Christianity* writes, "Since we are social beings created for community, we simply cannot be all God wants us to be if we live in evil social systems. That is not to forget that even the most oppressed person can accept Christ and be on the way to eternal life. But the slave, oppressed laborer, or malnourished woman cannot fully enjoy the dignity, freedom, and wholeness intended by the Creator."[4]

On April 12, 2015, Freddy Gray, a 25-year-old resident of one of Baltimore, Maryland's most impoverished communities locked eyes with a member of the local police department. A chase ensued. Somewhere between the time he was arrested and the time the police van arrived at its destination, Gray suffered a partially severed spinal cord injury. He lapsed into a coma and died seven days later. It was determined that Gray had committed no crime. Still, his life was stolen from him.

Baltimore exploded into flames and rioting following Gray's alleged murder. Television cameras on the scene beamed the images of local residents proclaiming that police brutality was a constant reality in their world. They also showed America multitudes of poor black people on an island of poverty surrounded by an ocean of boarded-up and foreclosed houses. Limited educational opportunities, chronic poverty, crumbling housing, and crippling violence have created a cauldron of anger and frustration in the city.

Baltimore is plagued by sin, not just personal sin but societal sin – sin that is in the machine that serves all of its citizens. The city is cursed with inequality clogged into the systems that determine the distribution of resources. It is sin in the hearts of people who benefit from a system that denies others the right to a livable wage, decent housing, good health care, or a competitive education. It is sin.

Some of us benefit directly from this sin; however, all of us participate in it to some extent.

Kalief Browder, 16 years old, was arrested and accused of stealing a backpack. Although he never stood trial or was ever found guilty of any crime, he spent three years in one the most dangerous incarceration centers in the entire country, New York City's notorious Riker's Island jail. He spent most of those years in soul crushing solitary confinement. Cameras captured two vicious beatings. One was administered by a prison guard; the second shows him being beaten by a gang of inmates as guards seemed powerless to stop it.

Earlier I observed that too often the skill of the lawyer, not guilt or innocence, is what wins the day in a courtroom. Young Kalief's family could not afford a "pay lawyer" to help free their loved one. Kalief refused the D.A.'s offer to plead to a lesser charge, insisting on his innocence. Finally, after three years the charges were dropped in their entirety and Kalief was sent home.

Kalief struggled to make up for lost time. He got his high school diploma and then enrolled in college. However, the struggle of those three years had broken something inside young Kalief. At the age of 22, he hanged himself in his parents' apartment.

Kalief was killed by a system that is broken, racist, and corrupt, a system that feeds on the flesh and blood of poor people, especially people of color. It stands opposite to everything that the Kingdom of God represents. It is our system. The question is, do we just turn away and say, "It's not my fault" or do we take ownership for Kalief's death? Do we do research on the events that lead to Kalief Browder's death? Do we write to the officials at the Riker's Island jail? Do we contact elected officials who have direct access to the controls of change? Do we get a petition going? Or do we simply turn the page and say,

"Rev, I ain't got nuthin' to do with all that. Stuff happens."

Kalief was killed by our sin, sin that is encased and entrapped in the structure of our system. Does it fall upon us to ask forgiveness? Does it fall upon us to do what we can to fix it? Especially you, Pastor?

In Isaiah 58, the prophet speaks for God, who addresses the ineffectiveness of their fasting rituals. God offers a new way. In verse 7, God says through the prophet, "Is not this the kind of fasting I have chosen: to loose the chains of injustice and untie the cords of the yoke, to set the oppressed free and break every yoke? Is it not to share your food with the hungry and to provide the poor wanderer with shelter; when you see the naked, to clothe them, and not to turn away from your own flesh and blood?"

Bible Truth for Our Times

What would the chains of injustice that need unloosening look like in the 21st century? Would it be the court system that hamstrings and shackles the dark and the poor at a rate unheard of anywhere else in the civilized world? Would it be the income and wage disparity or unequal education systems? Are these the chains that God is calling you to break? Who are the oppressed that need to be free? Do you share your food with the poor or work to get shelter for the homeless while you are fasting? Do you share your goods with those who have no coat or shoes? It is impossible to cross this out of the Bible. Jesus Christ came from this prophetic tradition – and he lived it.

Politics and Faith

A few years ago, I was invited to be a keynote speaker at a conference on human trafficking. At the time, I headed an organization called the Street Disciples, whose charter was to minister to women caught up in human trafficking and domestic violence. I was excited about speaking at this symposium. It was to be held at one of the most highly regarded institutions of higher learning in California.

The auditorium was packed. The young people had been fasting for the victims of human trafficking for a week. When I walked in, a riveting play about commercial sexual exploitation was in progress. Finally, I was introduced and took my place behind the lectern. The first half of the lecture went well, at least as I remember. And then I said something that caused the audience to stare quietly in amazement and eventually to break out laughing, as though I'd made a joke.

I had outlined four clear-cut ways to defeat human trafficking. Number four was politics. The young people broke out laughing when this hood preacher said that. What did personal politics have to do with religion? I broke it down like this: 1) Politics, at its core, concerns itself with the equitable distribution of resources; 2) Anywhere in the world where human trafficking flourishes, you will find poverty; and 3) One way to make a difference is to find out where the politicians you support stand on supplying educational, medical, and employment resources to areas where youth susceptible to human trafficking live.

Some of you don't agree with me. You believe that if we pass out enough copies of the "Four Spiritual Laws" or lay hands on enough people, the problems will crumble before us. I believe in both fasting and prayer ... deeply. I believe in repentance and soul salvation. I believe in the laying on of hands. However, I also believe that we have to broaden our pool of answers to the complicated problems that poor people face, not only in America's hoods, but all over the world.

Separation of Church and State?

My young friends at that prestigious university laughed because they had been taught about the line of separation of church and state. Isn't that what Jesus commanded when he said, "Render unto Caesar the things that are Caesar's, and unto God the things that are God's"? Dr. Leann Fletcher is the Academic Dean and Old Testament professor at the American Baptist Seminary of the West at the Graduate Theological Union in Berkeley, California. During an interview for this book, the noted theologian said, "In ancient Israel, the kingship and the priesthood were so intertwined that you could not separate them. The king is constantly involved with the priests. He looked to the priests for guidance before he went to war.

"In the New Testament, the Jesus movement exists in the midst of the Roman Empire. The Jewish nation had existed under foreign domination 600 years by the time that Jesus grows to adulthood. When Jesus says, 'Render under Caesar what belongs to Caesar and to God what belongs to God,' he is speaking within the context of the times. Jewish customs are still alive and strong and being lived out on a daily basis by this subgroup of the Roman Empire. *Pax Romana* (the peace of Rome) is brought about by the sword. If you start coloring outside of the lines, the troops will hunt you down and cut your head off. You have to stay in line with Roman laws in order to live a peaceful life. The Jewish population at this time has to toe the line as concerning Rome and at the same time be faithful to their own traditions.

"The Roman emperor had his own cult and at one time in history, if you refused to bow to his godship, there were negative consequences. Because of the strength of the Jewish traditions, some soldiers would burst into Jewish homes, request the sacred manuscripts, and then take them to be burned. So here, Jesus is saying, 'You have certain things that you must do to stay in harmony with

Rome, and then there is a temple with a Jewish government and rule.'"

Notes on a Preacher/Politician

Reverend Dr. Andrew Park is a native son of Oakland, a second-generation Korean-American and a founding pastor of Tribe Church. He is also running for a seat on the Oakland City Council. The push for the council seat, the pastorate, and his growing family and job take up somewhere between 16 and 18 hours per day. To get an interview with him, I had to meet him at a town hall debate and then travel with him to an outdoor crusade at the University of California at Berkeley.

As we turned the corner on two wheels, he said, "I was apolitical. I had no interest in politics at all. Politics can consist of professional politicians who are disconnected to people engaged in pay-to-play political maneuvers in their offices. As I started doing community organizing, which included fighting for jobs, safety, and housing, I found that being a local elected person creates the framework from which these things work. I found that the way to jump the chasm between the city and the community was to have a place in city government. I work hard at the grassroots connecting within the community. I work at building real, long-term relationships. I mean people to people, ground-level relationships. Who will benefit from the development that is taking place in Oakland today? Will it be the people who live here or the gentrifiers who are moving here in droves? A lot of that will be decided at City Hall. That is why I want to get inside the doors."

In 2014, Pastor Mustafa Muhyee and I hosted a political forum at his church, BASIC Ministries. We invited each of the candidates running for mayor to speak at a church that might hold 100 people at maximum capacity. Every single one of those candidates showed up except one. If Pastor Mustafa had said, "No, we're not going to open up our church for that political mess," what opportunity would people who live in the most crime-ridden, drug-infested hoods in the city ever have to dialogue with the Mayor of Oakland about job creation, access to health care, and improvement of the school system? Many of the folks in the inner city are not registered voters. That mayoral forum held at a church gave them that chance.

There were ballot measures about increased funding for inner city schools and whether the minimum wage should be changed. Should Pastor Mustafa Muhyee have said, "Let's hold a prayer meeting about your lack of finances," or should he have said, "You know, you might want to consider that ballot measure concerning raising the minimum wage by three dollars an hour. If it passes, that will change your whole life by helping you better provide for your family. It's your choice, vote for it or not, but at least look at the option."

Advice From a Fundamentalist Evangelist

I struggled with the concept of a social gospel early in my walk. When Reverend Jesse Jackson announced his run for president in 1984, the black community was ecstatic. Well, I should say "most of the members of the black community." I remember attending a Friday evening service in Brooklyn, New York, during that time. The minister jumped up from his seat and said, "Ain't no preacher got any business getting involved in any mess like that. The preacher's job is to preach the gospel and that's all!" The crowd in that storefront church backed him up with shouts of affirmation and hand clapping.

Years later, I had the opportunity to speak with a highly regarded "turn or burn" fundamentalist minister. I asked him what he thought about the politics and the social aspects of the ministry. I wanted to know how his theology reckoned with such things. He said, "Harry, recently I preached a crusade in Africa. And during that crusade, I had the opportunity to speak to the president of one of the nations over there. And it's strange because we had this very conversation. The president of that African nation was concerned about the apolitical stance that many Christians in his country took. Their colonizers had taught them words from a song that they'd internalized: 'Take The Whole World But Give Me Jesus.'"

This preacher took a good long sip of coffee. Then, he looked at me and said, "Harry, there are powerful people in political office with access to resources that could help your community. If you say, 'Take the whole world but give me Jesus,' that's exactly what they'll do. They'll take the whole world and give you Jesus.'"

This well-known clergyman did not have a public social justice message. However, in private that's what he said to me. He left me wondering about the balance between soul salvation and social justice. Just what was God's will?

Real Religion

Dr. Flescher says there is a thread common to both the early worshipers of Yahew and the Jewish movement. "Support of the widow, the orphan, and the foreigner were central to religious practice. In Job's legal material, Job's friends accuse him of disregarding this requirement. This would have been the first sign that he wasn't a faithful worshiper. Job later accuses God of not being faithful to this tenet.

"Widows were single women who had lost husbands. They could not hold jobs, own property, or hold bank accounts. They were completely dependent on a father, brother, or son. In the absence of a male family member, the community was responsible for her well-being. If a child ended up without a family, it was also incumbent upon the community to take in that child. Foreigners did not have property that could sustain life; therefore, the community became responsible for them. This was more than something people did to be nice. This was at the core of their religion.

"The story of Sodom of Gomorrah is about hospitality. God commanded that God's people care for the foreigners in their midst. Strangers and immigrants were to be shown mercy and given lodging."

Are We Sinners?

John Perkins worked for multinational corporations that offered aid to foreign countries. His guilt over the terms of this "aid" forced him to walk away. In his book, *Confessions of an Economic Hit Man*, he writes: "Is anyone in the U.S. innocent? Although those at the very pinnacle of the economic pyramid gain the most, millions of us depend – either directly or indirectly – on the exploitation of the LDCs [less developed country] for our own livelihoods. The resources and cheap labor that feed nearly all of our businesses come from places like Indonesia, and very little of it ever makes its way back there. The loans of foreign aid ensure that today's children and their grandchildren will be held hostage. They will have to allow our corporations to ravage their natural resources and will have to forego education, health, and other social services merely to pay us back. The fact that our own companies already received most of this money to build the power plants, airports, and industrial parks does not factor into this formula. Does the excuse that most Americans are unaware of this constitute innocence? Uninformed and intentionally misinformed, yes – but innocent?"[5]

Unforgettable Dream

Perkins wrote: "On my last night in Indonesia, I awoke from a dream, sat up in bed, and switched on the light. I had the feeling that someone was in the room with me. I peered around at the familiar Hotel Inter-Continental furniture, the batik tapestries, and the framed shadow-puppets hanging on the walls. Then the dream came back.

"I had seen Christ standing in front of me. He seemed like the same Jesus I had talked with every night when, as a young boy, I shared my thoughts with him after saying my formal prayers. Except that the Jesus of my childhood was fair-skinned and blond, while this one had curly black hair and a dark complexion. He bent down and heaved something up to his shoulder. I expected a cross. Instead, I saw the axle of a car with the attached wheel rim protruding above his head, forming a metallic halo. Grease dripped like blood down his forehead. He straightened, peered into my eyes, and said, 'If I were to come now, you would see me differently.' I asked him why. 'Because,' he answered, 'the world has changed.'"

For John Perkins, sin is more than ripping off that candy bar from the corner store. If you purchase goods that are made with slave labor overseas, you are partaking in social sin. If you benefit from a social system that condemns children to poverty and mis-education without fighting to make things right, you are in sin. And plainly here, if your nation benefits from the exploitation of another people's natural resources, then you are in sin. It brings new meaning to Paul's words: "All have sinned and come short of the glory of God," doesn't it?

America's Most Famous Hood Preacher Weighs In

One of the more interesting reality shows ever to appear on television was *Preachers of Detroit*. The opulence and excess many preachers live in there was highlighted through an opening montage of diamond rings, mansions, and luxury cars. Seemingly out of place in this over-the-top prosperity is a preacher – dressed in combat gear with Bible in hand and fitted baseball cap on backwards – who emerges from the front of an inner city row house: meet Reverend David Alexander Bullock, senior pastor of the Greater St. Matthew Baptist Church, Highland Park, Michigan.

When a verbal exchange with some of the city's most powerful and prosperous ministers began to get fiery, Bullock asked Bishop Charles Ellis, "How can you drive around in a Bentley in the city of Detroit? How does that work pastoring people that are in poverty?" In the same conversation, he asked another wealthy minister, "Do you think Jesus would drive a Bentley in Detroit?"

Reverend Bullock, a well-educated man, is clearly the people's preacher. In 2012, when the governor of Michigan decided to circumvent the democratic process by naming an emergency city manager to Flint, Michigan, Reverend Bullock came out on the streets with a bullhorn and warned of impending disaster. A few years later, phone calls began to come into Bullock's office asking for help ... something about lead in the city's water!

In an exclusive interview for this book, the reverend told me: "Members of my church went to Flint and took samples of the water and had them tested. I contacted folks in the governor's office. I was one of the first, if not the first minister, to get involved in the issue. We, as pastors, have become so disconnected from our own people; now it's all about higher praise and no longer about service. But folks knew that if they called me, they would get a response."

Said Reverend Bullock: "Yes, the people of the local church community need street cred. That is the definition of authentic witness in the community. Non-Christians and people who aren't a part of the church know who you are because of your acts of love and kindness. We're here to care for folk, to feed folk, to show folk love and kindness. That's what has given us the ability to impact the community. It has also made a community that was unsafe for others safe for me. The community cares about people who care for it. We had our air conditioning unit stolen a few years ago. The community began to police the community. They said, 'Don't mess with St. Matthew Baptist Church. That's our church.' Eventually, the air conditioning unit was returned.

"People just want to preach and teach," says Reverend Bullock, "but there's so much more to it than that." The reverend believes that a pastor must become involved in local politics, even going so far as to say that he or she should live in the city where they minister because their voice as a spokesman will carry more weight if they can personally vote on the issues that concern their members. "Pastor, you should begin by reaching out to your local elected official. Start a dialogue with that person. Find out their vision for the community. What is their platform? Build a relationship with the elected official. Become engaged in the political process. Learn what public policy is, how it is written, and then how to impact it. "First," said Reverend Bullock, "you must believe, and then you must become relentless."

Chapter 16

It's True But is it Relevant?

A few weeks ago, I wandered down a street filled with churches and noticed something interesting. Some of the once-vibrant churches were shuttered. When I looked into the windows of others, I could see people caught up in ecstatic rapture, but their shouting was bouncing off the walls of half-empty storefronts. Children played tag up and down the street, as though the churches did not exist. I had to scratch my head. The church has been entrusted with such a powerful message of hope in a world of desolation. This being true, then why are the churches empty but the streets filled with the lost?

Missions Sunday in the Ghetto

A number of years ago I received an invitation to attend a church in the middle of an urban war zone. The occasion was Annual Missions Day. I was excited. I think of missionaries as God's special-forces unit. They go to dangerous places to carry the word of God to people who are sometimes hostile. Missionaries, I was taught as a child, are bold, fearless, and one hundred percent committed to the gospel of Jesus Christ.

The church I was headed to that Sunday was located in a neighborhood that needed missionaries. The unemployment rate hovered around 70 percent. Houses were crumbling. It was easier to find heroin than a fresh pineapple or a mango in the stores. Crack and gang warfare had taken over. The sudden buck-buck-buck of nine-millimeter handguns made normal life impossible. Hope had evaporated. All that was left was this church.

I slipped into the back of the dark sanctuary. The thick stained-glass windows blocked light so effectively that no one outside could have witnessed what was going on inside the building. The drone of a pipe organ blotted out the ever-present hip-hop drums that boomed from passing cars. "Amazing Grace" drowned out the Wu-Tang Clan.

All eyes were aimed at the stage. As if on cue, the pastor walked in through a side door. He was followed by a cadre of austere ministers who wore the somber expressions of politicians who had been up all night working on the budget deficit. The man in the long black robe walked down from the pulpit desk and said, "Shall we rise." It was prayer time.

"Oh, God," he said. Those were the last words he spoke that I could understand. The rest was a garble of Shakespeare and Rimbaud, with some James Brown thrown in for good measure. It sounded something like, "We offer approbation and encomium to Thee, Oh, Thou magnanimous and effulgent tutelary ... Good God y'all ... on the good foot ... Oh, Thou prodigious, adroit... ."

The preacher spit and jerked as he hollered. He pressed his hand out in a *stop* motion as though he were trying to push back some overwhelming force. It was as though he had swallowed a dictionary and now it was coming out of the wrong end. "Ehhh, ehhh ... Oh, floccinaucinihilpilification! Oooh weee! We rebuke the degenerate antitransubstantiationists, in Thy Holy name, Oh, Lord the Baptist! Eh, Glory!!!" he prayed.

Ten minutes in, I broke a sacred church taboo. I opened my eyes during the prayer. I was curious. Were the other worshipers as bored and distracted as me? It was hard to tell since people were standing up with their eyes closed. I guessed they weren't. "Say your prayer, preacher!" a deep baritone voice behind me pleaded. Now that could have meant two different things. Was he saying, "Reverend, I am really feeling your words," or was he saying, "Man, would you please get it over with?"

The elderly lady in the silver wig next to me gave up. She plopped back down on the hard wooden bench, her eyes still closed. Thirty seconds later, I observed some light snoring. She would wake up from her slumber every two or three minutes just to push him on! "Say it, pastor!" she'd holler and then start snoring all over again.

I needed another shave by the time the preacher finally began to sputter out of breath. The man couldn't find a neat way to bring the thing to a close. He ended the prayer by saying, "Eternal One, hear this humble orison, this imploration – in Jesus' name, Amen." And that was the high point of the service. It went downhill from there.

While the musician beat on the organ again, the missionaries walked in two by two from the rear of the church swaying from side to side like the Supremes. They wore white nurses' dresses and white stockings. They topped that off with white head doilies and white corrective shoes. If the missionaries' goal is to blend inconspicuously into the mission field, they had failed Missions 101 most miserably. The people outside of the fort were walking down the boulevard dressed in sagging jeans, wife-beater T-shirts, and Chuck Taylor sneakers. I hadn't recalled passing a single soul with a doily on their head.

The main function of the mission society at this little oasis in the middle of the war zone was made clear early. It was certainly not to be salt and light in the troubled world beyond the doors of that building. The women came to the front of the church presenting fat envelopes, each stuffed with money. Lots of it. And the money was not to buy Bibles or food for the homeless. They had raised that money to send the pastor and his wife on a vacation cruise. And it wouldn't have been fair to send them on their way without any spending money, now would it?

You're saying, "Rev, I don't believe you."

Believe it. My imagination isn't sharp enough to make up something like this. Three hours later when the service was over, how was that community impacted? Oh, there was plenty of great food served. However, the homeless didn't get a scrap unless they scoured through the garbage can after we finished eating. No widow's rent got paid, unless she had the ingenuity to gather and recycle the soda cans that we had emptied. And no one in that neighborhood heard the gospel that afternoon.

Would Ghetto Storm have been welcomed here? If I could have dragged Ghetto Storm through the doors of that small castle, would he have understood anything the preacher said? I doubt it. I have two earned degrees, and the preacher lost me during the opening prayer.

There was something in the closing prayer that just raised more questions. The pastor cried out, "Oh, God, I pray that You were pleased with what we have done here in Your name today."

Was God Pleased?

I don't cuss at all in real life. I have friends who have known me all my life, and they will tell you that they have never heard me utter a cuss word. It somehow just pops up occasionally in my writings. So if you were to ask me whether I think that God was pleased with anything that happened in that church service, I would have to say, "Hell, no!"

The missionaries at that church weren't practicing out-reach. They were practicing "in reach." The entire extravaganza was created to tickle the flesh of the members. Everything was "our pastor this" and "our pastor that." I wanted to throw up. They talked about the pastor's goodness more than they talked about Jesus. There were no folks from the hood around the church building in the service, and no one seemed the slightest bit concerned that they weren't there.

Of the people in the church, 90 percent were over age 60. If they continue down the path of self-appeasement and pastor glorification, where will this church be in 30 years?

Holding the Line Between Hope and Destruction

I've seen so much beauty in the hood: little children grinning and smiling as they race their bicycles up and down the street, newlywed couples walking arm in arm, families dancing in the street at neighborhood barbecues, and young brothers trash-talking between layups and slam dunks in the park.

On the other hand, I've listened to one youth tell another, "When I see you again, I'm gonna pistol whip you." I've seen children sex trafficked in broad daylight. I've had brothers walk up to me and say, "Pray for me, Reverend. These brothers are out to kill me, and I feel that my time is at hand."

The only thing that exists between hope and destruction in the hood is the church. However, it seems to me that few churches are Heaven-bent on trying to use the mandate and power of Heaven to rescue those they are commissioned to reach. And therein lies the crisis.

Chapter 17

A Good Christian Death

 "The Black Church Is Dead." Princeton professor Eddie Glaude started a firestorm when he went public with that one. The wrath of the black religious elite raged hot on the editorial pages and beneath blog headlines. Angry pastors labeled him "the Uncle Tom who dared." Two prominent Anglo ministers answered Glaude's *Huffington Post* article with the release of a book entitled *What We Love about the Black Church*. Eddie Glaude was public enemy number one. Satan received better press in the black church community in the aftermath of his pointed public question.

Why this heated response to a simple blog entry? If some writer had declared the NFL to be dead, would the NFL owners blast him with searing editorials in the *New York Times?* No, the sheer absurdity of the thing would not deserve a response.

In 2008, Queens-bred hip-hop artist Nas released an album called *Hip Hop Is Dead*. There was no question mark behind his declaration. The statement was an obituary. Yet, little controversy was stirred. So, why were symposiums formed, books authored, and numerous blog entries created in response to Eddie Glaude's article?

James Cone addressed the furor in a *New York Times* article. He said, "The black church, like any institution, does not like criticism from outside the family. It wants to be prophetic against society, but it does not want intellectuals to be prophetic against it."[1]

The View from Life Support

Sure, that's part of it; however, that's not the entire reason. The truth is found in a point that Glaude did not even raise in the article: Black church attendance has been on the wane for decades. The pews are thinning out, and the heads are getting grayer. Some of its denominations have experienced dramatic membership decreases in recent years.

When Glaude released his article, some critics went so far as to scope out his religious background. "He's Catholic," they said. They argued that because Glaude was not Baptist, A.M.E., or C.O.G.I.C., he was, therefore, a non-affiliate of accepted traditional black religious culture as such. They labeled him an outsider, officially disallowed from offering any critique of the vibrancy of African-American religious life.

The same people might be a little harder pressed to deny me a say using that criteria. I am an ordained African-American Baptist preacher and a long-time member of one of the denominations I'm speaking about. I'm writing from inside the glass house.

Everything Changes

A few years ago, I attended a renowned African-American church here in Oakland. It was your typical church. A man in a black suit sporting a badge that said "Usher" met me at the door. He wore a white glove that shielded his hand from mine as we shook. He handed me a four-page church bulletin, alerting me to the date of the bake sale, the church leadership structure, and the upcoming revival meeting.

I took a seat in the back of the church and waited for the piano and organ to fire up. The choir wore long, blue robes. I stood up to clap along with their fiery spirituals. There's nothing like the soul of the black church when the people really believe what they're singing. They launched into "How I Got Over," one of my favorites: "My soul looks back in wonder, how I got over."

Attendance was sparse. There were gaps in the seating. Some pews were completely empty. And yet there were some special guests. Now, I had never been to that church before, and yet I knew that the people sitting in front of me were not long-time members.

What tipped me off? They were young. They didn't have on the ritual attire. They were sitting there staring into the Sunday school books from the last portion of the Sunday service. A young fellow of about 12 twisted in his seat, his eyes probing the ceiling for cracks. He whispered to a young woman who might have been his older sister.

Before too long it was time for the preaching moment. The pastor manned the pulpit. He stroked his gray beard and then shouted out a scripture. Some unidentified person behind him stood up and began to read. A chapter or so later, the pastor signaled for the hapless minister to sit down. The man of the hour was ready to take over.

The kid in front of me was two notches beyond bored. He took the little pencil placed in the holder for visitors and drew circles on his bulletin. He grabbed his sister's arm and stared at her watch. He huffed. Ten minutes into the message, the pastor had lost all of his visitors.

It's amazing what you can see from the pulpit. The preacher's eyes came to rest on the unchurched crew seated near me as they shifted in the seats, drew pictures on their bulletins, or just sat quietly with their heads back and their eyes closed as though trying to patiently out wait the verbal waterboarding. What I saw as a problem, the pastor saw as a challenge. God bless him.

The preacher became more demonstrative. He came out from behind the pulpit and strutted along the periphery of the stage. He made hand motions. I stifled a laugh. I thought he was going to break out into a moonwalk. The church members instantly recognized what the pastor was trying to do. (When you hear a man preach or teach more than a hundred times a year over a ten-year period, you don't have any trouble picking up on his cues.) Eyes flashed toward the back of the room. The pastor hollered, believing perhaps that if he simply amplified his voice, he could somehow reach that group of youth with his dry-as-dust sermon. It had the opposite effect. The louder he got, the more disinterested they became. I was embarrassed *for* him. Finally, he just gave up and brought the whole thing crashing to a merciful end.

I was among the first to hit the exit. I didn't beat the crew in front of me though. They were out of there like someone was handing out hundred dollar bills at the front door. All, that is, except the 12-year-old. He was trapped in the lobby. The usher with the white gloves had him pinned up against a wall. I stood back a little and watched. I know that's nosy, but what can I say? I wanted to see what was going to happen.

The usher's leathery brown face and thick mane of gray stood out in great contrast to the young boy's close-cropped hairstyle. The kid looked troubled, confused. There was just a trace of hatred in the usher's tight-lipped smile. Distilled fire tongues danced in his eyes.

"I saw you back there, boy," he said gruffly.

The kid was silent. It was like he was looking for space and the right moment to run away.

The usher was only inches from his face.

"What is to become of you, boy?" the older man asked.

"Huh?" the boy barely said.

"If you don't honor God, if you can't sit still while the word of God is preached, what will become of you?"

It was apparent to me that the usher and the young boy were strangers. The man didn't even know the kid's name. "I should take you in the back and whip your hide," the deacon offered. He was as nonchalant as a waiter asking, "Would you like cream in your coffee?" The kid's body language shifted. Survival mode kicked in. In the hood, every threat is to be taken seriously. "No, you're not!" the kid said. His voice was louder. He was afraid. Internally, he was preparing to defend himself. Even if he could not beat this man, he was ready to put up the best fight possible. I stood there trying to figure out what I would do if the usher indeed tried to drag this kid into the backyard for the tanning that he felt the boy so richly deserved.

The usher caught me staring. Embarrassed, he stepped back. He looked at me and gave a fake laugh as though he had been joking all the while. The kid saw his chance and bolted for the exit. I said nothing. Confident that the kid was safe, I left.

I understood both of them. The young boy did not have what we call "church manners." He didn't understand the appropriate times to sit or stand in a traditional church service. He had not learned that one does not talk in church, ever. And he had not learned how to pretend to pay attention even when he was being bored to the point of mind deadness.

The usher, on the other hand, came from a world where children were seen and not heard, where no one expected the preacher to be particularly interesting or relevant. If one grew bored, he or she simply popped in a starlight peppermint and counted backward from 100 to 1 to stay awake. He came from a world where if you were black and you didn't belong to a church, you were worse than a heathen. That deacon came from a world where Southern custom dictated that a stranger could take a child out into the backyard and whip the back of his legs with a tree branch for insolence or disobedience. However, he was now living in a world where that same kid could have returned with an uncle toting a .357 and a bad attitude.

The world has changed. The preacher couldn't understand it. The usher couldn't understand it. Neither could the church members, most of whose families had come to the San Francisco Bay Area from the Deep South long before the time of the Civil Rights Movement.

It's a Different World

That 12-year-old had been born into a world where television networks designed cartoons with quickly shifting images to capture the eyes of children who have a shrunken attention span of only six seconds.

Early MTV music videos were like short films. Today, directors never give the viewer time to focus on any one thing. Images are edited to jump cut from one to another, never allowing the viewer to focus in or concentrate. The director is battling the kid's urge to lose interest and switch channels. If a child can't sit through a three-minute music video without switching channels, what will he get out of sitting in a sauna-hot room listening to a senior citizen drone on and on for 45 minutes about Moses' genealogy? By minute 25, where is that kid's mind? Is he or she thinking, "My goodness, really? And then who was born after Pelage?"

Next Sunday, will the kid be saying, "Man, I just have to get in there today so I can get the second half of that sermon?"

Chapter 18

Consider the Future

 Back in the mid-nineties, I lived down the block from the Telegraph Avenue shopping area in Berkeley, California. Many was the Friday night when my friends and I would find ourselves among the crowd of window shoppers. We'd pass the time by strolling into the bustling, three-story Cody's Bookstore where we'd pray for an empty seat so we could sift through the new releases by our favorite authors. Then we'd drift over to the room that housed magazines from all over the world. I'd want to clap my hands when I found that my favorite hip-hop magazine had shipped its most recent edition. After Cody's, we'd glide over to the giant music beehive called Tower Records, sometimes waiting in line to pick up the CD by our favorite artist. We'd round out the trip by stopping at the Block-buster Video, where we'd rent two or three videotapes.

Do you want to know an amazing thing? Not one of those stores is there anymore. In 1999, somebody created a file-sharing system called Napster. This software made it possible to download songs for free and then send them to friends. It didn't mean much to me back then. Like most people, I didn't own a personal computer at the time. However, the multibillion-dollar recording industry was up in arms over this innovation. They could see the graffiti scrawl on the wall. Why would people buy what they could get for free?

You know how the story ends. In a few years, everyone owned a computer. File-sharing sites were all over the Internet. The entire recording industry crumbled. Artists who once sold ten million copies of a new release were fortunate to reach a half million in sales. The technology shifted from compact discs to downloads, the same thing for DVDs. Goodbye, four-story Tower Records megastores. Goodbye, Virgin Records behemoths. So long, Circuit City.

What those huge conglomerates learned (albeit too late) was that everything changes. People still listen to music, perhaps now more than ever. The fact is that the music hasn't changed that much, just the medium through which we hear it. Less than ten years after Napster was born, we were rocking iPods and listening to our music through portable telephones that took pictures. Kodak and Polaroid, welcome to life support.

Lessons from Berkeley

I was living in Berkeley when I saw a television show that featured a segment about Amazon.com. I found it intriguing, and I liked what I saw of Jeffrey Bezos. However, I didn't see how his idea would revolutionize the world. As I said, back then few people had personal computers, and most of us had little to no understanding of the Internet. Now, fast forward to today. Everyone owns a computer or has access to one. Amazon.com can send books to your house, and 90 percent of the time, they are far cheaper than the prices at your local bookstore. They also allow you to download the books instantly.

Amazon has changed the rules of the game. Books still sell, but the medium through which they are marketed, sold, and bought has changed. Originally, insiders in the book industry scoffed at Amazon.com. And then the day came that the giant Borders bookstore chain went belly-up, like a beached whale. I remember sitting in a book-store during its "Going Out Of Business" sale. The business heads of the once-thriving store were deeply engaged in conversation. The manager said, "We didn't see it coming. Nobody knew how this new model for sell-ing books would take off and what it would do to us." Once again I say, "Everything changes." Now, when I walk down to Telegraph Avenue in Berkeley, all that exists from my old Friday night routine is memories. The shops we frequented are closed up and gone.

The business world lives by the credo "change or die." Does that saying apply for the inner city church as well?

Change or Die

Pre-Disney Times Square was a gritty, seedy concrete jun-gle illuminated by a sea of neon lights and trampled by thousands of quick-moving feet. Quite a number of street preachers found their place among the hot dog vendors, porn peddlers, panhandlers, and pot dealers. They were often hard-eyed prophets of unmerciful gods who prom-ised vengeance and held out little hope for redemption.

In the early '80s, I worked in that section of New York City. Eventually, the raving pronouncements of the evan-gelists faded into the background like the sound of jackhammers breaking up asphalt or break-dancers spin-ning on cardboard for tourist change. However, there was one group that always unnerved me. They ministered in shifts so that the office workers and garment district seam-stresses could not miss their fiery preaching on hell, sin, and damnation. They were weary-looking men and women in tattered coats and run-over shoes who read aloud from the King James Version. They had blown-up full-color pictures of human fetuses propped up behind them to underscore their objections to abortion.

I never once saw a single soul stop to ask, "How can I be saved from the wrath that is to come?" The evangelists were undeterred. Perhaps in their minds they had classified most of those who walked by as burdened with reprobate minds and hardly capable of making a decision for Christ. They had sounded the warning. Their consciences were absolved. The blood was no longer on their hands.

We do the same thing when someone drifts into one of our churches, gets bored to tears, and then walks out just as lost as they were when they came in. We point to them and say, "It's their fault, the reprobates."

St. Paul, the master evangelist, had another view. Christianity's greatest apologist said in 1 Corinthians 9:19-23: "Though I am free and belong to no one, I have made myself a slave to everyone, to win as many as possible. To the Jews I became like a Jew, to win the Jews. To those under the law I became like one under the law (though I myself am not under the law), so as to win those under the law. To those not having the law I became like one not having the law (though I am not free from God's law but am under Christ's law), so as to win those not having the law. To the weak I became weak, to win the weak. I have become all things to all people so that by all possible means I might save some. I do all this for the sake of the gospel, that I may share in its blessings."

Paul had a powerful mission statement. His aim was not merely to preach the gospel but to "win as many as possible." He notes here that cultural barriers can keep people out of the kingdom of God. Therefore, his strategy is to shift from the cultural paradigm where he is most at home to a completely different social norm if that's what it takes. Before Paul expects someone to become something different spiritually, he recognizes that he himself first must become different culturally. He doesn't simply want to preach; he wants to persuade and do what he must to communicate from inside the other person's worldview.

Paul's Example

During his mission to Athens, Paul stood up in a public meeting and said, "For as I walked around and looked carefully at your objects of worship, I even found an altar with this inscription: TO AN UNKNOWN GOD. So you are ignorant of the very thing you worship – and this is what I am going to proclaim to you." (Acts 17:23)

Paul's message is not one full of abstractions. He starts his challenge with something tangible, something that the hearers could relate to and understand. Paul conjures up the mental image of an object that they might have walked past every day, something they might have wondered about for years. The evangelist does not ignore their culture; he engages it.

Later in the chapter, Paul clarifies a point about Christ by quoting Athenian poets. What might that look like today? If Paul were ministering in the 21st century, that might sound like, "Young brothers and sisters of Athens, I walked past a parked car at the In-N-Out Burger last week and someone was blasting a song that caught my ears. I asked homeboy what the name of the song was, and he told me.

"When I got home I jumped on the Internet and downloaded the lyrics to Plies's song, "Lord, I'm Tired of Lying to You." I cranked it up loud so I could catch all of the words. This gangsta rapper says, 'I told a [m.f.] if I died today, I don't know where I'd go / Cuz a lot of us out here that think we goin' to heaven and we just ain't gon' go / And some of us even go to church every Sunday, and still ain't gon' go / God, I lied to you too much / that's the reason I don't know where I'm gon' go... .'"[1]

Assuming he's talking to fans of gangsta hip-hop, Paul has just bought himself a broadened attention-span pass. He is clearly inside of the listener's worldview, and if he continues along this path, his audience will be receptive. From this launchpad, Paul could segue into quite a number of scripture passages. He could visit themes of mercy, redemption, judgment, or eternal life. He might not win the entire crowd, but it would not be beyond the realm of imagination to say that he would win some.

Fishing in the Hood

Jesus promised to make his first followers "fishers of men." I grew up on the seashore, so I can tell you that fishing is more complicated than it looks on TV. Certain boats go out to certain sections of the ocean where they are most likely to find a certain kind of fish. Experienced fishermen choose from a wide variety of baits, lures, hooks, and nets to catch the fish they wish to snare. And so it is with fishing for souls! The evangelist must be just as knowledgeable and inventive as the man or woman who makes a living on the sea. Where are you fishing, what are the tools of your trade, and what are you using for bait?

I don't care where you are in America, there's one thing you can count on. Eventually, someone is going to hand you a gospel tract. The next time they do, take a look at it. Often tracts are four-sided documents printed using a tiny 6-point font. I'm going to let you in on a secret. I'll bet most people take those tracts, ball them up, and toss them in a garbage can. Do they do this because they are irascible sinners? No. They chuck the tracts away because the little pieces of paper are boring. The form itself doesn't invite you to read them.

If tracts really worked, hamburger empires and clothing chains would be using that format to draw you into their box store outlets. Gospel tracts (with some exceptions) are unimaginative. They are poorly worded, dull, and uninteresting. They no longer reach the masses. They are a 20th century medium in a 21st century market! Jesus didn't often teach straight theology. He couched his message in parables, stories and sayings relevant to the culture He lived in. Jesus told stories about farming and fishing because he was speaking to people who made their living in the farming and fishing industries. If Jesus were living in the 21st century hood surrounded by crime, blight, poverty, police brutality, hip-hop and basketball, what kind of sermon illustrations would he use to capture the attention of people in the hood? What would his parables sound like?

Jesus knew that the secret to getting people to believe is to speak in a language they can understand and to make what you have to say relevant to their lives. All of the anointing in the world can't rescue a dull, irrelevant message.

You might be angry because your fishing isn't going well. Don't curse the fish; check the bait.

New School Bait

I once had a job as an employment counselor for emancipated foster youth. One day a young man came into the office and started filming me with his cell phone camera. Because he hadn't asked for my permission, I was furious. I sat him down near my desk and voiced by displeasure. In the middle of my admonition, I realized something. He never took his eyes off that phone. The entire time I had been lecturing him, he was watching social media clips, movies, comedy spoofs, pictures of his friends ... who knows what? As I watched him gazing down at that glowing, hand-held rectangle, something struck me. We're using the wrong bait.

Today, if you want to reach young people – like the kid sitting in that chair – you have to find a way to get the message inside of that telephone computer. The message has to be transmitted to him in a medium that he is apt to use. By the time you read this, there may be another medium, but the seed of the message still stands. Speak from inside their culture. Seize the medium that the people you wish to reach are using.

iPod Thinking

In the early 21st century, the teenager who appreciated music owned a suitcase full of compact discs and a portable disc player. Today, those disc players are relics that can be purchased on eBay as antique collector's items. As early as 2001, Apple chief Steve Jobs put a staff of people to work creating a small device that could download music. They called it the iPod. Music was transmitted to a portable listening device by electronic signal. There was no more need for the disc.

Whereas traditional record companies went belly-up with the release of new technology, Apple has continued to prosper. Why? Simply put, Steve Jobs and the Apple team understood early the threat that sites like Napster posed to the recording industry. They also understood that the new technology was not going to just go away. Hence, Apple created an online store where licensed music could be purchased via the Internet. The Apple squad understood the times, and they changed with them. There was really no alternative. The order of the day was change or perish. When confronted with those two alternatives, what will we, the church, choose?

So far we've traveled through the back streets of the hood to get an informed view of the issues, often hidden in plain sight, that impact a world. We've laid bare the hood's wounds and explored many of its greatest needs. Together we've considered the power of Jesus Christ and his gospel to bring not only change in the afterlife but in this one. We've looked at the misleading elements which have woven themselves into the teachings of Jesus and the great harm they have caused. Underneath all of this lies our challenge to reach people at a grassroots level.

In this next section, we'll look at some of the fundamental elements that will give a believer the street cred necessary to be an effective witness in the hood.

Chapter 19

Some of Your Most Essential Tools

 Victory Outreach Church of Oakland operates a men's home in deep East Oakland. The healing center is located far away from Oakland's major tourist attractions. No, there's no sightseeing going on down in that hood. You wouldn't come cruising through those winding streets unless you were actually looking for a street address. If you're the type who travels with a bulletproof vest and a .9 millimeter with a full clip in your lap, this is the type of place where you might need those toys. I once lived in this corner of America's second most dangerous city, and it's no joke. Trust me.

The Call of God to the Badlands

It's Saturday morning and these brothers are hosting a men's meeting. I've been asked to be the guest speaker. I go back with these folks and I am honored by the invitation.

You see, the Victory Outreach of Oakland Church is your bonafide hood church. Everyone is welcome home. I met some of the members of this church back when they were in the streets, before they knew the name Jesus Christ, back when they were on the block raising hell and I was a minister trying to get in where I fit in. We're practically family.

The Godfather Speaks

God has raised up a pastor to go after them when they are gang banging and slanging dope. His name is Pastor Larry Vigil. Pastor Larry looks the part. He is heavyset. He wears loc shades, a leather jacket, and a cool brim hat. He's an O.G. from the block who is claiming Jesus rather than a gang set. Pastor Larry is the type of guy who never has to walk into a room and say, "I'm the leader." He owns both the charisma and sense of spiritually that just make you fall in line. He's a very loving cat and a good friend.

When I walk through the door, I notice that most of the men sitting and waiting for the service to start are sporting homemade jailhouse tattoos. Most of them are Latinos. Some are black, others white. If I could add up the jail time these men have done, it would pass the century mark. And still, the miracle of our faith is in motion here. These brothers are lifting their hands to pray. They're praising God and calling upon the name of Jesus.

I notice some of the brothers are gathered around a young Mexican guy in the kitchen. They're laying hands on him. He's a heroin addict struggling to break free of one of the most vicious addictions known to humanity. When he's ready to surrender to Christ and recovery, he's got a place to live – right here. Until then, he'll come by to visit. The brothers here will continue to journey with him, pray with him, hope with him.

After the service, Pastor Larry and I sit down to chop it up over cherry Kool-aid and donuts. "Let me explain something to you about calling, Harry," he says. "I've had guys come up to me and say, 'My pastor told me that Oakland is a mission field that needs help, and so he sent me here.' See, Harry, the key word there is that their 'pastor' sent them. God didn't send them. And then you look around after awhile and they're gone. What they don't realize is that this is a demonic stronghold, and if God is not backing your play, you are literally going to face hell on earth. You need a sense of God's calling to be effective as a pastor. If your pastor calls you or you called yourself and Jesus hasn't, then it's not going to be pretty."

The term "call" can be ambiguous. People experience it in different ways. As Samuel lay down in slumber, he was summoned several times by a voice he had not previously known. Moses heard a voice from a burning bush. Paul heard a disembodied voice and saw a blinding light. For others of us it's the inescapable prompting of the Holy Spirit. It's a scripture that becomes emblazoned on the screen of the mind. Often there are steps of leading that might bring us over time to make a faith step toward a branch of ministry. Romans 8:14 says, "Those who are led by the spirit of God are the children of God." As we follow the voice, the calling, and the prompting of God, we can be assured of Christ's promise in Matthew 28:20, "… and lo, I am with you always even unto the end of the world."

Is God calling you to minister in the hood? Is God calling you to throw substantial financial support behind some organization or front-line soldier doing the work? Is God calling you to sew scarves or raise money for overcoats for inner city kids? Do the knee work. Acknowledge God in all your ways, and he will direct your paths. On some dark night that will surely come, that sense of calling will be your blanket of faith.

Vision

I have served beneath leaders who had a mission but no sense of vision. What is the difference? Mission is the overall reason for your ministry's existence. It's a broad-based directional blanket. You might tell me that my church's mission is to proclaim the gospel of Jesus Christ, create disciples, and engage in social justice. Millions of churches share that mission. What separates your church from them is a set of action steps unique to your gathering of believers. This year, we plan to reach souls. Really? How do you plan to do that? What will it look like? Your vision would be the bullet points that follow the mission statement. You would say, "We plan to carry out our mission in this calendar year by, let's say, hosting a community dinner in January, organizing a basketball tournament in February…." The vision would be the concrete steps that make the mission come alive in a given timetable.

I don't have a car; therefore, I often have to rely on buses for transportation. Just because a bus says AC Transit on it, doesn't mean it's the bus for me. Before I get on a public bus, I see if it plans to follow a route that leads it to my desired destination.

If I am a pastor and you're thinking of joining my church, you might want to ask me for my one-year vision. Tell me it's great that I want to reach the community, but ask me, "Pastor, what steps will you be taking to do that? May I see your vision statement and your plan?" Without a vision, I'm like man with a blindfold tossing darts at a target 20 feet away. I need a clear vision with expected goals. Without that, if my dart hits anything or even if blindfolded I throw it through an open window, I'll claim success. And that's not what you want is it?

The mission and the vision must be aligned. If your mission is to fulfill the Great Commission, your vision is the steps that you are planning to take within a given time frame to fulfill that goal.

Let me put it to you like this. Years ago I had a conversation with a friend who is a salesperson. I painted this picture for him. The Ever Rest Car Dealership decides to host an event. Their mission, of course is to sell cars. They reason that if they host a carnival at their car lot, they can lure kids. This in turn will bring in parents interested in purchasing automobiles. On the day of the event, helium balloons adorn the automobile showroom. The salespeople dress up like clowns. Busloads of kids come, but none are accompanied by a parent or an adult. Not a single automobile is sold. That Monday in the staff debriefing one of the salespeople says, "I thought the event went well. We were able to put smiles on the faces of those children, and we had fun, too."

I asked my friend how the supervisor might respond to that employee's reflections. He laughed and then replied, "The boss would say, 'Jim, you're in the wrong business. Perhaps, you'd do better making your living as a clown. The circus thing is just a tactic. Our real mission here is to sell cars.'"

What's your mission? If you lose sight of it, you might end up another clown down at the circus. Without a vision that includes clear tactics, you're just wandering around in the forest without a map. You need both mission and vision to succeed in urban ministry.

Courage

In the film *Troy*, an army of battle-scarred invaders land ready to take over yet another country. Instead of going to war in the usual way, they have a proposition. They have a ferocious fighting champion in their ranks, a giant of a man. If any of the native king's soldiers can best him in a one-on-one battle, the invaders will go back home the way they came.

A young boy is sent running. The king has sent him to fetch the legendary warrior Achilles. The destiny of the nation lies in the hands of Achilles. The young messenger approaches his tent and rouses him from slumber. He delivers the king's message. Achilles, played by Brad Pitt, rises to his feet. Purpose beams in his eyes. His footsteps are sure and quick. As Achilles mounts his horse, the boy says, "The Thessalonian you're fighting ... he is the biggest man I've ever seen. I wouldn't want to fight him." With his helmet strapped on, Achilles looks down from his horse's back, pauses, and states matter-of-factly, "That's why no one will ever remember your name."

Wow! What a line!

Courage, it's Biblical

If you hope to be successful in anything, you'll need a measure of courage. God told Joshua, "Have I not commanded you? Be strong and courageous. Do not be afraid; do not be discouraged, for the LORD your God will be with you wherever you go." Who can put it any better than that?

Pick out a single figure in the Bible that people revere so much that they would name their kids after. Ready? Do you have the person in mind? I guarantee one thing about this individual: The hallmark of the figure's personality was courage. Can you see David charging toward the giant Goliath with a sling and some rocks in his hand? Can you visualize Daniel being thrown into the lion's den because he refused to bow to an idol? Can you see a pregnant teenager named Mary walking through the streets of Nazareth? Can you see Paul hurled into the sea as his boat capsizes? Can you hear Peter singing in prison? Pastor, if you have no courage, you're going to have a problem here. Any of the people who followed God in antiquity either had it or came up with it. Hebrews 11 contains what Sunday school teachers call "faith's hall of fame." The courageous people on this honor roll obtained their faith through belief, surrender, and connection to the Lord. That faith produced courage.

God's Shepherds

In ancient times, the shepherd would face wolves and lions head on to protect his sheep. The shepherd's bed was the ground; his blankets were the stars and the wind above. The Scripture refers to pastors as shepherds. Consider the analogy. The pastor must be duty bound and fiercely committed to the protection of the flock assigned to him or her. Pastors must be willing – literally – to lay down their life if necessary to protect the sheep.

In the hood, the sheep face innumerable dangers. Therefore, one must not pick up the mantle of their guide and protector lightly, if one truly desires to serve as Christ commands. Like the shepherd of old, the hood preacher must be completely surrendered to the call.

Courage Puts a Leader Out in Front

A few years ago, a street ministry group I led was scheduled to embark on an evangelism mission. It was Saturday afternoon. I was scheduled to preach two services the next day, but I had completed neither of the sermons. A thought passed through my mind as I wrestled with what I should do. I contemplated calling the team and telling them that I would not be going out with them to the most dangerous hood in the entire city because I really needed to stay home to work on the sermons. And then I caught myself. What message would that have sent? If there is danger, you the leader must be prepared to face it first. That's the first indication you are genuine in your leadership. Nothing can make your co-laborers lose faith in you and your vision faster than perceived cowardice. The sermons would have to wait. I laced up my sneakers and got to stepping.

That afternoon I led the team on a mission to invite women caught up in domestic violence and human trafficking to a meeting that would be hosted at our church. I told them we would walk in pairs on either side of a busy street. I instructed them never to leave their partners behind. I also told them never to get a full block ahead of me.

At the end of the effort, we met in front of a local McDonald's to debrief. One of the sisters noted that one of the young men she'd tried to engage in conversation had a pistol lodged in his belt beneath his long white T-shirt. He didn't pull it out. But what if something had happened to one of the sisters on the afternoon that I had chosen to stay home to work on a sermon? How would I have felt upon hearing that news? What would that have said about my leadership?

If you are the pastor or the ministry leader, your responsibilities may stretch you so tightly that you won't have time to be a part of every single ministry. Leave the bingo game alone. Just say "no" to the golf tournament, the dinner invitations, and the fashion show. Say "yes" to the evangelism and outreach efforts. You'll touch your community. You'll learn a lot about it, and you'll have the respect and admiration of your members.

I once heard a sermon illustration about an army that landed on a distant shore to wage war. Things did not go well. The enemy drove the army back about a mile, then two miles. Finally, they backed them up so far that they backed into the general. If you are the leader, the troops should not be backing up into you. In fact, you should be out front. If you are the leader, your courage should go unquestioned. When you signed up to lead God's people, that meant you were willing to take this to the limit for the Kingdom of God.

This is no place for cowards. Go back and read the book of Acts if you doubt me.

The head coach of a professional football team was once sued by a player who claimed the coach had said he had no heart. (Heart is, of course, a synonym for courage.) When the athlete testified in court, he said words to this effect: "You can say that an athlete is slow. You can say that he is not strong. But when you say that he has no heart, you are denying the very thing that makes him a competitor. You are attacking the very thing by which he defines himself, the thing that makes him who he is." He won the lawsuit.

Courage as Testimony

Last summer, a local church called BASIC Ministries held an outdoor service in one of the most dangerous neighborhoods in Oakland. The worship team called down fire from Heaven. Pastor Mustafa Muhyee preached an intense sermon about Jesus' visit with Zaccheus. You could hear shouts from the worshipers who gathered in the big outdoor park. Occasionally, the din of a motorcycle would drown out the preacher's words, but it was only momentary because he was loud.

I closed my eyes and raised my hands as I felt God's spirit lift my soul. Of course, closing your eyes in a war zone is a no-no. Rapper Nas once said, "Sleep is the cousin of death." I was in Heaven. However, the sounds of screaming quickly brought me back to Oakland. I opened my eyes in time to see a mob chasing one of the worshipers through the park. They were gaining on him. They caught him, and it was on. That was the first time I had ever witnessed violence at a church service. Weapons were produced. I heard myself evoking the name of Jesus quite loudly as I moved to stand in front of our preacher.

The battered, bloody victim jumped up on stage and ran behind Pastor Mustafa. His pursuers were right behind him.

Pastor Mustafa had some choices that presented themselves in an instant. These choices would define his ministry for the community. He could have run. That would have been a reasonable choice, wouldn't it? Self-preservation is the first law of nature when a melee is running like a hurricane in your direction. Many pastors would have side-stepped it. Had he done so, his congregants would have fled in a stampede. They would have scattered in a hundred different directions. People would have been trampled. The attackers would have had a clear shot at the victim, and Oakland being Oakland, they might have killed him.

Mustafa chose door number two. He stood there on the stage. He called for calm. One of the believers stripped an attacker of her knife. The pastor told church members who were trying to physically intervene, probably to protect him, to back away. He spoke to the combatants and got to the root of the problem. Just then, some of the real Gs (certified gangstas), who had previously been smoking cigarettes and playing dominoes at the edge of the park began to race toward the madness. "No, not here!" They shouted. "These people are out here trying to worship God and have church. Y'all ain't doing this here." That gave the bloodied victim just enough time to scramble to his feet and race to his car.

Make no mistake, the brothers who intervened were not from the Sunday school convention. However, there is still a respect for the things of God here. After the victim had made his getaway, one of the block's shot callers (in the hood not all angels have wings) walked up to the pastor and shook his hand. I didn't hear the conversation, but I read his eyes. He was saying, "Where does your church worship? I'm coming there." Why? Because as was noted earlier in this book, the streets have a saying, "Real recognize real." And people who are deep in the streets can recognize courage and resolve in a believer. Those things have great value here.

If Pastor Mustafa Muyhee had run away in that critical moment, would that G be asking for the address of his church? Probably not. That gangsta realized that the preacher was doing more than delivering an entertaining sermon; he could see that if it came down to it, the pastor was willing to die for the sake of this Jesus that he was talking about. That kind of faith attracts people who live on the margins. BASIC Ministries is still relatively new in that community. In the hood, where word gets around quickly, that incident brought him a boatload of street cred.

Fear

God doesn't have any supermen or superwomen doing his will. Machismo and faith are not synonymous. If your faith never shakes, check your pulse because you are not human. If you've never found yourself in the Garden of Gethsemane sweating bullets, it's only because you haven't been doing this long enough. Just wait. One day you will have every reason to worry and a thousands reasons to turn around and walk in the direction opposite to God's call. One day you may wake up and realize that God is calling you to take a gigantic step that you just don't feel prepared for. One day God may tell you that it's time to step down from a position for which you have no more zeal or passion but, at the same time, not tell you how you're going keep the mortgage paid.

Courage in a spiritual sense is the ability to push past what you can see with your natural eyes and trust the One who lives in your heart. You find it in the bottom of your prayer closet on your knees.

Faith is also contagious. Hang around people who talk about God's tremendous capability to do the impossible. Put the naysayers out of the room when it's time to put your faith to the test.

Crippled By Fear

Years ago, I spoke at a men's prayer breakfast. As part of my presentation, I showed a film clip of gang members shooting the breeze and trash talking on a sunny day. They looked threatening in their bandanas and wife-beater T-shirts. The young thugs threw gang signs at the camera. Some of the very middle-class gentlemen who had commuted into town for the free grub and prayers recoiled in horror.

At the conclusion of the video, I grabbed my Bible, went to the podium and then did my best to explain to the believers that it was incumbent upon them to form a strategy to reach lost young people like the ones in the video. One of the elders raised his hand and said, "All our lives we've been taught to avoid people like the ones you pointed out in the video, and now you're telling me to leave the safety of this building and walk out in this neighborhood to speak to people like them ... at night no less?" Yes, that's exactly what I was telling him.

One night I put out a call for some of the brothers to join me at dusk in front of the church. Three of us showed up. The night air was hot. Sirens whined. Polic helicopters swooped down out of the sky. We went to a hot corner. Heroin was everywhere around us; dealers and dope fiends were making hand-to-hand transactions at lightning speed. I didn't see any guns, but they were there. Dope and hammers go together like grits and eggs.

The three of us from the church stood out on that corner like sheep in a lion cage – especially one of the deacons. He was a classy gentleman in his late seventies. He was neat and well pressed, dressed for the golf course rather than the dope track. When the shot-caller emerged from the crowd to find out who we were, the deacon didn't back down. He said his name was Deacon Joe Lewis, and then he gave the name of the church that we were affiliated with.

The brother from the block introduced himself as well. He gave a street name. I hadn't come out to the block with a hard-sell program in mind, but the conversation grew serious right away. The shot-caller had a message for us. He said, "There are plenty of us behind bars. We're invisible to you, but we still need hope." He also said, "I believe in God. I know that what we're doing out here isn't right. Sometimes, on Sunday morning I'll give money to someone headed to your church and tell them to put it in the offering basket for me."

We shared Christ's love for him and the plan of redemption that culminated with blood on a Roman cross and an empty tomb. He wasn't ready to make a commitment to the King of Kings just then, but he did agree to pray. He walked us to the next corner, away from the drug trade. We held hands in a circle and each of us from the church said a prayer. When we concluded, the shot-caller said, "I want to pray." And he did. He prayed for us. And that night as we headed back to the shelter of the church, he hollered, "Don't forget about us out here." And I never have.

Why did he pray for us? He realized that he and his friends needed help and that they would need people with Deacon Joe Lewis' courage to come out to that corner toting Bibles. He needed believers that would have the faith in Christ to overcome fear.

Fear, next to apathy, is the greatest enemy of urban evangelism or community outreach.

Passion

I was riding the bus up Haight Street in San Francisco some time back when I saw a crowd gathered ten deep outside the front door of a bar. Hundreds of unblinking eyes aimed themselves at the TV screen in the front of the establishment. Manny Pacquiao and Floyd "Money" Mayweather were swinging at each other for all they were worth in one of the richest prizefights in history.

Boxing must require the most intense preparation of any sport. Months before the bout, fighters run a dozen miles a day, torture themselves in the gym by doing endless pushups, jumping rope, and sparring in the ring. Before the first bell has rung, they have put in dozens and dozens of man-hours and been punched in the face hundreds of times. And then it begins for real. The body and mind must work together to ignore pain while taking advantage of milliseconds-long openings in the opponent's defense. As the fight goes into the middle round, only sheer will pushes the great fighters; there's unexplainable energy, a force that causes them to press on even when fatigue makes their muscles feel like sandbags.

Former heavyweight champion Ken Norton, a decided underdog at the time, broke Muhammad Ali's jaw in the ring. To have one's jaw snapped is excruciatingly painful. When asked at what point in the fight it happened, Ali said that it occurred in the first round of a 15-round bout. Naysayers doubted that. They said there was no way a man could withstand that kind of pain over 15 rounds of boxing. But they didn't understand Ali's passion.

Passion is an intense driving, overmastering feeling of conviction. It is an emotion sometimes defined as fervor, ardor, enthusiasm, or zeal. It is a deep stirring within one's inner being. Webster's dictionary calls it "an emotion that is deeply stirring or ungovernable." A famous song called "Impossible Dream" makes it even clearer: "To fight for the right without question or pause / To be willing to march into hell for a heavenly cause."[1] Yes, that's passion.

Unmistakable Passion

Passion is something that cannot be counterfeited. If you spend an appreciable amount of time with someone who has passion, you will feel it. It will be in their speech, where they spend their time, in their checkbook, even where their eyes roam. If that person is a pastor or the leader of a faith-based organization, the point of their passion, whether it's to save the whales or to rescue children from the clutches of human trafficking, will be revealed in their sermons. The passion of the heart speaks through the mouth. It shows up in the budget. It proves itself in where the leader's feet go. We are all drawn to people of passion.

Years ago, I was watching an ESPN special about the New York Jets. The athletes rose at the crack of dawn. They pushed their bodies beyond the point of exhaustion for 12 hours a day at the height of hot, humid summer days. And as the sun set, they curled up their bruised bodies in hotel room corners and stared at X and O patterns in a playbook. That is passion.

Jimi Hendrix's manager once recalled a group of young fans that told him they thought Hendrix had magical powers that allowed him to play the guitar with such fluid dexterity. The manager laughed. He said that Jimi would pick up a guitar as soon as he got out of bed. He would be playing his guitar with one hand and eating his cereal with the other. Some friends said that Jimi would sometimes fall asleep at night with his favorite Fender Stratocaster guitar curled in his hands. That is passion.

John Knox, one of the fathers of the Protestant Reformation prayed, "Give me Scotland or I die." Today, passion says: "Lord, give me this hood or I die!" Based on the examples above, what would passion for *your* ministry look like?

Making a Dent in the Universe

If you believe in the mission and then give it your all, the chances are great that your passion will ignite a spark in others. The film *Pirates of Silicon Valley* focused on the lives of the men who pioneered desktop computers. Steve Jobs says in the opening line of the film, "I don't want you to think of this as just a film – some process of converting electrons and magnetic impulses into shapes and figures and sounds – no. Listen to me. We're here to make a dent in the universe. Otherwise, why even be here? We're creating a completely new consciousness, like an artist or a poet. We're rewriting the history of human thought with what we're doing. That's how you have to think of this."[2]

Steve Jobs changed the world with three instruments: vision, courage, and passion. Consider his words, "We're here to make a dent in the universe. Otherwise, why even be here?" As Christians, we must say, "We, as a people of God, meet in this building to make a dent in this community for the Kingdom of God by all holy means necessary. If this is going to be just another church or another non-profit organization, why even be here?"

Your passion for the ways of God, the things of God, the word of God, the vision, and the people – not only in the church but in the community – that's what will make the difference. That kind of passion will make a dent in the universe.

People might not like the way you part your hair, but they should never be able to question your commitment. Pastor, the members may criticize the way you deliver your sermons, but there must be one thing beyond question: your passion. When you walk by, even if they say it grudgingly, people must admit (as we say in Oakland) "she's about it" or "Like him or not, he's in with both feet."

When his crew threatened mutiny, explorer Hernando Cortez and some trusted loyalists went on a stealth mission to the seashore and destroyed all of the boats that had brought his navy from Europe. Doing this, he left only two options on the table: believe or die.

Now, I wouldn't recommend that you go out to the parking lot while service is in session and firebomb the vehicles in the reserved spaces, but you get the message. Cortez was unwilling to even consider the notion of mediocrity, and he would not let his followers accept it either.

When Passion Reaches Zero

May I share my personal heartbreak with you? I have seen too many pastors, church leaders, and church members without passion. They play the game. They suit up for the role, and yet there is no passion. They are doing what they do based on a paycheck. I told a friend of mine some time back, "Your pastor ain't nuthin' but a hustler." I never apologized for that comment, because I meant it. Years ago, a rock and roll band called Dire Straights had a song called, "Money For Nothing," and that's how that pastor is rolling.

You can get away with things in ministry that would never fly in any other employment field. For the next four weeks, try coming to work for only two of five weekdays. On the two days you do show up, take a two-hour lunch. Come back on both days with your hands filled with shopping bags from the clothing boutique of your choice. Go ahead. I give you permission. Write back to me and tell me how well our little experiment goes over with your supervisor.

Of course, I'm just kidding! Don't do that! You'll get fired. However, in the church world, things work differently. I have met pastors who extract huge full-time salaries from churches. Nowhere in the Bible does it say that the pastor has to walk around in a loincloth and bare feet. However, these jokers may not set foot on the church premises more than twice a week, and even then never for more than six hours at a shot.

They spend more time massaging the TV clicker in their den than actually preparing sermons or visiting sick and shut-in church members. They might manage a prayer on your behalf during a commercial break. Still, every few months they have the nerve to arm-twist their poor congregants for a pastor's anniversary "gift" or a birthday "love offering."

Church member, these characters are playing you like a back street pool shark plays a mark. Put all of their "godspeak" and church slang on mute for a minute. Passion is measurable, so open your eyes and measure it!

Your pastor may be a hustler slanging Bible verses instead of crack rock. And the moment anyone begins to ask any probing questions, he or she will start shooting scriptures at them out of context. They've been doing this for so long they almost believe their own bull spit.

Come Sunday morning, they'll copy a sermon off the Internet, print it out, read it to you verbatim from the pulpit, and then dare you not to shout, amen! And at the end of all that, they'll meet you at the door, throw their arms around you, and shout, "I love you."

That's like the wolf kissing the lamb on the top of the head and saying, "I love you" when what he's really thinking is "I love you on a plate with salt and pepper next to a slice of buttered bread and a glass of chilled white wine."

Christian Commitment Costs

When I first became a believer, a woman I respected in the Lord had a phrase that she would repeat to me often. "Every little thing we do is precious in His (God's) sight." But is that true? Time and time again in the scriptures Jesus outlined the depth of commitment it would take to follow Him.

In John 6:53 Jesus says, "... Verily, verily, I say unto you, Except ye eat the flesh of the Son of man, and drink his blood, ye have no life in you." Jesus was talking about a "consuming" relationship with Him. Nothing about those words makes me think of a religious social society or an Elks Club with a prayer component.

A famous preacher ends his television broadcasts by asking viewers to pray a four-line mantra behind him for soul salvation. I'm afraid that it's a little more complicated than that. Jesus told people to count the cost before they followed him because, indeed, a cost is involved.

What is the difference between a good idea and a passion? We might talk about a good idea, even debate over it. If something is your passion in the faith realm, more than likely you're willing, if need be, to die for it. Passion drives real preachers and ministries. Passion draws people. It sustains the fight in the darkness.

One of America's Most Courageous Pastors Weighs In

At the beginning of his pastorate at the Allen Temple Baptist Church in East Oakland, the Reverend J. Alfred Smith, Sr., received an odd message from his secretary. Sister Marie Johnson said, "Pastor Smith, don't come in today. Frank Rucker was here with two men."[2]

"What did he want?" Reverend Smith asked.

Rucker had said, "You tell that preacher to stay off East 14th Street. Tell him to leave East 14th Street to us. His place is down here at the church."

But that wasn't all. Sister Johnson said, "Pastor Smith, he said that he and those hoodlums are going to run up here next Sunday, drag you out of the pulpit, and beat you down in front of the entire congregation. What are you going to do, Pastor?"

Frank Rucker was a drug dealer who, it was said, had already done time on a murder charge. As you can see, he was not exactly enthused by the new pastor's outdoor evangelism crusade, which he saw as costing him money. The battle lines were clearly drawn. To what had to have been Frank Rucker's shock, Pastor Smith immediately went down to the bar where Rucker was known to hang out. When the barkeep told him Rucker was not there, he said, "You tell Frank Rucker that J. Alfred Smith, Sr., pastor of Allen Temple Baptist Church, was down here looking for him."

Reverend Smith's members began dressing him in a bulletproof vest. Church members served as bodyguards. The police put out a warrant for Rucker's arrest. One night, the pastor received a phone call from a Richmond, California, clergyman. He said, "Frank Rucker is here. He wants to speak to you at my church. Come alone."

Against the pleadings of family, friends, and church members, Reverend Dr. J. Alfred Smith, Sr., walked through the doors of that dark, empty church. Frank Rucker met him there and apologized. But the story did not end there. Again, in the face of vehement opposition, Reverend Smith had the complaint against Rucker dismissed. If this wasn't enough, he told the church deacons that they were to give Frank Rucker a job as a church custodian. In the coming years, Frank Rucker would become a born-again Christian and then a minister of the gospel.

In an interview for this book, Reverend Smith said, "If you don't have passion, you can't have perseverance. If you don't have passion, you don't have the courage to be defiant. Defiance is often missing due to the lack of courage. You have passive proclaimers who pray long prayers expecting God to perform the miracle, whereas God has, in fact, called *them* to be the change makers! I can pray long prayers and I can preach properly and write essays on justice, but in writing, justice is a verb, not a noun. It becomes a verb when I have the passion and the courage to act."

Be a Hood Monastic

Most of the time, prayer is just something we do to get God to go along with our agenda. So often, in public settings it has become entertainment. Rev, this isn't the direction you want to go. Learn how to listen to God. Find yourself in places of quiet where you can discern God's voice. Consider God's leading. Read God's word. Ponder divine "coincidences." Create spaces in your weekly schedule to be alone with God. Make Christian retreats a part of your connection activity to the divine.

In the urban setting, it's hard to find the quiet garden or the mountainside where one can seek God in quiet. The sounds of sirens and barking dogs seem to blot out holy silence. You must seek out this silence. Prayer is the most important element of any ministry. Is it any wonder that Jesus would commune with the Father before dawn in a secret place? Touching hands with the Father came before touching the hand of the leper.

There's a big Catholic church about three blocks from my apartment. They open the chapel during the day for community members who wish to pray and meditate. It's quiet. The church sits back from the street, and three of the walls have no windows. More of my ministry has been crafted in that quiet room than on the block. That space has been the incubator for divine intervention in my life. There have been moments where I walked into that room and said, "Father, do something!" There have been other times where I just sat back for an hour and listened in dim light, quiet, and stillness, praising, meditating on the word of God, and seeking God's fire and direction.

Seek God without an agenda. If God truly called you, God has more for you to do in a hurting world than to holler "amen" on Sunday morning. Go back and listen to God. Sit at God's feet for awhile. Do it daily.

You Can Make a Difference

I have met some astonishing people along the journey. I want to talk briefly about two of them.

Daphne Phung is a gentle, unassuming lady who was sitting at home watching a television broadcast on MSNBC about human trafficking. She was completely unaware that something so atrocious could be so widespread in America. It moved her so deeply that she knelt in prayer and asked God why He hadn't moved to eradicate this great evil. God spoke to her heart; He told her that *she* was to combat human sexual slavery.

Ms. Phung's background was not in social service or advocacy. In fact, she works in finance and accounting. Undaunted by her seeming lack of expertise, she began to study the issue and seek out teammates to create a bold step. Daphne Phung founded California Against Slavery and partnered with Safer California Foundation to sponsor Proposition 35, also known as the "Californians Against Sexual Exploitation Act."

If passed, it would increase prison terms for human traffickers, require pimps to register as sex offenders, require criminal fines from convicted human traffickers to pay for services to help victims, mandate law enforcement training on human trafficking, and require all registered sex offenders to disclose their Internet accounts.

Proposition 35 passed in November 2012 with more than 81 percent approval, making it the most successful ballot initiative since Californians began this voting process in the 1914 election. With more than 10 million votes, it was the first initiative in California history to pass with more than 80 percent of the vote. One person with a burden from God and a passion to see change come for "the least of these," made a huge difference.

Soccer Mom Warrior

Some years back, following a conference on human trafficking, I met Genice Jacobs, a woman with an engaging smile and long, curly red hair. Genice thought often about her Jewish forebears who had perished in the Holocaust. She said that she would like to believe that, had she been alive during that time, she would have been a part of the underground resistance, that she would have hidden other Jewish people in her house under threat of death if need be. Genice sees commercial sexual exploitation of children as akin to the Jewish Holocaust or the African slave trade. Her conscience would not let her sit in silence after she discovered that children were being trafficked in her city. She raised money to have billboards placed all over California decrying the evil of human trafficking. She sponsored public service radio bulletins about the issue. This suburban soccer mom goes into the public schools and warns children about the dangers that pimps and other sex traffickers pose to their well-being. Today, she is one of the leading abolitionists in the city of Oakland. She has never lived in the hood. No one in her family has ever been trafficked. She simply cares. And one person who cares can make a tremendous difference, as her life proves.

During the campaign, Genice said, "One day future generations will read about the plague of human trafficking and wonder about all of the good people who knew of its tentacles into society but did nothing. I refuse to be counted among that number. I have to act."

I can't think of anything more poignant than Genice's words. The hood needs ministry, *real* ministry. It's time to act. The willingness to do rather than just talk is what separates those with street cred from the posers. The struggle is out there in those streets. It's time to move into action. People are counting on you. One person can make a difference. Do something.

Chapter 20

Nuts and Bolts

So far, we've dealt mostly in concepts and ideas. In this chapter, I'm going to offer some practical ideas that might help you press into action. Some of these ideas, if put to use, can lift a person out poverty. Sometimes you can save a life with a simple phone call; I've been there when it's happened. Put into practice, the principles listed below can save you a world of heartache.

Never ever divulge graveyard secrets.

"I could be killed for what I'm telling you... ." I remember the first time I ever heard those words. It took a few seconds for them to register in my cranium. The person seated across the desk from me was actually shooting dice with his mortality, gambling on whether or not he could trust my integrity as a minister. If I repeated to the wrong person what he was telling me, he could indeed be murdered. And it wouldn't be the last time someone would sit across from me and open a conversation with that phrase.

If you do urban ministry, people caught up in all kinds of situations will need to be able to trust you. Can you keep what is known as a "graveyard" secret, so named because it's something you will take to the grave with you?

Gossip is the preacher's kryptonite. It will unravel everything you are or ever want to be. The first time one of your members realizes that you've passed along something they shared with you in confidence, your ability to speak into their life is dead. You're unlikely to get a second chance. The ability to keep a secret is a discipline. Human nature doesn't make this your first inclination. Some things you hear will be so amazing that you'll want to share them with somebody. Don't do it. Learn early how to keep that secret between you and God. Your ability to be trusted is as important as your ability to preach, perhaps even more so. As a minister, people have confided in me about everything from adultery to ... well, let's not go there.

Confidentiality does have its boundaries. If you work for a faith-based organization or a non-profit organization, you may be required to disclose anything that happens in the course of your duties to a supervisor or pastoral board. That being said, the confided information still should never leave the offices.

Preacher, you are also a mandated reporter. If an elderly widow whispers in your ear that her caretaker is stealing her social security check and is threatening to break her arm, you are legally required to report the abuse. (You'd best check the laws for mandatory reporting for your state.)

One of my favorite gangster movies is *A Prayer Before Dying*, starring Mickey Rourke and Bob Hoskins. In the film, a priest witnesses a mob hit. The killer, a backslidden Catholic, slips away from the scene of the crime only later to sneak into the priest's confessional booth. In the secret space between priest, God, and man, the hit man confesses his sin – the murder that the priest witnessed. The priest is incensed. He races to the other side of the confessional, flings the door open and orders the penitent out. However, because the evil deed was shared under the seal of the confessional, the priest cannot reveal to the police what he has heard. It becomes the premise for a great movie.

"Has anything like that ever happened to you?" you ask.

What? Do you think I'd tell you? You might as well forget everything I just wrote!

Suffice to say, if you're going to be effective in urban ministry, learn how to keep your mouth shut. The ministry you save might be your own. The life you save might be someone else's.

Be who you say you are.

"Pimping and hoing is the best thing going." Those are not my words; nor did I make up that statement. On the street corner where this book was conceived, that credo is stamped into the sidewalks with a fiery brand.

One afternoon I stood in the hot zone watching a young pimp holler at a teenage girl across the street. She quickened her step as he offered to show her how she could make some real money out on the track. Many fall for the lure. Some get kidnapped. For some reason, watching that 30-second interaction birthed the idea for this book.

Pimping carries serious legal penalties, including having to register as a sex offender. If you get hit with one of those California penal code 266 charges, we'll see you in six years. That's why a pimp stomps the fear of Satan into a woman. He wants her too terrified to testify on a witness stand. He also needs a trusted co-conspirator. So, one of those women becomes his "bottom b———." She's completely bought into his psychological manipulation. Her job is to make sure the other girls stay in line and produce money for the boss player. As sick as that sounds, in that world everyone knows their role, and in that game, they play out their job descriptions – especially the pimp. He has a street name, and 9 times out of 10, he's living up to it at the very bottom of the evil scale. There are no illusions about who he is or what he does.

Many pimps are real about their trade. They're second- or third-generation flesh peddlers and enslavers. Of course, that's not how they refer to each other. They call themselves "sporting men" or "gentlemen of leisure."

I remember my jaw dropping at the sight of a lost-looking girl in her late teens, standing in the back of a local convenience store. Her black skirt was so short it barely covered her vital parts. A woman with silver gray hair glanced at her and shook her head. The young woman had a phone pinned to her ear. I couldn't hear the other end of the conversation. I didn't need to hear it to discern what was going on. Her pimp was giving her instructions for the evening. Why didn't he come in the store and just tell her face-to-face? The pimp is smart enough to realize that he has to avoid ever being photographed on a security camera with one of his girls.

Pimps are real. They study their craft. They study their prey. They study the clientele. They study the laws. They study the routes and routines of law enforcement officers. The pimp is a career criminal dedicated to his craft. A pimp will risk prison or death over a dollar.

Christian, what are you willing to risk for the sake of the gospel? Minister, missionary, evangelist, God has called you to be out on the same turf in a life-and-death struggle to reach the same people that the devil is using these merchants of death to ensnare. You see that cat with the pistol in his pocket whispering into that child's ear? You are his opponent, his enemy. Do you think God called you into this so you could call out numbers at the church bingo game or show off your shiny new clubs in the church golf classic? Are you kidding? If it were that easy, Jesus never would have had to tell people to count the cost before they chose to follow him. Read the newspaper! Being a Christian is dangerous! In other parts of the world, to claim the name of Jesus is to become an enemy of the state. It is to face torture, imprisonment, and execution. And you're running around here shouting "I'm a Christian because I wear a floppy hat, hang a cross around my neck, tip God when the offering basket is passed, and put in my hour-and-a-half on a hard pew every Sunday." Are you serious?

I'm going to challenge you to do an in-depth study of the book of Acts. Paul spent more time in prison than on the tennis court. Stephen didn't receive trophies and all-expense-paid vacations from the enemies of the cross.

Pimps are real about the game. How real are you about the gospel?

A real gangster doesn't walk out of the house to play it safe. He or she will do whatever they feel they have to do to come up (gain money). They don't necessarily worry about whether they will survive the night or end up in a cell. There are consequences to the game, and the true hustler is ready to pay them if necessary.

Again, I must ask, "How far are you willing to go with this?" I can hear someone saying, "It doesn't take all that." You're wrong. Go back and read your Bible. It takes all that and more. If you're not willing to pay the price to reach the lost in that hood where your church is situated, who will? Are you for real, or do you just enjoy a good shout and a rousing hymn?

Be yourself.

A former high-level drug dealer called me one night. Someone had given him my phone number. He had written a book and, since we both aimed our literary works at the same market, he suggested that we do some book-signing events together. After we had been conversing about book marketing for awhile, he switched the subject in mid-sentence. His voice sounded puzzled. "You don't sound like no gangsta," he said.

And there's good reason for that. I'm not a gangsta. I'm a Baptist minister. Rule Number 1 in the streets is: Be yourself. Don't feel as though you'll get hood points for trying to be somebody you're not. Walk like yourself. Talk like yourself. Pray like yourself. Teach like yourself. Fellowship like yourself. Be yourself.

I was thrilled to see one of my young mentees walk out of jail one day. He and his cousin had jumped on a total stranger at a train stop. Later I asked him what had caused the conflict. My young friend said of his victim, "He wasn't about what he said he was about."

There's a lot of fronting, faking, and perpetrating in the hood. Unfortunately, it doesn't stop there. Open the church door. How about you, Christian? Are you real? Are you really who you say you are? Authenticity is three-fourths of street cred. Be yourself. Keep it real. In the end, people will almost always respect that.

I wasn't born knowing how important it is to "be real," to be myself. In fact, I remember distinctly the conversation I was having when three words brought it home to me.

The construction teacher stared at me with a smile and a glazed-over look that said he couldn't believe what he was looking at. I had applied for a position at a school for kids who had not been "a good fit" for the local school system. Some had been expelled; some had dropped out. These were tough kids, many who would fight at the drop of a hat. Some came to school draped in gang colors.

The teacher looked me in the eye and said, "I don't think you quite know what we're dealing with here, and frankly, I don't think you'll make it."

His blunt assessment stunned me. "You mean because I have salt-and-pepper hair and I tend to smile a lot?" I asked.

"Bingo. That's exactly right," he said.

About then, a late-model sports car pulled up in front of the school. Hip-hop thumped from the 15-inch woofers in the trunk. A young Latino kid got out of the passenger seat. He didn't look in our direction as he headed into the school, late for class.

"You know who he's down with, don't you?" the teacher asked.

How could I know? I had never seen him before. The teacher mentioned the name of a notorious multinational gang. I'd seen a television special about them the year before; they were, indeed, notorious. When it was time to leave, I shook the teacher's hand. He stared at me as though he was looking at a shooting victim on the other side of the yellow tape. I have to tell you, his gaze was unsettling.

A few days later, I was scheduled to speak at a correctional facility for high-risk kids – actually, the kids deemed by the courts in this particular county as the most incorrigible. When I arrived at the location, I met a smiling, heavy-set, African-American man with salt-and-pepper hair. It was like looking in a mirror.

Turns out our appearance wasn't all we had in common. He was a Christian as well as a deacon at his home church. It wasn't quite time for me to address the incarcerated youths, so we sat down to share a meal of hamburgers and fries. During the course of our conversation, I also shared my concern over the words the construction teacher had spoken and the look he had given me.

The deacon thought for a moment and then said, "Just be yourself. Don't try to out-tough them. Some of these kids have stared death in the face. Since they were in the cradle they've been in violent situations you can't even imagine. Nothing you ever say or do is going to scare them, so if you get that job, just be yourself."

I watched him that afternoon at the correctional facility. Kids from the hood who had done everything from arson to murder would come up and put their arms across his shoulders. They loved this guy. I never heard him raise his voice; nor did I ever see any of them defy him. They had a ton of respect for the deacon.

I took his words with me when I left. I got that job and I put them into practice. And I got the same response from the kids at the new job. So I share his advice with you: "Just be yourself."

Real recognize real.

If you're a drug dealer, you learn early on that who you buy or sell to could mean your freedom or your life. You learn to develop a heightened sense of awareness regarding the authenticity of the people you do business with. In the streets they say, "Real recognize real."

Crime is not a stable job. The odds of rising to the level of billionaire are slim indeed. In real life, even celebrated criminals like mafia legend John Gotti end up in prison or in the graveyard. The only way you survive in an industry where you can't trust anyone is to partner with people who have sworn to live by a certain code of "honor." It gets tricky when you consider that part of a criminal's resume must include the fact that she or he is a world-class liar. However, loyalty is part of the code of the streets.

How does a bank robber find someone who will keep the getaway car in "Park" even when sirens whine in the distance? How does a high-level heroin dealer find someone to work a certain territory for him, trusting that he won't turn him in if caught? Criminals live by a twisted sense of honor and loyalty. Of course, people tell on each other and sell each other out to cops and enemies all the time, but that's not the ideal. People who have crime and mayhem coursing through their blood stream can usually spot other people who are real about who they say they are and what they do – and they respect that.

In the streets, where nothing is what it appears to be, a high currency is placed on being authentic. At some point, if you need an introduction to someone higher up the food chain, the person making the introduction is going to vouch for you by saying something like, "He's solid. I can co-sign for the dude. He's a stand-up brother." Or, "Yeah, he's real."

When I was in seminary school, I met a minister who lamented something to me. He said, "I've always felt sort of bad because I don't have a background. I've never been bad. I got saved as a boy. I've never done drugs. I've never been arrested. I married young and have remained faithful to my wife. The only thing I know is Jesus. I don't have a testimony."

My jaw got rug burn. After I had picked up my mandible from the carpet, I said, "You don't have a testimony?" What better testimony than to be able to say that God kept your life pure, to be able to say that you managed to avoid many of the pitfalls that ensnare others? How much more real can it get? Why make up a story?

Being real doesn't necessarily mean you need a resume that allows you to walk out on the block and say, "I used to be a gangster." No, being real means that you are living your authentic self. Nothing is a greater turn-off than hearing someone who hasn't been there imitate hood speech or seeing somebody adopt a gangster limp because they want to be accepted in the hood. Better to wear polka dot high-water pants and Coke bottle glasses and be able to say "This is who I am" than to adopt some persona that is untrue to who you really are so that you can fit in.

You might ask why I would spend time telling you something as simple as "Just be yourself." It's because that doesn't always come as easy to people as you might think. In truth, nothing can cost you more in your search for common ground than to adopt a swagger that you really don't own or a false back story.

Each summer when I was a kid, my mother would fill up a school bus full of inner city kids and cart us off to camp. Miracle Camp was nestled deep in the Maryland woods. After a dozen or two rambunctious kids disembarked from the big, red church bus, we were assigned to camp counselors. These suburban, Anglo teenagers would be our surrogate parents for the week.

One summer I drew Elmer as a counselor. Elmer had a pot belly and skinny, pink legs. He had eyes that flitted hither and fro like two brown marbles in a bottle of turpentine. He led us to our dormitories, rectangular wooden barracks coated in peeling gray paint. The door made a creaking noise when I opened it, like the haunted house at the amusement park. There was enough dust on the floor to challenge Lawrence of Arabia. Bunk beds filled the room. I sat down on my assigned bunk. The mattress had a curious design, as though Picasso had been there as a child experimenting with urine rather than pastels.

In the dark of night, instead of ghost stories, counselor Elmer chose to regale us with crime stories from his past. He had been a gang leader in his hometown. He had run with fast women, been stabbed in a bar brawl, and once faced down 10 men in a dark alley with a lead pipe. How odd! Counselor Elmer had no visible scars, except the ones caused by acne. In the dark, he bore an uncanny resemblance to Bill Gates without his glasses. As Elmer finished his story with the day he was converted to the faith, I shrugged and went to sleep. Something about it didn't exactly ring true, but surely a man of God would not lie about the circumstances surrounding his conversion. When the lights went off, I turned over, forgot about my questions, and went to sleep.

The next morning on the way to chapel, Slim, a fast-talking kid from inner city Baltimore grabbed my arm. We were the only two black cabin mates. Apparently, he had forgotten rule number 18, on the "Thou Shalt Not" list at Miracle Camp because he said, "Hey, Harry, that m.f. is straight bulls——-tin'. The only drive-by he ever did was on a lawn mower at the country club!"

"But why would a preacher lie about his background?" I asked Slim.

"M.f. be lyin', trying to get you to respect him behind some ole bull—-t. It's a puzzle, homie."

Years later, I was walking the crowded passageways of a bus station when a homeless man shook a wrinkled copy of the *Street News* newspaper in my face. Next, he shook his palm, I assumed in request for some coins. We made the exchange. Minutes later, as I sat back in the reclining chair of my bus seat and read, something drew my attention like a magnet.

An ex-member of a once-notorious gang was writing his memoirs in installments. He wrote the gruesome details of his life adventures in the 10-page paper. And then he said something that raised the hair on my head. He noted that a famous evangelist who had claimed to be a member of his gang in a famous autobiographical bestseller was actually a fraud. He had never, in fact, been a part of the gang. And if memory serves me, the *Street News* writer noted that hush money had been paid to the gang members after the book's bestseller status brought the preacher to prominence.

I stroked the hairs on my chin as I mulled over the matter. It was then that I saw holes in the preacher's story, not necessarily noticeable at first read of his autobiography. The preacher had said that he was, simultaneously, a church youth group leader, a chess champion, and leader of one of the most notorious street gangs in New York City.

As a kid, I had believed the story without question. Now I began to ponder the details. As leader of this gang, he would be infamous, the kind of person that people would point out as he walked down the street, the kind of person that would give parents thoughts of sending their kids up the stairs when he approached. How could a teenager hold that kind of power and weight in the streets and have the people in his local church be completely oblivious to his status as an outlaw? How could he have been an arch criminal and not just an ordinary A student but the leader of the student counsel at the same time? The whole thing made me think of Slim's assessment of the camp counselor's testimony: "M.f. be lyin'; trying to get you to respect him behind some ole bull—-t. It's a puzzle, homie."

The author had fooled a lot of people in evangelical circles over the years, but he couldn't fool the streets. As I said before, "real recognize real." And in the streets, people can spot a phony from as far as the moon is from planet Earth.

Earlier in this chapter, I wrote about the position I landed at the second-chance high school in the San Francisco Bay Area. Among my responsibilities were keeping order and, if necessary, breaking up fights. One day I stopped a young girl from jumping on a teenage boy. Fury contorted her face. "What did he do?" I asked. She said, "He says he's from (a notorious San Francisco housing project), but he's not from there like that." Let me translate "like that" for you. The young man might have shared a residence in that housing project with his grandmother. However, he was not a member of the gang that assumed the project's name; not by a long shot. When he said he was from that housing project, he was leading people to believe that he was affiliated with the notorious thugs who were feared all over the city. In actuality, he was half a step from being a choirboy. In the angry girl's opinion, he was a fraud. Real recognized real.

Put your platinum hood card to good use.

Simply put, people who respect no one and nothing often respect men and women of the cloth. I rarely wear a tie. You couldn't tell me from anyone that lives in my neighborhood based solely upon my clothing choices. And yet, if I walk down my block, people nod in my direction respectfully. They might censor their conversations. They'll pick up the dice from the asphalt. They'll hide the 40-ounce bottle of beer behind their back. Someone will respectfully utter the greeting, "... Morning, Preacher" or "Hi, Rev."

If they offer that respect to a hood preacher in Chuck Taylor sneakers and an Oakland Raiders T-shirt, imagine how they'll treat you in your clerical garb with black shoes and a round, white collar! Even after the social cataclysm that has shaken the inner city in the past 40 years, the minister of the gospel is still the most respected individual in the community.

Look at the facade of your building. There's a good chance there's no graffiti on it. Think with me. Why is it that everything in the hood is covered with graffiti – except your house of worship? Chances are great there's a respect level that frowns on vandalism of a church.

A few years ago a funeral in East Oakland was interrupted by a shootout. Gang rivals came together at the wrong time and place, and they started exchanging lead inside the church walls. Church mothers in black straw hats had to dive for cover. Police set up a perimeter around the house of worship as thugs took the opportunity to reload. At the end of the day, no one was grinning or laughing about that. No one involved had anything to brag about. Even the heavy hitters in the hood thought it was scandalous. That is where people draw the line. The church is a neutral zone.

Pastor, you are the only universally respected person in a neighborhood where people sometimes do not respect anything or anybody. Use your platinum hood card. Go out to the street and make the presence of God in your life be recognized. Does that mean you need to stand on the corner with Bible in one hand and bullhorn in the other? It might, but that's not exactly what I have in mind.

Go and spread the light of Christ in the world.

I had a rough time in seminary. I transferred from the American Baptist Seminary of the West in Berkeley, California, to Palmer Theological Seminary in Wynnewood, Pennsylvania. I found that I would need to do some hardcore, intense work if I planned to graduate within my desired time frame. I overloaded myself with classes. On top of that, I traveled back to Asbury Park, New Jersey, once a week to do my internship. And somehow in between, I eked out time to write my first published book. My schedule was murderous.

In the midst of that grind, a ray of sunlight shone. A soul food restaurant opened about two blocks from the seminary. The people who opened it were loving and sincere. They were a wonderful couple that made more than soul food. They created a home away from home for me. One day while I was having breakfast, a white man in a priest's vestments walked through the door. He looked like Saint Francis of Assisi with glasses, and we just struck up a conversation. As I got up to leave, I realized I had left home without any money. Now, since I was in the restaurant all the time, it was really no problem. I told the proprietor I was headed to downtown Philadelphia and that I would return later with the money to pay my bill.

When I returned a few hours later, ready to make good on my breakfast bill, the owner put her hand up and shook her head. She said, "No need. That priest paid your bill as soon as you left."

The priest and I became friends, and that's how I found out that it took almost half his month's stipend to cover my breakfast bill that morning. When I offered to reimburse him, he refused to take the money. I felt bad, but he didn't. The responsibility that his order had given him was to simply leave their housing quarters each morning to spread the light of Christ in the world. Can you imagine that? His job was to make Jesus Christ known to the world through kind words and deeds. As far as I'm concerned he was a resounding success. Something like that is dangerous, you say? I shouldn't even have to address that statement at this point, but I will. Being a Christian is dangerous. Paul was heckled, whipped, shipwrecked, and according to church history, beheaded. I can't find a single scripture in the Bible that reassures you that if you put it all on the line for God, nothing negative will ever happen to you. However, I *can* tell you that if the Spirit of the Lord leads you there, God's will be done. I can also promise that your life will have meaning and fulfillment that you might not even be able to imagine right now.

Understand racial differences before you speak.

You might be an Anglo called to a black community to do ministry. Can it work? Sure. The people you've met in this book are from every spectrum of God's human rainbow. They are black, white, Asian, Latino, and bi-racial.

The first church that gave me an opportunity to come aboard was almost all white. I was the only black man in the building. Other churches joined our youth group for weekly Bible studies and fellowships. Soon the majority of people I ministered to were Southeast Asian.

One night after Bible study, two of the teenagers rushed into my office. The older said, "Do you know there's a difference between me and him?" One was Hmong; the other was Cambodian. I had said something that they found insensitive in my sermon. It shook me. I listened as they gave me an in-depth teaching session on their different cultures. The next day, I went to the library.

That experience taught me that it is the height of arrogance to walk into the community without humbling oneself to listen to the people who live there. You want to walk into their reality and give them spiritual directions, but you haven't listened to them first. You haven't made yourself a student. This is a big no-no. Those young men will always be better experts on what it means to be Hmong and Cambodian than I will, but still, I had to immerse myself in books about their culture. I had to sit at *their* feet, if I really intended for my journey with them as pastor to be a meaningful one. I valued their words. I treated their viewpoints and ideas with reverence, and they recognized it. It worked.

Be a servant to the homeless.

Anybody can end up homeless. The San Francisco Tenderloin (or the T.L. as many call it) taught me that. The Tenderloin is one of the worst drug ghettos in the United States. Everything from heroin to pain pills is sold right out in the open, day and night. Homelessness is epidemic in the Tenderloin.

In 2005, through the grace of God, I landed a job as a case manager (akin to a social worker) at the Glide Memorial Church health clinic in San Francisco's Tenderloin district. When the nurse practitioners and psychotherapists entered an area outside of their resources and expertise, I got the call.

Homelessness can try your soul. I can only speak on it from the outside. It's one of those things you have to experience to really understand. As a case manager, I listened to stories from those who came from all over the world only to find themselves trapped in the mean streets of the T.L. I fought to find them housing, transportation back home, legal status, and about a hundred other pressing needs. I trained interns to do the same thing, and some are still working in the hood today serving the struggling poor.

How do you become homeless? Here's one example. Let's say you've been piecing together something resembling a living in America's most expensive city by fusing the income from two jobs. One day you lose one of those jobs due to downsizing. You have no savings. You have no family. You have no friends who can take you in. One day you come back to your residence and find that the key won't turn in your door. Management has changed the lock. So, not only have you lost your job, you've lost your bed, since they now own all of your possessions. Good luck getting them back. Welcome to the streets. Once you fall through this hole, it's hard to get out of it.

Many homeless folks have drug and alcohol problems. They didn't have their problems when they first became homeless. Over time, however, they turned to substances just to cope. The nights find them sleeping in the hospital emergency room, in doorways, in abandoned cars, and in the city-run shelters – if you can get a reservation for a bed.

On a cold night in Frisco, many people pitch a tent in the park or stretch out a sleeping bag in front of a brightly lit building rather than go to a shelter. Shelters are plain and austere inside, and some are even infested with lice and bed bugs. It can't be easy sleeping in the bed next to a snoring, total stranger. One man told me that he tied his cell phone to his wrist before he went to sleep. When he woke up, the phone was gone. The cord had been cut with a knife while he slept.

Many homeless people end up with legal problems. In San Francisco, if a cop catches you with an open container of beer, he can cite you with a ticket. You don't have a mailbox, so you don't respond to repeated notices to pay the ticket. The ticket turns into a warrant. One day you're stopped for jay walking, and then they see that there's a warrant out on you. You're going to jail. And it all stemmed from the fact that you lost a job through no fault of your own.

Sadly, it's not just the grown folks that are homeless. I have shaken hands with homeless children. Even now, it's hard for me to write about it. I was serving at a church one afternoon when a phone call came from the school down the street. The call involved a destitute family whose children needed food. I said, "Send them over." Thank God I was serving at a church that cared enough to help people in distress.

The knock at the door came 5 minutes later. My jaw dropped when I opened the front door. A short woman with a forced smile stood in front of me. Her children ranged in age from infancy to high school. There were 12 of them. They were sleeping in a relative's mobile home down the street, a temporary situation, I was assured. It's their eyes that I remember most. They were bulging with hurt, suffering, and humiliation. I can only imagine the teasing the kids took at school.

We broke the bank to feed them that night. The next day they were back. It takes a lot of money to feed 12 children and 2 adults. Right, 2 adults. The husband never came to the church to shake my hand. Perhaps his male ego made him too proud to beg for help, so he sent his wife instead.

One day, the children expressed their thanks by gathering in front of me, like the hood version of the Partridge Family. They sang a medley of Motown hits for an audience of one. Where did kids their age learn those songs? Mom told me. When they lived in places where there was no electricity, no heat, and no television, singing was the communal exercise that kept their spirits high and their minds off their hungry bellies and cold hands.

One day, they just disappeared. I never saw them again.

TRULY CARE FOR OTHERS. While working at the Glide Health Clinic, I served with nurse practitioners who would use tweezers to pick lice out of homeless people's hair. I saw them give up their lunch break to strategize how they might help a client who had urinated on the floor and cussed them all out. At a gathering called Homeless Connect, I watched servants of humanity connect to basic resources that save lives. I've seen people go the extra mile and then some. I've been blessed to meet some of the most compassionate people God ever made. They're walking wonders, filled with love. If you're going to walk in their footsteps, love must glow from the pores of your skin.

Struggling people know when you like them – or don't. They caucus outside the doors of your office, sharing the names of the people inside your work space who really care. They'll walk past three or four desks to get that one person. Serving the poor has to be more than just a good idea, a good job, a way to start up the ladder. If this is not in your soul, get a job working at the Post Office. I've seen people who work in places where love should be the number one job requirement. It's sad that it's that way because people suffer as a result of their lack of compassion.

SEE EQUALS. Never look down on someone who has less in the way of material things than you do. When someone has to journey from office to office and desk to desk seeking survival resources, it doesn't take long to figure out how people on the other side of the desk see you. Bureaucrats do not necessarily live by Jesus' command to love. They often treat the homeless population like criminals. When I worked as a social case manager, I made a special effort for people to know I was excited to see them. My standard greeting is "Whass up, family?" And I meant it.

One day a man caught in a state of homelessness told me, "The worst thing about being homeless is the fact that you become invisible to people. They don't look you in the eye."

I have never had to live in the streets, but I do know what it is to be invisible. A few weeks ago, I was returning from a weekly Bible study I teach at Glide Church. I dress like anyone you'd see walking in the hood. On chilly California nights, I wear jeans, sneakers, and an oversized flannel shirt. Nothing about my dress says, "I don't belong in this hood." Unless you know me, you wouldn't know I'm a minister, not by my clothes.

That night, as I crossed from the San Francisco Tenderloin to the downtown shopping area on the way home, I ran into a couple of people I knew from Oakland. "Reverend," they said, "they're having a grand opening at the museum down the block. And they're serving free food." I thanked them and made my way there. I love museums, and let's face it, the free food offering wasn't exactly a deterrent.

Who should I see as I entered the building other than Brother So and So, an upstanding Christian figure that I recognized. He was engaged in conversation, but I leaned over and waved at him. He didn't wave back. "That's odd," I thought. I tried as best I could to mingle with the tuxedo and evening gown set, the folks giggling and telling inside jokes as they sipped their martinis. Nostrils flared at my sneakers. I saw a well-known black leader standing in front of a second floor exhibit. "Hi, So and So," I said. She looked at me as though I were made of glass. I made a second attempt to get my Christian brother at the front door to at least acknowledge me. Not even a sneer.

Yes, I know what it's like to be invisible. Let me put it to you hood style, "Don't do people like that, Christian." They say that clothes make the man. That paradigm doesn't hold up in the world where you want to serve. Love everyone with the love of Christ, and stare at people as though you are transfixed on Jesus. My guess is that if Christ were here in human form today, he probably wouldn't be walking around in a tuxedo and $900 shoes.

Bring your hard hat and lunch pail.

Serving is hard, blue-collar work. You'll need to give your all. When it's time to serve, be prepared to do everything in your power to help this person that God has placed in your path. Act as though she is your mother or a beloved sibling sitting in the chair across from you. Like my late mother would have said, "Go to town."

One day, at the end of a work shift, a man came to my office and said he needed help with something that would have required me to leave the building and confront someone in the neighborhood. I was tired. I almost told him I couldn't do it that day. And then I asked, "Bruh, what's your name?" He looked me point blank in the face and said, "Jesus." Sure enough, that was what was on his chart.

My mind instantly went to St. Matthew 25, where it says, "In that you have done it unto the least of these my children, ye have done it unto me." I hollered, "Somebody hand me my jacket!" I was out of there in a flash. I took care of his problem and almost ran back to the office to get back to Jesus with his answer.

I've often met the real Jesus, and you'll meet Him too, every time you look into the eyes of someone who is struggling or hurting in the hood. The prerogative will always be there to tell Him to show up at a more convenient time. I wouldn't suggest that though. For further directions here, open your Bible and read Matthew 25:31-46.

Always keep your word.

Some of the people you are serving expect you to lie. Everyone else has lied to them. Why not you? Therefore, do not promise lightly. Make sure you can deliver when you give your word.

Keep an updated list of resources at your fingertips.

People are going to come to you for everything from baby cribs to domestic violence housing. You'd be surprised at how many resources are available. Search the Internet. Network with other local churches and service providers. Don't wait until people walk through the door and say, "I need help." Gather these resources and have them at the ready before you actually need to share them.

Before you give someone a resource referral, make sure you've checked it out first. Make sure it can work for them. Nothing can be more discouraging for a person than to go to a resource and find out that it's gone out of business or moved. Check it out first.

One day, a young man asked me for the address of a place where he could get dental care. Easy enough. I looked in a resource book and said, "Go here." He flipped. Veins popped out on his neck. He halfway rose from his seat. "Look at my tattoos! I'll get killed going there!" he hollered. Sure enough, he was a gang banger and the dental clinic was in enemy territory. If I had paid just a little closer attention, I might have figured that out. That episode taught me that I needed to do my homework.

When I first became a believer, I gave a gospel tract to a girl who worked as a receptionist on the floor where I worked. The next day, she didn't speak to me. I thought little of it. She was usually so friendly, so perhaps she was having a bad day. By the third day of icy silence I knew something was wrong, so I approached her and asked, "Did I say something that offended you?" She shouted out two words, "I'm Catholic!" The words hung there in the air. And then it hit me. I quick stepped back to my office. I opened up my desk and then pulled one of the gospel tracts. Sure enough, it was a Catholic-bashing diatribe. I ran back to the young lady and tripped over an apology that she wasn't really willing to hear. I lost her friendship. It hurt, but I learned a valuable lesson that day. Be sure of your resources before you share them. Never give anybody ANYTHING that you haven't read or investigated first.

Be a powerful listener.

Preachers earn their reputations through their ability to skillfully deliver powerful sermons. Every theological library has a section on sermon preparation. However, the minister's greatest gift to the wounded individual is often not the sermon but the ability to be present and to listen. To be known as a great listener is far better than to be known as a great speaker. Nothing helps people heal their inner selves faster than running into someone who can listen with energy and compassion.

I've had people talk with me for 20 minutes about the weather, and then they'll slip in a sentence like, "Something happened yesterday that I just can't deal with." Then, they'll go back to talking about the weather. If you have zoned out thinking about your grocery list or your TV picks, you might have missed the one thing that could save their life.

Can you listen without interrupting? Can you listen without throwing in your opinion or saying, "Let me tell you about the time that happened to me"? The most valuable thing I learned in seminary was not the rudiments of sermon preparation; it was how to listen and share presence. Far too many people on the margins have no one to listen to them. Everyone wants to be their voice. No one wants to be their ear.

Reverend Dr. Karen Oliveto, Senior Pastor of Glide Memorial Church in San Francisco, explains it like this: "For me imagination is the ability to dream, the ability to see the world differently. To see it as it is, but to be able to also imagine it transformed. And I think the same thing with the self. To know the self but to also imagine how the self could be different.

"The hardest thing is that people have had their imaginations broken. If you can't imagine yourself any other way, if you can't imagine how you walk in the world any other way, how can you effect change in yourself? I think when we talk about transforming lives, part of it is giving people the safe space to feel the brokenness in their own lives in a space, but then to be able to do enough healing so that people can dream again. "Listening is the most important piece of my pastoral care. It's being fully present with someone. Nell Morton used to say, 'We hear each other into speech.' And for people who have had their lives discounted and their experiences not trusted, allowing them to give voice to their lives and to be able to utter the most terrible things that have happened to them and their secret longings is a profound gift to give to someone.

"I must stay open, not let my judgment enter in. I cannot let my feelings of being comfortable enter in. That someone has been carrying this and they are risking so much to share it with me, I just have to keep open and receive it. There's healing in the telling and having someone to be a witness for them.

"People who have been injured as children are stuck at the level of brokenness where it occurred. Whenever we are broken, our development gets stunted.

"As a minister, one needs to keep open to people, keep loving, and keep offering them grace. How can we invite people into a fuller life and equip them for it as well, with the support and the love of a community, so that when they feel like they're starting to slide, there are people who have been there?"

Never donate something you wouldn't want yourself.

A few years ago, I was asked to begin a ministry to women who were caught up in domestic violence and human trafficking. An idea came to me. Once a month, we would have a women's-only service at the church. Here we would offer clothing, hair styling, and manicures, all free. Of course, food would have to be served.

Unfortunately, there was little money for all this in the budget. Where would we get the food? It wasn't hard to make that decision. I walked up the street to a local soul food restaurant. I met with the owner and asked for a deep discount – to which he agreed – on a meal for my sisters. Why did I pick out my favorite fried-chicken-and-fish spot? Easy. I often ate at that restaurant. I wanted the sisters to eat what I like to eat. I can't even begin to tell you how well that worked out!

In one place that I ministered, one of the congregants would tell me how blessed they were by my sermons. Once a month, they chose to share their gratitude. When it was time to clean out the refrigerator, they would bag up all of the food items they no longer desired to eat and hand them to me in a plastic bag. Some of those "love offerings" were rock-hard stale or covered with green and white mold. Don't get me wrong; I like my T-bone steak! I just don't like it gray and dried out. (Hmmm, come to think about it, maybe she didn't like the sermons that much after all.)

I once served a church that had many congregants who called the area beneath a bridge in a forgotten part of town, "home." Often, after I'd preached a sermon, these struggling church members would shake my hand, smile, and walk off without so much as a word. As our hands parted, I'd realize that they had pressed a piece of paper – sometimes as much as a five dollar bill – into my palm. Five dollars to them might have been like five hundred dollars to you. To refuse it would have been an insult. Those people were teaching me a lesson about generosity.

Never do for people what they can do for themselves.

This is the universal rule for urban ministry of social service. Don't let your love and mercy cripple someone in an iron vise of dependency. If they can do it, even it means making a phone call or filling out a form, insist that they do it. This is the base principle of empowerment.

Never lose your sense of gratitude.

The only thing that separates you from the people you serve is a set of circumstances. You had a parent or a loving Sunday school teacher who told you that you could, when they had no parents and an entire world around them who told them they couldn't. You didn't have a big brother who offered you that first hit. You were never separated from your family and passed around from home to home as a foster child. Right now, I challenge you to take the front door key out of your pocket. Hold it in your hand and then say, "God, I thank you." Someone you desire to serve does not have this blessing. Don't you dare take it for granted.

Understand that people will try to beat you.

When you read the word "beat," you instantly associated it with violence, didn't you? To beat someone has another meaning in the hood. It means to take advantage of an individual by misrepresenting the facts (or straight-out lying) in an attempt to separate them from money, merchandise, or services.

Imagine you're in the downtown area of a major American city. A man with stringy, brown hair and a tattered beard walks up to you jingling pennies in a beat up paper cup. He says, "Would you please throw a crisp twenty in this bag so I can buy a balloon of heroin?"

How would you respond to that request?

No!

Exactly. And that's why he's not going ask for money that way. He's been on his hustle for 10 years, and he's got it down to a science.

He's going to say, "Do you have any spare change?" Some of you, especially tourists, will either give him that twenty or help him toward it. He'll be thankful for your ten (even your five), and so will the dope man. That individual may well plan to buy food with your money. Then again, he may use it for his wake-up shot. In which case, your twenty will go toward buying the neighborhood drug dealer a brand new pair of Air Jordan sneakers. (He thanks you, by the way.) Your new friend says he's hungry. Is he standing in front of a restaurant? If he's really hungry, why wouldn't he stand in front of a fast food joint and ask people to bring him a cheeseburger on the way out? People out here in the San Francisco Bay Area are both liberal and generous. They'd more than likely get you that cheeseburger. Panhandlers with discriminating taste even stand in front of high-end steakhouses and ask for doggie bags! You can trust that they're going to eat that food. It's when people ask for spare change that I start wondering. In a world where most of us don't have any spare change, where is it going?

Years ago, I took a walk through downtown San Francisco on my lunch break. I spotted Doris. She had a sign in front of her that said, "Trying to raise money to get back home to Denver. Any amount will help. God bless." Doris even had her pet poodle sitting next to her looking doe-eyed and pitiful. I almost felt sorry for the two of them, except for one thing. I knew that Doris lived on Turk Street, three blocks away and had never been out of San Francisco in her entire life. I wondered if she even knew what state Denver was in. When I walked up to her to say, "Hello," we didn't even discuss the sign. Our conversation went to other things. She was scamming. She knew it. I knew it. Everyone except the tourists knew it.

One thing you'll have to remember is that even some of the people you serve will try to beat you.

Years ago, a young man walked up to my desk, excitement in his voice. "Rev," he said, "my son and his football team just won the championships. They're going to the playoffs in Las Vegas. We're trying to raise money by selling candy to pay their way."

The proud father produced a sign-up sheet and a colorful page with the different kinds of available chocolates. I'm a chocolate-covered mints kind of guy, so I ordered a tin of them as my contribution.

After a month or two, I began to wonder when he would deliver my mints. One day I ran into my former client and asked him about the candy. Perhaps it was guilt that struck him. Who knows? But he decided to come clean. He said, "Rev, there really was no trip to Las Vegas. I used your money on some get high."

Oh.

Best not to loan out your car keys or give out money. These things can complicate your relationship. Why not have a system set up in your nonprofit where people can fill out a form and requests for aid are evaluated. Have a team of people who have resources that can be shared. Let them say "yes" or "no." It's not good to say, "I have to make a decision personally about your request." If you need to say, "no," that may leave you in a bad light.

Some people will always have an emergency. Beware. They operate on the squeaky wheel principle. They will raise Cain to bring attention to their situation, knowing that you might be willing to do most anything to get things quiet again. Don't give in to that. Ask questions. Be nosy. After all, you are a steward over that money.

Don't take money out of your pocket and put it into someone's hand. Not good. People will tell their friends that you broke the code and hit them off. The next time their friend needs money, they may say, "Well, you helped so and so, why not me?"

You say, "This person loves me. They would never steal from me!" Well, they might love you, but that might not stop them from stealing from you. People in the streets live in survival mode. They might do something and think about it later. A client used to come visit my co-worker almost every day. My co-worker was kind to her, going overboard to help this person through their tangle of issues. One day, my co-worker asked, "Did anyone see my phone?" Only one person could have stolen it: the young lady into whom she'd poured out so much love and affection.

Not everyone will do this sort of thing. In fact, probably 90 percent of the people I've served, even if they are caught in the game, would never take anything from me. They will honor that outpouring of mercy. Beware the other 10 percent. It's not necessarily that they're bad people; it's just that they have lived in survival mode for so long that when an opportunity comes along, they can't switch off the "go" button.

Find ways to help without giving money directly. Buy the groceries. Give the money directly to the landlord. And don't be afraid that they might not like you and that they will pull the string that unleashes the recording, "And I thought you were a Christian."

Not everybody is going to be your friend. Don't let people use and take advantage of you. It's not good for *them*. Don't let them use street psychology on you, probing for your weakness and then using it against you. For example, someone whispers in your ear: "You know you really should be the supervisor here. I like you better than that guy. I don't like the way he looks at you." That's called "staff splitting."

I could write another book about all the scams, cons, and hustles I've seen over the years. You feel like a jackass once you realize you've been stung, but don't worry. It happens to all of us.

There was a gentleman down the street from my job who used to sit in his wheelchair with his hand extended. Compassion caused people to dump quarters into his palm. They felt sorry for dude. One day I was coming out of work, and to my great astonishment, what did I see? It was the guy in the wheelchair. However, he wasn't sitting in that wheelchair. He was on his feet pushing it up one of the steepest hills in San Francisco. Either he'd experienced a miracle of Biblical proportions or he was making an excellent living scamming half the city. I stopped seeing him at his usual spot not long after that day. I wonder why? Maybe he retired to the Bahamas!

It's not only regular folks who will try to beat you. If you have deep pockets, people with expensive suits and letters behind their names will try to beat you in the name of the Lord. They'll write grants for projects that they don't have the ability to execute. They'll take your money and put friends, church members, and relatives on the payroll who may or may not have the required skill base. Meanwhile, some group of people huddled in a storefront might be able to use that money to save lives but lack the necessary skills to make the proper presentation or the money to hire a top tier grant writer. They'll be putting pennies together to keep the lights on while your scam artists are flying to Paris on your dime.

Someone reading this book is in a place to change the world for a Zip Code full of people by sending an envelope full of money that they'll never miss. If it's you, don't do this lightly. Follow the words of Ronald Reagan when he commented on his willingness to discuss disarmament with the Soviet Union. He said, "Trust but verify."

Help people escape poverty by dismantling the sense of entitlement.

There's a tightrope between knowing you've been born into an unjust situation and adjusting yourself to live in it forever. If you're journeying with folks in the badlands, your aim is to help them escape poverty, not adjust to it. Some folks tend to idealize the oppressed and the impoverished. They cease to be "Bill" and "Suzy" and become the noble poor in our family and church conversations, as if that were a good thing! Not good. There is nothing noble about learned dependency. Your goal is to help people find the tools and the power within themselves to escape poverty, not perpetuate it.

Veronica Boutelle and I have labored side by side as social case managers in inner-city settings. She owns a well-respected voice in the social service community. More than once I've heard her use this phrase: "Entitlement is the devil." Once, when I asked her to explain, she answered: "Entitlement is when there's a lack of personal responsibility and an expectation that things are given to you without having to work for them. It's the idea that people owe you something just because you've suffered."

She went on to say, "I've worked with clients who were given gifts during the holiday season. Without fail, when Christmas would come around I would hear the complaint, 'I didn't get what I wanted. I only got a $100.00 gift card. Why didn't I get two of them?'

"Entitlement is the devil. It's learned helplessness. It comes from a place of oppression and living in an oppressed community. Privileged people give you a hand out, not a hand up. There's no accountability. It's just, 'Give me.' You don't learn how to do anything.

"Poverty pimps just give to people. They don't create a situation where there's real, sustainable change. In this paradigm, the same homeless people will be staying around 20 years from now in the same place with their hands open.

"The system disables people. I think of one client I worked with over a period of time. She asked herself, 'Why do I have to work?' She learned that the system would reward her for being helpless, not for bettering herself. After all, the agency serving her would always rescue her before she could hit bottom. There's no personal responsibility, there. The more of a derelict you are, the more benefits you reap. What's the point of helping and giving if they aren't improving their existence?

"You have to build your movement on the idea of change. If you don't do this you will keep people imprisoned in the system. In my experience, people have to feel that they have something of value to contribute in order to access that part of them that wants to get better. They need to accept that if you've been receiving services, you need to provide services in return."

So how do we dismantle this cycle of dependency?

"Find out what people's strengths are. What are they good at? It could be something as simple as smiling or making people laugh. Make them the greeter at the community meeting," Veronica said.

"You need to demand that people be accountable for doing something in return for the services they are receiving. If they don't follow through, there should be consequences. You need to let go of the outcome. You teach people how to do things and stand back to see if they're going to follow through. You can't keep throwing money in a pit. At a certain point, you have to let them either sink or swim. If you are a helper, you are doing something for someone that they can't do for themselves. If you do not demand that they expend energy on doing what they can do to help themselves, you are you enabling them. That's not empowerment.

"In the end, you want the people you serve to be able to rise above their circumstances. I've seen that happen many times. Its a beautiful thing."

Get the people's opinions.

Many years ago, I served as a case manager for formerly incarcerated people. I can still recall the morning that a young man came into the office and sat down in the chair adjacent to my desk. He had recently returned to society after having served five to ten years in prison.

After some light chit-chat, I got down to business. My first question was: "So what do you need?"

His eyes instantly became moist. He tried to blink back the tears. He leaned forward and said, "No one has ever asked me that question before."

I met many like him: state-raised, born into the system. They traveled from the maternity ward to foster care, to Juvenile Hall, and then to state prison. They were told where to stand, where to walk, what to eat, when to squat, and where to sleep. No one ever asked about their needs, goals, and desires. So when I asked, "What do you need?" the young man was overcome by emotion.

Too often the church and Christian-based non-profit organizations have become the religious welfare system. We don't ask people in the community what they need; we drive through the neighborhood on our way to the church parking lot, glance around, and make assumptions. We then look at some statistics, call in the grant writers, twist a friendly politician's arm, and then build whatever it is we think they need, expecting people to come, claim it and use it. We spend a fortune without ever asking the people themselves what they need.

Before you have the blueprint drawn up, hire the contractors, or even name the thing, please talk to the community members. Go out to the senior center, the pool hall, the PTA night, the pick-up basketball game, the neighborhood watch meeting, the sneaker shop, the supermarket, etc., and ask people in the community for their opinions. Ask them what they need.

Next, get the community members involved. Give them some ownership. Make them partners in their own deliverance. Say, "Come, let us do this together." At the end of the day, let them have the joy of saying, "Look at what we did!" The alternative is to leave them in the place where they and their children must bow down in humility and say, "Look at what you did for us, Oh, Great Sir (or) Great Madam!" They'll never treasure "this blessing" if you take the welfare approach because "this blessing" will be yours – not theirs. Bring them to the table in the beginning. Let them partner in the process. Share ownership of the end product with the people.

ABCD

Deficit thinking causes us to look at community members and judge them based on what they don't have and then figure out what must be done for them. Dr. John McKnight, Professor Emeritus of Communications Studies and Education and Social Policy at Northwestern University, pioneered a concept called "Asset Based Community Development." ABCD, as it is often called, requires that service providers see the community from the perspective of its assets rather than its deficits. Everyone has something to add, something that can be contributed to community building. That skill could be anything from the ability to cut lawns to the skill to teach trigonometry. Instead of people just receiving, their ability to give back creates a mutually beneficial interaction.

One day, a man walked up to me as I was crossing the church parking lot. He was swinging a little girl by the hand. He said, "Mister, my check comes tomorrow but my little girl is hungry now. Do you have some money so that I can get us some groceries?"

I said, "Brother man, here's what we're going to do. I'm going to give you money for groceries; in turn, you're going to come back here tomorrow to sweep this parking lot."

He agreed. And sure enough, the next day he returned to the church with his little girl, asking for the broom. I got it for him. How did he feel as a man having the opportunity to work in exchange for that food? What vision did his daughter get of her daddy, as she saw him laboring away there? What would she have thought of Daddy if he had just accepted money from a stranger for food and offered nothing in return? Giving people the opportunity to give back bestows dignity.

Having a community barbecue? Give the neighbors the opportunity to arrive early and put up the chairs and unpack the groceries. Invite them to stay to help clean up. Give them an opportunity to give back. We weren't built to simply receive. Empower the people by giving them the option to contribute. Sometimes you'll have to require it. Like medicine, they might think it's bitter, but in the end, it'll do them good.

Pray with your eyes open.

Don't be fearful, but do be aware of your surroundings at all times. I was walking down the street with an intern years ago when a man we didn't know struck up a conversation with us. Moments after we left him, I looked back to see him fighting off a robbery attempt. Never get so comfortable in a high crime area that you neglect to look around yourself with the knowledge that bad stuff happens to people everyday in the hood. When people ask me to pray for them in certain areas, I literally pray with my eyes open. I don't get caught "slipping," as they say.

Listen for God's guiding word.

I wrote earlier, in several instances, about the need for courage in ministry. Urban ministry, by its very nature is going to demand that you take some risks, but understand this: Steps of faith and steps of foolishness may look similar, but they are not. I live by the law of reasonable risk; if in doubt, don't. This is a good one to remember. You don't have a thing to prove to anyone. You can get into a lot of trouble trying to live up to someone else's ideals or expectations. That's why urban ministry's Number 1 component is prayer. God may very well say "yes" to your sense of calling; however, give Him room to say "no" if His plan differs from yours.

Chapter 21

Be Present: Examples to Emulate

 I've lived in the same location for about 8 years now. I rarely wear a clerical collar or a preacher's black garments. In fact, you're more likely to find me in a pair of jeans and a T-shirt than a suit. Still the people on my block call me "Rev." When I walk by they might tuck that can of beer behind their backs out of respect and say, "God is good," to which I, of course, reply, "all the time." People have asked me on occasion to pray with them right in front of my apartment building. They talk to me about victories and fears. Occasionally, they come to me with hardcore, hood issues. Why? Because I'm both a preacher and a neighbor. If there are a spate of break-ins, drive-by shootings, or just excessively loud parties happening in their world, I'm already involved, because it's my world too.

And it's not one-sided. They watch my apartment when I'm not home. They encourage me when I'm down. When I fell ill once, I literally leaned on them as I walked up and down the street. They drove me to do my errands. On a holiday, they might show up at my door with something good to eat.

It would be difficult for any preacher coming here once a week from out of town to make that same connection. It took a few years for that bond of trust to build.

Once people realized that I live here, that I know everything that goes on in this hood, and that I could kick it with them without judgment, the gigantic wall between us came down.

Every conversation doesn't start with, "And Jesus said… ." Lots of times, we bemoan the abysmal state of the Oakland Raiders or talk about our predictions for the Oakland A's. Sometimes, it's something as simple as the weather. And then there are other times when I've talked people out of doing something (shall we say naughty) to someone who has done them a terrible turn. Now, often *those* conversations *do* begin "And Jesus said… ."

At the bottom line, we're here together.

Being There is Half the Battle

There's a donut shop not far from my house. Here, the O.G.s sit down and talk about the meaning of life, sports, politics, women, etc. In the middle of the bunch is a fellow that I recognize for his mission efforts. When I see him around the hood, he's wearing a suit and toting a briefcase. He's also trying to dispense his quota of *The Watchtower*.

Now, in that donut shop he's not preaching to the fellows. He doesn't wear a suit. He's got on a casual warm-up outfit. *The Watchtower* is nowhere in sight. He's not here to preach. He's here to make friends. And I suspect that his agenda is to get those friends to visit the Kingdom Hall where they might become Jehovah's Witnesses converts. For once people buy into you, they are much more likely to give a genuine hearing to what you say you believe. For this reason, my friend the missionary is strategically present in the community that he seeks to evangelize.

As you can imagine, I disagree with the guy from the Kingdom Hall on a great number of theological issues. However, you can't help but admire the fact that he makes an effort to be present with the very people he desires to reach. Jesus used that model. He was recognized and known by the very people he chose to minister to. Are you present in the community you wish to impact for the Kingdom of God?

Here's another example, though far less exemplary. In the hood, the first of the month is called "Mother's Day." Welfare checks, Social Security checks, and pension payments all come in at that time. The first is the busy season for your local drug dealer. He or she is going to be heavy on their grind. Day and night you can find them out where they do business. If they absolutely *must* close their eyes to rest, they may sleep for a few hours in the back of their car. That individual may wear the same clothes for three days in a row, but they aren't going to move away from the spot where that money is flowing in. There's a commitment there. This person is rooted and grounded in their mission, and if that means they have to stay in one place for three days without a shower, so be it, they reason. Everybody knows them and what they do because they are present among the people they want to reach. What would it look like for the people of God to use this model?

The Office

Most churches are isolated islands disconnected from the communities around their buildings. There are several ways to make your church or faith-based organization a more integral part of the community. I call one of them the "office."

I have a running joke with my friends and community partners. When it's time for a face-to-face meeting, I tell them to meet me at my office. My office is not in a church or an office building. It's actually the back room of a coffee shop located on a main street in East Oakland. I meet with people in the community in an easily accessible public place. In fact, I am writing this paragraph in my office right now.

I am not the only person who has had this idea. One of the local politicians used to set up informal meetings here once a week. The public servant would set up a cardboard placard on a table inviting people with issues or ideas to come over to chat. Here's the thing. The politician had a traditional office two blocks away from the coffee shop. However, to create dialogue with people as well as presence, she committed dedicated time to being where her constituency spent leisure time.

In the hood, I have had people walk up to me searching for help with everything from how to find an anger management workshop to help locating a missing loved one. Often, I tell them to meet me at my office. I have planned demonstrations with community members in the coffee shop. I have counseled people here. Shoot, I even plan on having a signing party for this book here in this very coffee shop.

For me, it's the coffee shop. Your public office might be in the burrito spot or the soul food restaurant. It's any place that you plan on being on a regular basis where you might rub shoulders with the people in the primary community where God has placed you. When Jesus met the woman at the well, he was in a place where regular folks gathered. If Jesus would have seen his ministry as being primarily inside of building, he would have never met her.

The office is your well. Pray, pray, pray before you go there. Ask God to anoint that time in your life and create the divine appointments. Don't make things happen. Let God do that. Just make sure that you show up in the same spot on a regular basis and watch God do the rest. Make the office a part of your weekly schedule. Pastor, let the people in the neighborhood see you. Let them know who are and not just once. Are you meeting with another local pastor? Don't go to the Four Seasons Sushi

Emporium. Meet at the office. Bring some cards. Shake some hands. If the door opens, make some invitations.

There is just one caveat. Make sure that you buy food and drinks at your public office and insist that anyone who joins you does the same. The person who owns that cafe or restaurant has a rent payment to make. Don't sit up in there four hours drinking the water, eating the free crackers and occupying space reserved for the paying customers. Part of the ministry is sharing resources for people who are providing resources for the community. Make sure that the owner benefits from your ministry.

New Neighbors

There's a movement that's transforming the parameters of ministry in the inner city. Some call it the "emergent church"; others call it "missional" ministry. The movement was spearheaded by Dr. John Perkins, an African-American minister who fled the South because of segregation and racism. Eventually he returned to Mendenhall, Mississippi, to create a community-based ministry and, subsequently, the CCDA (Christian Community Development Association).

Reverend Perkins lists three pillars upon which the ministry rests, all three of which begin with the letter "R."

- Relocators are people who may not have been born or raised in a community but move into the hood to do ministry.

- Returners are people who leave the hood because education and economics allow them to do so, but they return to live in the community to share in the life of those who have less.

- Remainers are people who could have fled the hood but didn't do so because they wanted to serve the community.

Missional believers practice what they call "incarnational Christianity." The gist of it is that believers move into urban neighborhoods not so much as missionaries but as neighbors. Just as God became man in flesh and established himself as a community member in a distinct geographical area, the missional settle in the mission field. They don't commute in. They live in the places where they serve. They become involved in the life of the community. They might send their children to the neighborhood schools, and they try their best to live out Christian testimony in the places where they are planted. Some pastor churches, others start nonprofits, and others work regular 9 to 5 jobs. Theirs is a ministry of presence. Missional evangelists live to be salt and light. Often, they live lives of material simplicity, getting by on the bare necessities. They are more likely to ride skateboards than drive Rolls Royce automobiles.

Missional collectives that I have connected with in Northern California tend to be comprised of people who come to the Bay Area from all over the United States. Most of them tend to be young and white.

Patron Saint of the Missional Church

A great number of the young people who find themselves drawn to ministry in America's ghettoes can trace this call back to a single book, *The Irresistible Revolutionary: Living Life As An Ordinary Radical,* by Shane Claiborne. Shane has been the subject of a documentary film entitled: *Jesus For President: Politics for Ordinary Radicals.* He has been mentioned in *Esquire, SPIN, Christianity Today,* and *The Wall Street Journal.* He has been interviewed in media as diverse as Fox News, Al Jazeera, CNN, and NPR. Harvard, Princeton, Brown, Liberty, Duke, and Notre Dame have all called upon him to give academic lectures. He gave the following interview exclusively for this book.

Shane Speaks

There is a certain humility that mixes in with Shane's Southern twang. This is a man who has sat at the feet of Mother Theresa and has been a John the Baptist figure, attracting thousands of followers and propelling them into selfless Christian service. His story is unique.

"I grew up in East Tennessee," Shane told me, "in a small town far outside of anything urban. When I graduated from high school, I wanted to have my world expanded a little bit. However, my mama said, 'If God wants you to go to Philadelphia, Pennsylvania, God can pay for it!'

"I was always interested in the world. At Eastern University, I learned about issues of inequality and justice. There, I learned about Karl Barth, who said that one must hold the Bible in one hand and the newspaper in the other. My professors taught me that faith is more than a ticket to Heaven."

The Fight That Lit the Fuse

"In 1995, everything started taking shape. A courageous group of homeless mothers and children began organizing themselves. It was a difficult time for them. They had no housing, and the Section 8 wait list was years long. One hundred of these folks moved into an abandoned cathedral at 8th and York in Philadelphia. We read about it in the paper. This struggle was being waged just one hour away from our university campus. Lots of questions arose, like: "How can we worship a homeless man on Sunday and ignore one on Monday?"

"Some of my fellow students and I went to inner city Philadelphia to meet the folks who were making this courageous stand. These people became our mentors. We read about the early church and saw it lived out. It wasn't perfect, but it was surely powerful.

"It wasn't long before they got a threatening notice. It said: 'You have 48 hours. If you don't get out, you'll be arrested for trespassing.'

Moving In

"One tenth of our campus got involved in some way. A group of us starting moving into the community. In 1998, I moved into the Kensington area of North Philadelphia. Everything emerged out of that movement. I didn't choose the neighborhood. It chose me. It changed the course of our studies and our lives. We've been out here ever since.

"When we moved here, we became part of what was going on. We already had a relationship with the folks who lived here. It wasn't about starting anything new but building on to the neighbors' ideas, including a food-distribution project. They said, 'We're hungry.' We said, 'Let's start a fish restaurant.'"

The community that Shane moved into was one-third African-American, one-third Dominican, and one-third white. They encountered some obstacles of racial bias. Shane and his friends were brought before town meetings. They went back and asked themselves, "How do we love our neighbors as ourselves? How do we build bridges?" They were determined that they would never put themselves in a position where someone would be asked to carry their bags. They were completely averse to that mindset and social arrangement.

A great number of Shane's friends considered him a hero for shedding power and white privilege to move into a crime-ridden inner-city neighborhood. They looked up to him as being "sacrificial" even "messianic." He resisted these laurels with a high level of disdain. However, it could hardly be avoided. He said there was a "powerful narrative there that attracted a ton of journalists."

The Real Story

Some of the long-time residents of the community began to raise eyebrows and ask questions. Still Shane insists, "The story is not about a bunch of suburban kids who came here and changed the neighborhoods. I have a buddy who is going to college. He plans to return here to bring gifts and skills to the neighborhood. We've always said that the people who are the most impacted by injustice tend to be the best to lead.

"Incarnation is one of the fundamental ideas of our faith. One of the neighbors told us that we make it too complicated. She called the concept "con carnita" or "with meat." For Shane Claiborne and his friends, the believers in the inner city represent the presence of Christ, the body of Christ, that people can touch.

Shane said, "Jesus came to listen, to learn, and then earn the right to speak. Jesus sits and listens to the woman at the well. He asks for water before speaking. This shows us that we should be slow to speak but quick to listen. We don't always make space for other people's voices to be heard. That doesn't represent Jesus well. As we move a little closer to the pain and injustice, something significant happens. It's a beautiful thing."

The Missional Movement Confronts Urban Violence

In 2014, gun violence rocked Philadelphia. There were 22 homicides in the first 20 days of the year. Montell, a 19-year-old whom Shane had befriended, died on his doorstep. Much of the blame lay with a local gun store. In the wake of the shooting, Shane's community began to host demonstrations outside this notorious gun dealer's lair.

On Good Friday, young men from the community carried a giant cross and set it down in front of the gun shop.

Community members laid roses at the foot of the cross. At the conclusion of the service, a mother who had lost her son to gun violence told Shane, "I know that God understands my pain because God saw His own Son get killed." Through prayer and strong community activism, the Kensington community fought to have the gun shop closed. Today, a bicycle shop stands in its place.

But that's not the end of the story. The community brought in blacksmiths to transform weapons of war into ploughshares. Said Shane, "We've literally turned AK-47s into farming tools." He recalls the day that a mother, who had lost her son to gun violence, took a hammer to the molten, red-hot barrel of a pistol. As she was beating the hot metal she hollered, "This is for my son."

The Fight to Stop Gun War Goes Global

Shane said, "I've told kids here in Philadelphia that I can't speak out against the violence in the ghetto without speaking out about the impact of violence all over the globe. I've been to Iraq. I've been to Afghanistan. I've met kids in Kabul who are 15 and 16 years old. For their entire life, their country has been at war. They are so tired of violence. These kids have been studying King, Ghandi, and other champions of peace. They all wear this one blue star. They want two million friends in other parts of the world to wear a matching blue star.

"We set up a Skype account so that kids from the hood in Philadelphia could talk to kids in Kabul, Afghanistan. They were calling and talking and dreaming of a world where their friends could live in peace without fear of having their lives snatched away by random gunfire. There were days of listening. People got to hear stories from the ground in Kabul.

Once there was a NATO strike that killed two 8-year-olds tending sheep. Kids in Philadelphia went into the streets carrying blue scarves in honor of the fallen.

"Every morning," Shane told me, "I curl myself into a little ball, and I listen to Jesus tell me how much He loves me, and that gives me the courage to get up. We are not trying to be the church. We are community. We surround ourselves with the people we want to become. The element of community is really important. There's a critical mass of people keeping this alive. If the community is cynical, it's going to put out our fire. The fire is contagious when you've seen people put down guns or heroin. There's no age to it. We're as old as our cynicism, and we're as young as our dreams."

Creating Ministry With Genuine Results

Nate Millheim, founder and executive director of Oakland Leadership Center said, "When we moved to East Oakland six years ago, we came with the idea that we were going to live here indefinitely. We came here to learn and start slowly. We wanted to connect with people who are doing good things in the community.

"My mission was to learn the culture, learn people, volunteer with other people's organizations. It's been a roller coaster ride since then. We've lived in the same house and have done a lot of different kinds of ministry with young people and young adults."

According to Nate, "A lot of people say they want to be change agents in neighborhoods like East Oakland but don't interact with the young people who are most at-risk and most vulnerable in the neighborhood. In our basketball league we have 18- to 25-year-old men who attended schools that did not serve them well. Some of the young men are on probation because of things they got caught up in where they grew up. Many are underemployed or unemployed. Others grew up in the game, having lived in families where there were guns in the house and family members sold drugs.

"We want to be there for them, to connect with them. Some of those young men are the ones who go on to become leaders. We can empower them to be leaders of their own peers. One of the young men in our league was doing quite well. He had walked away from gang life. He had a child. He was in community college and being recruited to play basketball for a four-year college. A few months ago someone walked up on his front steps and shot him to death. This pushes me even more to connect with these guys.

"Not a lot of other churches or organizations are reaching out to these guys and helping them. A lot of people are scared of them. Dreadlocks and baseball caps cause people to assume that these young men are no good and that they are trouble. It's hard for me sometimes, too. I've seen people shot in front of my house. My extended family is sometimes not entirely supportive of us living where we do in the neighborhood.

"Though the ministry is rewarding, it's not easy. It takes commitment over the long term, and I don't know if everyone wants to do that. It takes a lot of work, energy, and passion to connect with young men in the inner city. But these are young adults who are caught up in a vicious struggle; for them there will be no overnight successes either. It's going to take awhile."

Understanding the Dynamics of Race

Nate Millheim learned that people of color view the world through a different set of lenses. One morning he picked up a group of youth to practice basketball at a community gym, only to find that the space he'd rented was locked. He pulled on the door briskly three times. The last tug set off an alarm. It was almost a relief for Nate. Now, someone will come, he thought. The young men who had been beside him had the opposite reaction. They were startled. They split up and began to run and hide. When they heard alarms they thought, police. The fear of being accused of wrong-doing by law enforcement and all that might entail for a young black man sent them ducking and dodging.

Resistance from the Old Guard

Finding a headquarters for the Oakland Leadership Center was an arduous chore. Nate went on a journey through Oakland's inner city neighborhoods seeking a church that would rent space to him. Many of the churches were open only for Sunday morning services and Wednesday night prayer meeting, all told, less than 8 hours a week. However, when Nate laid out his vision of bringing young people inside their walls when the building was vacant, they scoffed. They wouldn't even consider it. They considered the youth incorrigible and, one by one, denied them use of their facilities.

Nate recalls, "There was one church in the community where I live that had a fairly large meeting space. I went to the front door and asked to speak to a pastor. Some workers pointed me toward a stairway; the pastor's office was at the top. I climbed the stairs and walked into the open office. The pastor just glared at me, kicked a chair toward me, and hollered, 'You got five minutes.' That was it. No, hello. No, nice to meet you. No, what's your name? We ended up renting from him because that's all we could find."

Light in the Darkness:
I Want You on My Team

Later, Nate went to a recreation center to play basketball. He was the only white fellow in the entire gymnasium. It wasn't long before he saw some of the players whispering and pointing in his direction. Nate assumed they were wondering out loud what a white guy was doing in that gym. He was wrong. A few minutes later, the young men asked him if he would like to join in on a game of pickup basketball. The fellow said, "Hey, I've seen you shooting around. You're good! We were just arguing about who would get you to play on their team."

Chapter 22

Hip-Hop: Urban Ministry's Bullseye

 "I want to do authentic inner city ministry, so why do I need to know anything about hip-hop culture?" Is that what you're asking? Honestly, that's like taking flying lessons, sitting in the cockpit of a jet, and asking the instructor, "Why do I need to know what the wings do?"

A couple weeks ago I walked up to an at-risk youth at the program where I now work and said that my dream was to reach young people like himself. He said, "No, offense O.G., but I don't want to be reached. I'll reach myself." That took me back. I didn't expect that answer.

Later in the day, he was standing around in a cipher (circle) with other young people trading hip-hop rhymes over instrumental beats. At one point, he looked at me and said, "Let me hear you, O.G.!" I eventually showed him a hip-hop video I had made in one of the worst hoods in Oakland. It changed our relationship completely. You see, he didn't want to hear another lecture from a concerned elder. However, he was open to hearing what I had to say in the language he could best understand – hip-hop.

You may tell me that you have no idea what hip-hop artists are saying. To you, it all sounds like noise. You'll never be able to rap or even have the desire to rap. Fair enough. However, if you want to reach folks in the hood, especially young people, it would be best to understand the music they listen to, the culture they live in, and the importance that both of those play in their lives.

Somebody Scream

Hip-hop is a powerful and pervasive force today. It influences political thought, style, taste, fashion, communication, ethics, and literature. In the hood, hip-hop is everywhere. It's blasting from every other passing car. Kids are listening to it through headphones as they walk down the streets. Commuters defy the signs demanding that music not be played on public buses. People watch hip-hop videos on television. They listen to it on the radio 24/7. They have hip-hop lyrics tattooed on their arms. They name their children after hip-hop stars. Macy's sells hip-hop fashion wear. Government officials use hip-hop slang in their speeches. I recall hearing a white Air Force pilot discussing the success of an aerial mission. He said, "We cold, smoked the b———." That was a term straight out of South Central Los Angeles.

Movie moguls seek out top tier hip-hop artists to either star in their films or create the soundtracks (sometimes both). Hip-hop artists sell out coliseums. The music is used to sell everything from soap to automobiles. Consider the fact that hip-hop artists in Egypt relayed the message of Arab Spring through the medium of hip-hop music. For you to say, "I want nothing to do with it" is to secure your place in the infamous museum of irrelevancy, as far as youth and urban culture is concerned.

Hip-hop is more than music. It is the language, the visual art, the pulse, and the heartbeat of several generations of people all over the globe. It is the mode through which they express every emotion from love to hate. The song topics can vary from the gospel to gunplay.

Hip-hop is comprised of five elements: turntablism (djing), rapping, graffiti, break dancing, and knowledge. The music is all about the hypnotic beats that cause one's head to nod. With the advent of social media, American hip-hop music and its artists are beamed all over the world from Miami to Mogadishu from Brooklyn to Brazil. In 2008, when then-Senator Barack Obama's first Presidential bid began to stall down the stretch, who did he reach out to for help but Jay-Z? Hip-hop is more than music; now it helps turn political elections.

Rock and roll has had a broad influence on international culture. No question. However, hip-hop's influence transcends the boundaries of class and race. At the height of rock and roll's lure, you probably wouldn't have found thousands and thousands of Black kids all over America demanding that their radio stations play the Beach Boys or Led Zeppelin. It's not that they didn't like the Beach Boys. It's just that the impact wasn't there. You weren't going to walk up 125th Street or Crenshaw Boulevard and see teenagers with striped shirts toting surfboards.

On the other hand, you can hear Ice Cube's music banging from dance floors in Dubai to the dope strip in Detroit. In Singapore, kids are spinning on their heads. In Cuba, female rap stars are shaking the nation. In Somalia, young people are doing wild-style graffiti. In Brazil and Germany, hip-hop music is everywhere.

No longer can you hide from hip-hop. Oakland pastor and hip-hop recording artist Mustafa Muhyee once said, "The shepherd always knows what the sheep will eat." Pastor, if your sheep live in the hood, your sheep eat hip-hop. If your sheep are white kids living in suburbs, I have some news for you. They are probably eating the same thing, because 85 percent of all rap music is purchased by white kids. Guess who's paying $100.00 a ticket to see the top-tier rappers perform? Hint: It's not kids in the hood.

Snoop Dogg is perhaps the most famous rapper in the world. He's sold millions and millions of recordings. He's performed around the globe several times. He's survived wars and street battles that destroyed the lives and careers of a number of hip-hop's most notable celebrities. As a Long Beach Crip, Snoop is perhaps the most recognizable gang member on the planet. I guess if we're going to start anywhere in our discussion about hip-hop, we probably need to start with Snoop.

Funky Fresh in the Flesh

The San Francisco ballroom was filled with thousands of waving arms floating in a cloud of marijuana smoke. Soon enough the smooth-talking, Crip-walking, hip-hop phenomenon strolled onto the stage. Like a ghetto griot, he railed against Babylon, the prison industrial complex, and, of course, anyone who stood between him and his desire to smoke weed. Spotlights swept the auditorium as he performed the classic "Gin and Juice." My boy, Dave Aron, stood at the sound board at the rear of the auditorium, twisting knobs and sharpening Snoop's voice.

From My House to Snoop's House

Life takes us through some strange places. When I first met Dave Aron, he was a little kid with a red Beatles-style mop haircut. Come to think of it, the Beatles might still have been on the chart back then. Dave and I were both students at my mother's Good News Bible Club. Dave was 6 and I was 9. He came up to my shoulder. Times have changed. Now, it's me who comes up to Dave's shoulder, and nobody has heard from the Beatles in a long time. Dave has been Snoop's sound engineer for nearly 20 years, producing his records and making his live shows sound tight.

Now, I don't look for much in life. My heart's unspoken desire that night was simply for an opportunity to take a photo with the rap icon for my Facebook page. Needless to say, I wasn't really prepared for what was to follow when Dave said "Follow me," and gave one last knob a twist to wrap things up.

As we approach the backstage, I can see that it's flooded with hangers-on, groupies and 9-to-5 stooges with a desire to touch the hem of the Dogg's khaki's. Two bodyguards, who look like human mountains in sneakers, guard a stairway that leads to what looks like a treehouse in the back of the auditorium. After some discussion, the two mountains part, wave us upstairs, and then close ranks to re-form into a two-man phalanx.

A closed door opens at the top of the stairs. We walk inside. There are two rooms. The first one contains double-stuffed Oreos, chicken drumettes, beer, and pizza. In the other room stands a tall black man sporting sunglasses with dreadlocks sprouting from his head. He wears a red San Francisco 49ers jersey, unusual, I suppose, for the single-most-recognizable member of the Crips, a gang universally associated with the color blue. I stand in the first room and just stare.

Dazz Dillinger, Snoop's first cousin sits at the far side of the room texting and filming. People walk in and out of the room, but I stand back in the tiny room, munching the delicacies and watching the most famous rapper ever hold court in the next room.

I feel as though I know him. My mind races back to the refrain of his first hit, "yeahh, ya don't stop/Cause it's 1-8-7 on an undercover cop." I remember his contributions to Dr. Dre's album, *The Chronic*, which sold 35 million copies worldwide. My mind drifts from there to his duo with Tupac, "Gangsta Party." I recall him throwing up the Crip gang sign at the Grammy awards. I remember watching his body collapse in a pile of relief after the judge pronounced him "not guilty" in a gang homicide case. I recall his interaction with Denzel Washington in the film,

Training Day. He had outlived and outlasted them all. And there he is, sitting in the next room.

Reverend?

Eventually, Dave walks into the room where I'm scarfing down the chicken wings and Coca-Cola and summons me with a wave of his hand. I walk into Snoop's dressing room to be introduced. "Snoop, this is my dude from back home. He's a reverend. His mother led me to the Lord," Dave announced.

The smile retreated from Snoop's face when he heard the word "Reverend." He stuck out his hand and in his trademark drawl he said, "How you doin', Reverend?" The word "Reverend" seemed to stick in his throat as though it was something distasteful. I wasn't the only one who noticed. Dave quickly stepped in to clarify himself. "Oh, he's a *real* preacher, Snoop. He's the type of preacher you'll find out in Tenderloin or chopping it up with gang members or people caught up in all types of s——."

Snoop's face softened. The smile returned. "Oh," he said.

When he said, "Oh," the jigsaw puzzle of my life seemed to snap together. I'm not a "highly respected" clergyman in the community, *per se*. I don't have many of the creature comforts that you would associate with main-stream respectability. I don't drive a Cadillac; in fact, I haven't owned a car in 20 years. I don't own a house. I live in an apartment with a bullet hole in the wall. The chances that your local pastor is going to invite me to preach at your church is, shall we say (and I'm sure you'll agree, having read this book thus far), slim. However, that does not mean that I'm without respect in certain circles. The late author, Piri Thomas, was the first to ever call me a "street preacher." I wasn't smiling when he said that.

However, in reality, there is no other way to describe who I am and what I do.

At that moment, Dave snapped the Facebook photo of Snoop Dogg and me.

Chopping it Up With Snoop

I had to work the next morning, so after running through more than my share of Snoop's pizza, chicken wings, and desserts, I decided it was time to make my exit. Plus, we were in San Francisco, and I had to get back to the dark side of Oakland in the wee hours of the morning, when it was least safe. I bid my new friends adieu.

"No way, man!" Dave said. "It's early. You can't leave yet."

The bodyguards threw out a few of the after-party guests who had overstayed their welcome. At Dave's invitation, I scooted into the now almost-empty room and took a perch just a few feet away from Snoop Dogg. I just listened. He spoke about people like beloved Pharrell and Stevie Wonder like family members. He talked about an event where they were together in a room. Pharrell said he wanted to play a song he'd written about Los Angeles for Stevie, a song that he wanted him to perform on but was intimidated by his fame. Snoop encouraged his friend to make the step. He said, "He know we got love for him, man!" (Many months later, when I heard the song, "California Roll," I recalled that moment.)

He then launched into a medley of TV theme songs: "The Jeffersons," "Good Times," and then "Gilligan's Island." We all sang along with gusto. And then he turned the corner completely. Snoop Dog led us in a very reverent rendition of the Negro National Anthem, "Lift Every Voice And Sing," the song of struggle that had originally flowed from the pen of Civil Rights stalwart, James Weldon Johnson. The walls shook. It was as though we had gone back in time to the days when black men swung from trees in Louisiana bayous instead of fading away from bullet wounds in the hood.

When it was finished, Snoop looked at a blond woman behind me who had had a sip too much to drink and asked, "You don't know nuttin' 'bout that, do you?" She didn't answer.

Feeling relaxed behind doors and out of camera range, Snoop took off his sunglasses. He sat back and puffed his chronic weed, unwinding from another night in the spotlight. "Snoop," I said, "my favorite song you do is 'Conversations,'"a gospel-tinged piece, with Stevie Wonder providing the hook.

Right then and there, Snoop started nodding to the beat of invisible drums. And when the cue came in, the world's most successful hip-hop artist launched into the song. "But the race ain't to the swift or the strong, the wise or the rich/But to them that can endure it to the end and win…. When you feel your life's too hard/Just have a talk with God."

Briefly Snoop and I discussed my call to bring the word of God to the streets. He said, "That's what you supposed to do. God blesses you with gifts for a reason. God blesses us so that we can help others, but it's always your choice whether you're going to do that or not."

Ghetto Communicator

Snoop has his finger on the pulse of young America. He understands how to communicate thoughts to a broad demographic of young people. His music and his video image send his message all over the world. As I stared into his eyes, I wondered if even he understands the scope of his influence. Hip-hop is an incredibly powerful tool that impacts several generations all over the globe;

Snoop has the mic to which millions will listen. Where did this phenomenon come from?

In the Beginning

How many hundreds of thousands of hip-hop recordings have been made? Who can even venture a guess? What we *do* know is that Kool Kyle, "The Starchild," was only the 18th person to ever record a rap record. "Do You Like That Funky Beat?" was rocking the clubs in 1980. His follow release, "It's Rocking Time," was just as powerful. As a testament to hip-hop's relevancy and longevity, Kool Kyle recently received a phone call from London, England. A young kid who wasn't even alive when Kool Kyle was signed to Enjoy Records called to tell him that he thought he was one of the greatest rappers of all time.

"How he got my number, I'll never know," said Kool Kyle.

Kool Kyle the Starchild agreed to be interviewed exclusively for this book. He has been involved with hip-hop since 1976. He recalls those early days.

A Hip-Hop Pioneer Breaks it Down

"New York City was broke, so the city's leadership reached out its hand to Washington, D.C. Gerald Ford, who was the President at that time, said to New York City, 'drop dead.' The South Bronx was a furnace. Landlords couldn't pay the insurance premiums because people weren't paying their rent. So the landlords would have the building torched so they could get insurance money. The whole place looked like a war zone. When you got on the train, you could look down and see whole city blocks turned into empty lots because of fire and devastation.

"At the time, New York City was a cesspool of gang activity. Hip-hop was one of the few conduits we had access to. It's something we did because we lived here.

Whether you were middle class, upper class, or lower class, this is something you wanted to be part of. And then there was the music. Afrika Bambaataa was one of the leaders of the Black Spades, one of the largest gangs in New York City. The Bronx River Housing Projects were their Mecca. Kool Herc might have begun the whole thing. Grandmaster Flash was perfecting his quick mix, but because of his ties to the Black Spades, Bambaataa had a following.

"When Bam created the Zulu Nation, you couldn't come around him talking that gang talk. He no longer wanted that negativity around him. "Bambaataa's stand was revolutionary. You see, in the early '70s, gangs were everywhere in the Bronx. You walked past gang members when you walked to the store and when you went to school. Sometimes, they would jump on you, take your sneakers, tell you what colors to wear, and announce that you were now a member of that particular gang."

So, when one of the most feared and respected gang members in the city of New York puts down his colors and creates an organization built on peace, love, unity, and having fun, things are going to change. Bambaataa went from being a gang warlord to becoming known as the "peacemaker" for his uncanny ability to bring warring gangs to the negotiating table to resolve conflict.

Meeting the Godfather of Hip-Hip

Kool Kyle met the godfather of hip hop, DJ Kool Herc, through a female emcee named Sweet and Sour who used to perform with him. As his own career began to take off, he persuaded the owners of a club called the T-Connection to allow him to throw hip-hop parties. He reminisces: "I was the house MC. I did stuff there with Herc.

Kool DJ Herc's parties rocked because he did not play the disco hits popular on the radio. He played songs with break beats, the stripped down rhythm segments that made

partygoers go wild on the dance floor. Partygoers nicknamed it "break beat" or "b-beat" music. Dancers who
grooved to it were called "b-boys" or "break dancers."

Hip-Hop's First Star

Back in 1976 this style of music wasn't called "hip-hop."
According to Kool Kyle, it had no name, but it had a star.
His name was DJ Hollywood. Around January of 1977,
a young lady Kyle was seeing asked, "Do you know who
Faye's boyfriend is?" Kyle shrugged. "DJ Hollywood"
was the answer. One day, Faye called Hollywood and put
Kyle on the phone. His jaw dropped. He was invited to
go down to the 371 Club in Harlem where DJ Hollywood
held court.

"I couldn't believe my eyes," said Kyle. "It was so
crowded. People were mashed together in there. Hollywood had complete control over that crowd. He'd say,
"Throw your hands in the air!" The crowd would do it.
If he had said, "Smack your neighbor," they'd have done
it. It was hot. What an amazing vibe! The famous DJ
June Bug was DJ-ing that night as DJ Hollywood did his
thing on the mic. During a break, Faye introduced me to
him, and then DJ Hollywood said, 'Do you want to get
on the mic?'"

Kool Kyle recalls, "It was like going to Madison Square
Garden when the Jackson Five were at their peak and
Michael hands me the mic and says, "Sing." I had never
performed before a paying crowd. June Bug played three
or four records and I rapped over them. When my
moment was ended, DJ Hollywood said, "Yo, you did a
good job, kid."

From there Kool Kyle was on his way to fame. He performed with early rappers like his old high school
classmate, Kurtis Blow. Grandmaster Flash would enlist
him to take the place of a member of the Furious Five if

someone couldn't make a performance. And then one hot evening in 1979, a car drove past him with the R&B summer smash, "Good Times," playing from its radio. Someone was talking over the music. Kyle ran through the streets and caught the driver at a red light. "What is that?" he asked. As it turned out, what he was listening to was "Rapper's Delight" by the Sugar Hill Gang.

The Game Changes

"When the record came out, the whole game changed," said Kool Kyle the Starchild. Hip-hop, which had originally been centered in the South Bronx and Harlem, spread to all five boroughs of New York City. Promoters began to look for rappers who had made hot records. The old-school stars that performed in parks and small clubs faded into obscurity. Kool Kyle signed to Enjoy Records, perhaps the first independent label to score hip-hop hits. His first hit, "Do You Like That Funky Beat?" released in 1980, allowed him to travel to places he'd never been before.

The Fall of the Old School

"Rap is the only idiom that doesn't care who you used to be," said Kool Kyle. "The Rolling Stones are in their 70s, and they're still selling out stadiums. Country music stars can stay around forever. However, L.L. Cool J has been kicked to the curb. Rap is the only legitimate form of music where the label will tell you that you have a shelf life of three years. They aren't going to even touch you without incredible street cred.

"You also have to be young. You have to have moved a lot of product out of the trunk of your car and be able to prove it. They'll use you up and then you're gone. The next 50 Cent is down the street. No, he's actually down the hall. They'll just call him 49 Cent. Let's move him in and throw you out!

"My father, who had been a rock and roll studio musician, came into my room once when I was a kid and asked, 'What are you doing?' I said, 'I'm saying rhymes to the beat of a record.' 'That's just a fad,' he pronounced. That was 1977. It's the 21st century and hip-hop is still here.

Consider its Power

"Hip-hop is a powerful, subliminal tool designed to get into your consciousness. Any music that can do that has a certain power. Teachers can take something like lines from Shakespeare, stuff kids wouldn't give five damns about, make them repeat the words with a hip-hop cadence, and before you know it, they know it!

"Hip-hop is the main, cohesive genre in all kinds of music. It is this universal power. It boils down to the funkiness, rhythm, beats, voices, and drive. When it's done right, it's irresistible. The preeminent elements are impossible to resist. Hip-hop has bridged cultures and joined people that never in a million years would want to be with each other.

"If I was a psychologist, I'd be working at Sony making two million a year. Hip-hop is designed to infiltrate an area of your brain through rhythm and repetition. In the past 10 years, it's been the best selling genre of music on the planet. Kids all over the planet want to dress like rappers."

"A Place Called Harlem Was My Home ..."

Rappers have a nasty habit of not voicing their support for their peers. I am going to break that mold right here and now. Hip-hop might not exist in the form you know today without the talents of Kurtis Blow. Blow was a ladies' man with show biz charisma. I remember him on stage in 1981 dressed in a white leather suit and sporting a diamond necklace that spelled "BLOW." In the words of L.L. Cool

J, Blow was "cooler than snow under a polar bear." Was he the king of rap? Who else could have gotten away with recording a song called, "If I Ruled The World"? The first hip-hop star from the ghetto, Blow hit the scene first with "Christmas Rappin'." And then there was "The Breaks," the first certified gold hip-hop record of all time. He also became the first rapper to receive an endorsement deal that led to a television commercial for Coca-Cola. Back when rap was still relegated to the streets and after-hours joints, Blow was touring with acts like Bob Marley and the Wailers and the Commodores.

Kurtis Walker (a.k.a. Blow) was born and raised in Harlem, New York. He lived right next door to Dr. Betty Shabazz, Malcolm X's widow. In an interview for this book, he said: "The earliest beginnings of hip-hop? I guess it has to be about 1972 or '73, about when disco was just getting to mainstream America.

"We were part of a rebel group, along with people like the Isley Brothers and The Jimmy Castor Bunch, that grew on the Motown sound and all of that stuff. We were rebels, musically speaking, because we didn't relate to the thump, thump, thump monotonous European disco beat. To us it was a contradiction because we'd grown up listening to Aretha Franklin, Sam Cooke, and Wilson Pickett. Our music in the 1970s was old school stuff. That idea, that we would play this music in a world of disco music, spawned hip-hop. From there, you had DJs, emcees, b-boys, break dancers, who would just go out to that type of music. It also spawned the kind of DJs who would play only that type of music, that playlist. That's what later motivated emcees who got to make rap records. We tried to make music that was funky and that was motivated by soul music; we played it in spite of disco.

"In 1979, the Sugar Hill Gang's smash 'Rapper's Delight' was all over the radio. Producers Robert Ford and J.B. Moore decided to use a young Curt Walker to go into

the studio to make a rap song because this new phenomenon was playing everywhere – on every bus, every train,
every car, every taxi, every boom box, every radio station,
every record player, 24/7. They wanted to get in on it.
Said Blow, "Christmas Rap is kind of like a miracle.
Here it is – a young college student, Curtis Walker, 18
years old who gets the opportunity to make a song. The
idea of it being a Christmas rap, something that would
play annually, was unheard of.

"It was God's plan that I made this song. My first song
was about the birth of the most famous, the most incredible man in the history of humankind, our Lord and
Savior, Jesus Christ. I was the first rapper from the ghetto
signed to a major label. I was in London, Paris, Belgium,
the first to introduce hip-hop to this world. It was like a
dream world."

When Kurtis Blow was in his late 20s or early 30s, in
semi-retirement, he faced a life change. "I got married,
bought a house, had kids, and got bored. One day I just
picked up the Bible and started reading. Lord have mercy!
It became a mission. I wanted to read the whole Bible. I
had to do this once in my life. I started in Genesis and
starting reading the stories of the Old Testament. I read
about Abraham, Isaac, Noah, Moses, David, King
Solomon." Blow had been captivated by Bible-based
movies as a child, and now he was reading them in the
Word for himself.

He said, "Then I got to Revelation, the most incredible book in the Bible – just the awesome imagery of it,
the visions. I don't want to say that it scared the hell out
of me, but I started saying to myself, I have to start
going to church before Jesus comes back. My wife and
I started going to church. We got saved at Church on
the Way under the leadership of Pastor Jack Hayford in
1994. We started having Bible studies in our home.
Wow, how God transforms you and the changes that

come! I see God in everything, in every-day miracles. Today, I'm just loving on everybody; loving life more to the extreme every day."

Kurtis went to Nyack Bible college, where he majored in communications. Although he still performs his secular hits on the global stage, Kurtis Blow now also records gospel hip-hop and is considered a pillar in that community.

The king of rap uses Proverbs 18:21 to counsel rappers who influence the world through the vehicle of hip-hop. "Death and life are in the power of the tongue: and they that love it shall eat the fruit thereof."

Keeping it Real

Authenticity is essential to the hip-hop ethos. The term "keep it real" is heard in almost any discussion about the music. It's unique to the culture. After all, no moviegoer expects Robert DeNiro to continue be a gangster after the final credits roll. No one expects Al Pacino to show up on the front page of tomorrow's newspaper in handcuffs accused of taking part in a drive-by. However, in hip-hop the audience expects the rapper to *be* the character they're presenting in the song.

No one illustrated hip-hop's thirst for authenticity better than Christopher Dorsey. B.G. (short for Baby Gangster), one of the greatest rappers to emerge from New Orleans, was known for his graphic gun talk in songs like "Chopper City." (A "chopper" is a machine gun.) In his classic, "Kill or Be Killed," the rapper boasts about his prowess and skill as a killer.

B.G., one of the highest earning entertainers in the rap genre was pulled over by the police in 2009. They found guns in the car. He and his friends were arrested. The prosecutor's goal was to give young B.G. a 25-year prison sentence. He pointed out that B.G. gave shout-outs to the city's highest profile killers on one of his videos. Fans disagreed. They mentioned first amendment rights and artistic license. U.S. District Judge Ginger Berrigan, who would decide B.G.'s fate on gun possession charges, did not share the opinion of the rapper's fans. She believed that B.G.'s artistic endeavors may have influenced killers to commit murder. B.G. was given 14 years.

Street Cred. Really?

Rick Ross, who recorded albums like "Hood Billionaire" and "God Forgives, I Don't," exemplifies the image of the high-flying street figure. His songs are about drug importation and the elimination of rivals through street justice. His heavily tattooed body is photographed draped in expensive jewelry, surrounded by beautiful women, and at the wheel of expensive sports cars. He looks at the world through black lens sunglasses. But did Rick Ross cut some corners to advance his hip-hop career? Freeway Ricky Ross, California's famous ex-drug lord, seems to think so. In fact, he took Rick Ross to court for the theft of his name. Undeterred, the rapper created an album entitled *Teflon Don*. Teflon Don was the name given to the late Mafia chieftain because charges never seemed to stick to him.

Late Mafia kingpin John Gotti's grandson, Carmine Agnello, took offense. It's widely known that "Teflon Don" was a moniker bestowed on his grandfather, John Gotti, because prosecutors seemed to never be able to make charges stick. Gotti's grandson said of Ross, "He should have asked for permission. A standup, respectable guy would come and ask if I could use the nickname... . I think he's a great artist, but you just can't start calling yourself that to sell records. He wants to go for that whole image, but hey, be yourself. Only in American can you go from being a corrections officer to calling yourself Teflon Don."[1]

Oh, (forehead slap) did I leave that out? Rick Ross was a corrections officer given oversight of incarcerated people before he became a superstar hip-hop artist extolling the greater glories of the dope game. No matter, in hip-hop, image is everything.

The Seduction and the Turn Out

"Man, you're 19 years old. How did you end up with bullets in you and a long list of drug trafficking convictions?" I asked. He uttered a single name, the title of a well-known rapper, and then he just stared at me.

"And?"

He went on to tell me that this rapper's music had exercised a profound influence over his life. He listened to him when he rose from bed and played his music all through the day. Sooner or later, he was convinced that his only way out of poverty and hunger was the dope game. Unfortunately, the rapper didn't talk about the consequences of the game. There was no mention in his songs about solitary confinement, cavity searches, or prison rape, only gold chains, free sex, and fast cars.

This young man had no father to guide him. The rapper he idolized was more than a guy in a sound booth somewhere creating entertaining records. His lyrics, guidance, and insight fed into this fatherless kid's need for a father. When my young friend was shot, the rapper was just as responsible for the bullets in his body as the gunman who pulled the trigger. The hip-hop artist presented a hard, macho look that the young man took as real. He bought into the image and the authenticity. Although many hip-hop artists never actually live the life they talk about, many young people buy deeply into the image.

Conscious Rap

Back in 1981, I was standing in front of the Bronx River Housing Projects with Afrika Bambaataa, founder of the Zulu Nation, when a senior citizen approached him. She began to talk with Bam, not about break beats but about environmental racism in the area and how they engage the political machine to combat it. This woman saw him not as a hip-hop figure but as a community leader. At that moment, I realized the power potential that the hip-hop community possessed.

In 1980, Brother D produced a song called, "How We Gonna Make the Black Nation Rise?" In an era where hip-hop was almost exclusively party music, the rapper said:
"People like Malcolm lived and died
... Warning us about genocide
While you're partying on, on, on, on, and on
The ovens may be hot by the break of dawn
Your party may end one day soon
When they round the niggas up in the afternoon... .

Brother D's opus was a classic, but three years later Grandmaster Flash and the Furious Five changed the world with the release of the "Message." *Rolling Stone* later named it the greatest hip-hop song of all time. Its poignant reporting about urban city life, insistent bass line, and powerful chorus stayed in your head long after you'd heard it for the first time. "Don't push me, cause I'm close to the edge/I'm trying not to lose my head/It's like a jungle sometimes/It makes me wonder how I keep from going under."

In 1986, a hip-hop collective, called Public Enemy, released, "Yo! Bum Rush The Show." Public Enemy was from another planet. Rapper Chuck D's sonorous voice collided with hip-hop street dude, Flava Flava, over a sonic collage created by producers known as the "Bomb Squad." The Bomb Squad specialized in borrowing tiny bits and snippets from David Bowie, James Brown, or anyone who had sound that would work and then squeezed the samples together over a beat. They were artists and magicians. Back in the 1980s, all rappers were using samples from classic records, the more obscure the better. Few if any were as effective with the medium as the Bomb Squad. In 1987, Public Enemy released what some call the "greatest hip-hop album of all time." It was called, "It Takes a Nation of Millions to Hold Us Back." The inside poster shows Chuck D, Flava Flava, and the S1W paramilitary wing of the group standing on top of the American flag.

Hip-hop that is socially aware and politically grounded has spurred revolutionary movements in countries around the globe from Mauritania to Haiti from El Salvador to Cuba to Kenya; hip-hop is giving a voice to the unheard. Artists like The Roots, KRS-1, Lupe Fiasco, Immortal Technique, Talib Kweli, and Common are not only rocking the airwaves, they are addressing students on major college campuses. Drugs, debauchery, sex, and violence are the formula of mainstream hip-hop dreams. However, mainstream radio is leery of rappers who preach empowerment and tell people to think. Still, some of the conscious rappers, through the underground, are selling more music than their contemporaries.

Chapter 23

Killer Rap

 In 1986, I signed to Pow Wow Records as a recording artist. My record "Back To The Scene of the Crime" was released on London Records in Europe. The B.B.C. filmed a video of the song. Its success allowed me the opportunity to go on a brief tour overseas. I was fascinated by London. I had never been that far away from Harlem, where I was living at the time. That first night I went for a long walk. Pretty soon, I realized that nothing looked familiar. I was lost so far away from my hotel. A young black fellow and his girlfriend were walking in my direction. I stopped him and asked, "Say, brother man, can you tell me how to get back to such and such a street?" His jaw dropped, and he said in his cockney accent, "INCREDIBLE MISTER FREEZE!" That was my hip-hop name. What a bizarre moment, to be on another continent and have someone recognize me.

Westside, Baby!

I idolized the Harlem/Bronx hip-hop legends back then the way a British blues musician might look up to a blues player from the Mississippi Delta. The first uptown star I ever met was Afrika Islam. He was known as the "son of Bambaataa, none hotter." Some say that as the captain of the Zulu Beat Radio Show, he was the first hip-hop DJ to rock turntables on the airwaves. Back in 1986, if you were a hip-hop fan like me, Islam's 2nd floor, South Bronx apartment was like the Legion of Superheroes. Artists like Grandmaster Melle Mel, Bronxstyle Bob, and Donald Dee hung out there. You actually never knew who was going to walk through the door.

One afternoon, I noticed a couple new faces in DJ Afrika Islam's living room. They were West Coast cats, from L.A., to be exact. The more talkative of the duo was a light-complexioned cat with his hair in a ponytail. Like a great white shark, his eyes hardly moved, and yet they saw everything. He had "hustler" written all over him (ironically, one day he would create a hit song by that title). He and Islam had both landed bit parts in a hip-hop B movie. They met on the set in Los Angeles and hit it off. Now it turned out that this guy had a record contract with a major New York label. He was an anomaly. A California rapper! I had never heard of such a thing.

Up to that point, 95 percent of hip-hop artists didn't come from just New York City; they came from a small sliver of New York City – Harlem and the Bronx. What did Los Angeles know about rapping? (Actually, the first time I saw Ice-T perform in the South Bronx, I realized he knew plenty!)

Ice-T did not create the first gangsta rap record; however, he was the first to effectively package the underworld lifestyle and sell it to the streets. His magnum opus was a song called, "6 In The Morning." Officers are at his front door to serve a warrant. The protagonist escapes through the bathroom window to live out his life in the streets of the ghetto and later the county jail. Ice would go on to star in blockbuster films and TV series, but not to make platinum-selling albums. Although his music was rooted in the streets, it had a strong degree of social consciousness. His songs are cautionary tales that always include the terrible downside of street crime. His song, "New Jack Hustler," is one of hip-hop's greatest triumphs. In that song, he is an urban folklorist in the skin of a teenage drug-dealing sociopath.

Niggas Wit Attitude

Ice-T rose to fame in an era of black consciousness in hip-hop. The Native Tongues, which included A Tribe Called Quest, Black Sheep, Queen Latifah, and others, spoke about black pride and rocked Africa medallions. Public Enemy, the Black Panthers of rap, were headlining basketball arenas by 1987. And still, 95 percent of all hip-hop was coming out of New York. A band of discontents from a place I'd never heard of, called Compton, was going to change all that.

It's difficult to believe that the vast majority of hip-hop records contained no profanity at all in the golden age of hip-hop – until August 8, 1988, when five Los Angeles rappers produced *Straight Outta Compton*. The group's name was N.W.A., which stood for Niggas With Attitudes. The cover picture featured the five rappers standing in a circle peering down at the listeners, with one of the rappers, Eazy-E, pointing a pistol at the viewer.

That first album contained hits like "Gangsta Gangsta" and "Dope Man." However, it will be forever remembered for the underground atom bomb, "F—- The Police," which has been an anthem for every uprising from the L.A. riots of 1990 to the fiery 2014 demonstrations over the killing of Michael Brown in Ferguson, Missouri.

There was nothing polite or politically correct about N.W.A. They cursed in their songs and they used the word "nigga" without repentance. The group brought L.A. gang culture – the dress, the hairstyle, the classic low-rider cars, and the West Coast hood ethos – to the world. Eventually, the F.B.I. sent them a letter stating that the agency was unhappy with their stand against the police. Instead of toning it down, N.W.A. used the letter as a marketing tool. They began to call themselves "The World's Most Dangerous Group."

The Fallout

Others disagreed with N.W.A. on one matter or another. One of those was Bay Area hip-hip radio personality, Davey D. Listeners asked why he was willing to play speeches by Malcolm X and Martin Luther King, Jr., and at the same time play N.W.A. Davey D got the point. He eventually refused to play N.W.A.'s music.

In an interview for this book, Davey D said, "There was much debate around Oakland about this new music. I got Cube and Eazy on the phone, and Eazy-E said, 'What are you saying man? You're not going to play our records? What's up with that?'

"So I said, 'Well, Easy, you know the instrumentals are good. I like the beats, but the words, we just can't play them.' And so he said, 'F— it then; we'll just send you instrumentals,' and he hung up the phone.

"Cube stayed, and he talked about wanting to put context to the songs they were doing. Ice Cube had wanted to publish disclaimers and commentary about why they were doing certain songs. Both of them had said they were reporters. They were talking about the realities of what they had seen and what was going on in the streets, and Cube felt they could take it another level deeper. He said that he had been overruled by Ren and Dre at the time and that they were more like, 'Let's just keep it raw.'

"So, unbeknownst to me at that time Cube was having issues with the group and eventually left it. When I learned that I remember thinking, 'Wouldn't it be great if Cube was to hook up with Public Enemy. And I remember running into Cube in L.A., and he said, 'You know I'm going back to New York and hooking up with Public Enemy.'

Many of the things he talked about wanting to do with N.W.A., he did on his first solo album, *America's Most Wanted*. Hip-hop music would never be the same.

One rapper was quoted as saying that his goal was to create a "worldwide westside." Others had the same vision. L.A. gang culture was transmitted through the music, dubbed "gangsta rap," that was coming out of L.A. In coming years Crips and Bloods were seen in places where they had never before existed. There was no doubt that the emergence of the crack trade spurred the migration of enterprising L.A. gang members all over the country. (Listen to Ice Cube's song "Summer Vacation.") Still, no one could discount the free advertising gang culture got from gangsta rap and its fallout. Artists like the Game, YG, Chief Keef, and a host of others still propagate the spiritual holocaust unleashed by the godfathers of gangster rap. Can music kill? Twenty years ago, I would have answered, no. Today, I know better.

But as N.W.A. said so many years ago, there is an "Appetite For Destruction." When N.W.A.'s biopic *Straight Outta Compton* hit the screen in 2015, it outsold big-budget summer blockbusters like *Mission Impossible* and *The Man From U.N.C.L.E.*

Biggie and Tupac

I met Daddy-O in the mean streets of East New York, Brooklyn, in 1983. I can actually remember the day. He was rehearsing in the recreation room of the Unity Plaza Housing Project with his crew, Stetsasonic. Over the years, I watched him go from rhyming in the projects to rapping on MTV and recording with Queen Latifah. In a recent conversation, he recalled the rise and fall of two of hip-hop's greatest talents.

"You can't really understand Biggie without knowing who Un was," said Daddy-O. In the early days, Biggie wasn't jiggy with it at all. Un lived the King of New York life that Biggie dreamed about. All of that high fashion urban wear that he talks about in his songs was actually in Un's closet. Back in those days, hustlers didn't like to take one dollar bills. Un would come back from a trip out of town and give a garbage bag full of ones to Biggie and them. It was Un who came up with the concept of Jr. Mafia as a hip-hop group.

"I remember the first time I was in the studio with Big. I was at the boards messing around. Big was clowning with his boy, Ceas. When I got everything ready, I told them I would play the track a few times so that Big could write his rhymes to it. Un said, 'He's ready to do his verse. He don't write nuthin' down.' Sure enough, Notorious B.I.G. walked into the booth, put the headphones on, walked up to the mic, and with the track playing, he said, 'I'm surrounded by criminals, heavy rollers/Even shiesty individuals... .'

"God gives people talent and they just have it. I had to work at being a great rapper. Biggie was never whack. He was born with a gift."

Who's That With Big?

Daddy-O said, "I used to live on Fulton Street [in Brooklyn, N.Y.]. One day I saw Big coming down the block with Jr. Mafia. They weren't a rap group yet. They used to walk around with bubble jackets that had '666' patches over the chest. That day they were coming down the block, and there was a little dude in front of them. He was a dark skin guy. His gold chain was swinging. He was waving his hands up and down. He was very animated. I said, 'Un, who is that cat?' Un said, 'That's Tupac. Biggie love[s] that nigga.'"

Years later, Tupac would blame the Notorious B.I.G. for having him ambushed and shot up in the lobby of a New York recording studio. This would spark an East Coast/West Coast rap war. According to Daddy-O,

Tupac's allegations about Biggie were wrong. He said, "I was in the studio when Tupac got shot. I remember coming downstairs, and there he was on a stretcher. Puffy and Big didn't have anything to do with it."

Encountering Tupac in Vegas

Daddy-O recalls his exposure to Tupac's music early in the legend's career. He said, "I was in Las Vegas one time while I was working for MCA. They would have these showcases where new artists could perform for record company executives. Tupac was on the showcase. While you are eating the dinner they put the first acts on. Some of the older executives would leave early. Some of the young execs would stay around and watch the rest of the showcases.

"Tupac was one of those guys on the bill that night. The show wasn't that interesting to me. When I got up to leave with some of the young execs, a guy stood up in front of us, his coat folded over his arms. He had a gun in each hand. He said, "If any of you guys try to leave and disrespect my man Tupac, I'll shoot."

Daddy-O and his friends reconsidered their decision to leave. They retook their seats and watched Tupac's performance to its conclusion. I imagine they clapped heartily at the end.

Remembering Tupac

Recently, I visited Davey D, an Oakland based hip-hop radio personality, at his home. During our conversation, he recalled that "Tupac sat right up there on that staircase when I first met him. He came into the house with his brother, Mocedes (also known as Mopreme), who lived right next door. We used to have a piano that sat right where I'm sitting now. Shock D came over one day and Tupac was with him. I said, 'What's your name?' 'Tupac,' he replied. Shock was playing the piano, but 'Pac didn't say anything. He was very quiet.

"It might have been several months later that I ran into 'Pac at a North Oakland club called the Oasis. N.W.A. were there. They were in town, but not to perform, and 'Pac came through. He had gotten beaten up by the police because he demanded that they know his name. You could see the scars on his face. He was talking about, 'These guys are going to pay.' He was much more animated that day, and I was thinking, 'Oh yeah, that's the dude who was at my house.' It was no big deal. I would see him from time to time at what used to be Lucky's Grocery Store.

"And then I saw him after he had shot *Juice*. It hadn't come out yet. And he lived up on Harrison Street. And I remember going over there to interview him with my boy. And he had a gun sitting there. And I remember asking him, 'What's this gun for?' And he answered, 'Well, this is what's out here.'

"I thought that was a bit over the top. I always thought that 'Pac was very theatrical, but very smart. He had a lot of heart in the sense that he committed himself to the role he was playing. Even if he wasn't a gangster, he committed himself if that was the role he was going to play for that day. He was willing to kick up dust. He was willing to challenge. And he was willing to bond with those who were unreachable. He was very, very complex."

In the Event of My Demise

On the night of September 7, 1996, Tupac was ringside as his buddy, heavyweight champion Mike Tyson, took apart contender Bruce Seldon. However, that would not be the only violence of the night at the MGM Grand. Tupac and his entourage ran into an enemy, a Crip gang member, in the lobby. It's alleged that the gang banger had stolen a prized Death Row Records medallion. A fight ensued. The Crip was beaten and stomped.

A few hours later, a white Cadillac pulled up alongside the late-model BMW owned by Death Row Records boss, Suge Knight. An arm poked out of the window. A pistol pointed at the BMW's passengers. Gun smoke filled the air. Bullets ripped through doors and windows. In a desperate attempt to escape, Tupac tried to climb up and flip over into the back seat, but the seatbelt held him down. It was all over in seconds, leaving only the screech of car tires and the scent of burning rubber. Tupac was badly wounded.

It was a tragedy but not a shock to many, least of all perhaps to Tupac himself. He spoke of his impending death often in his songs. In "Life Goes On" he said, "Bury me smiling with g's in my pocket/Have a party at my funeral, let every rapper rock it… ."

Twenty-five-year-old Tupac had survived a prison stretch and a shooting incident, but he would not survive Las Vegas. He took his last breath there on September 13, 1996. It was said that his crew, the Outlawz, smoked his ashes after the funeral ceremony.

Connection to the Streets

What I'll remember most from those days is this: as Tupac Amaru Shakur lay dangling between earth and afterlife, hundreds descended on Las Vegas University Medical Center. These were the inner city young people who had breathed in his lyrics like food. Some of them, tattooed and scarred, shed tears for their fallen hero as he battled for his life. Tupac was their voice. He was them. The numbers don't lie. Tupac's music continues to sell. To date, he has sold 29,235,000 copies of his recordings.

Hip-Hop in Print

When I was young, I picked up a paperback autobiography entitled *Pimp: The Story of My Life* by Iceberg Slim. Until then, I had attended private school and lived a very sheltered and protected existence. I read books like *Rebecca of Sunny Brook Farm* and *My Side Of The Mountain* before a barely repentant career criminal named Iceberg Slim, with a loaded pistol in one pocket and plastic baggie full of cocaine in the other, took me on a literary tour of gambling dens and introduced me to hired killers and armed robbers.

There had been others who had written about "the life." None however, who offered the reader a front row view of the dark side of urban life with such a flair for detail. The street credo goes, "The game is to be sold not to be told." Well, Iceberg Slim sold it and told it, and I found it fascinating.

Iceberg Slim's literary protege was Donald Goines. Goines was discharged from military service with a heroin habit that he financed by writing books about the game. Like Iceberg Slim before him, his tales of sex, violence, drugs, and incarceration sold to an audience hungry for ghetto realism.

In the early 1970s, blaxploitation films like "Superfly," "The Mack," "Willie Dynamite," and "Shaft" took the hood stories to the big screen. Then, in 1999 there was Sister Souljah. The Harlem activist created a work of fiction to connect young people she was mentoring with the powerful life lessons she was sharing with them. She penned a novel called *The Coldest Winter Ever*. It became a blockbuster bestseller. Young people from urban America saw their world in that book and purchased hundreds of thousands of copies. *The Coldest Winter Ever* also birthed a publishing bonanza in the community. Folks from the streets and the prisons began to write their own tales. When they couldn't find major publishers to take on their work, they simply self-published them.

This new wave in black literature became known as "street fiction" or "hip-hop lit." Just like hip-hop music, hip-hop lit has its heroes, people like K'wan, Ashley and JaQuavis, Nikki Turner, Terri Woods, and Treasure Hernandez.

When I first arrived in Oakland, I realized that young people had eyes and ears for two things: hip-hop music and hip-hop lit. An idea sparked in my mind. I realized that if I could write an urban fiction book, I too might be able to reach young people with a message.

In 2008, my first novel, *Straight Outta East Oakland*, was released. The cover showed a thug pointing a Mossberg shotgun at the reader. People in the streets and in the prison system loved it, and they understood the underlying points. In 2011, I followed up with *Straight Outta East Oakland, II: Trapped On The Tracks*. That novel dealt with the trafficking of teenage girls in Oakland.

When *Straight Outta East Oakland* first came out, a store owner complained to me that my novels were being shoplifted. He said, "They only steal *your* books, no one else's!" Those books weren't stolen by Sunday school children; they were ripped off by their intended audience, who valued them so much that they risked imprisonment to get copies. I was more than happy to replace the books that had been stolen.

The Church That Chose to Ignore Hip-Hop

Some years ago, I went on a tour of a church back east that had been a stop on the Underground Railroad. It was fascinating. A secret chamber beneath the church had hidden the escaped slaves until arrangements could be made to get them to freedom.

The church building itself was a huge gothic structure with three tiers. I asked the tour director, "How many people were here for church services last Sunday?" He didn't answer. What he said was, "The numbers have gone down. The young people don't come here anymore. I figure one day they'll get over that old hip-hop nonsense and regain a taste for the grand, old classic hymns."

When I told a young friend – an unrepentant hip-hop-head who was studying in seminary – what he'd said, she sneered sarcastically and said, "Well, let him keep waiting."

I know what she was saying. It's more likely that that church will die from hemorrhaging members, before youth lose their taste for hip-hop music. However, many churches refuse to allow hip-hop music within their sanctuaries because they do not consider it possible for God to use hip-hop as an instrument of worship, evangelism, or social justice. To put it bluntly, they say, "It's not church music."

What is Church Music?

Recently, I had a conversation with my senior citizen mentor, Ms. Irma, about this idea. She said, "Church music is the old-fashioned music we used to hear in church down South about Jesus, God ... something that will give you hope, love. It touches your soul. It has to have a piano or organ in it. Individuals can get up there and sing, and it'll tear you up on the inside like Mahalia Jackson. Like I used to like Bishop G.E. Patterson. Oh, my goodness. Every Sunday morning I used to watch him on TV and listen to him sing. Those songs make you tingle."

"Do you like the song, 'Precious Lord,'" I asked.

"Oh, yes! I love the song, 'Precious Lord.' That is good church music, the way we used to sing it."

Good church music, huh?

The Rebel Roots of Religious Music

The fact is that the church considered Thomas C. Handy "Public Enemy No. 1" when he released his magnum opus, "Precious Lord." Traditionally, there had been a broad line between gospel music and the blues, which was considered "the devil's music." Blues tunes were played in gin joints and on late night radio. Good Christian people shunned it completely, and the more liberal among us at least didn't play it in the house on Sunday. In 1938, Handy crossed blues music with gospel lyrics and came up with "Precious Lord."

Of course, "Precious Lord" was radical for its time, but is it still considered the "devil's music"? Does it still cause a firestorm of controversy when it's played in churches? Hardly. In fact, today "Precious Lord" is often heard at funerals where its words and melody bring comfort to the bereaved.

In the early 1970s Andrae Crouch was also considered the demon seed. He billed himself as a preacher and yet took the stage in an afro haircut and bell bottom pants. His band resembled and sounded more like Sly and the Family Stone than the Five Blind Boys From Alabama. And yet many, many people came to Christ through his music. And just like "Precious Lord" of a generation before, Andrae Crouch's song, "Soon And Very Soon," considered radical in its time would one day be sung as an anthem of comfort at funerals. Instead of leaving this earth as an agent of rebellion or a reprobate, Crouch left a legacy as a pastor and a statesman of the Christian church.

And so what should we say of hip-hop? I would encourage you to at least keep an open mind. It might sound like fingernails scratching on a blackboard to you, but the young people in your circle may love it. It speaks to them. Ignore what they love at the peril of your relevancy. Locking hip-hop out of the conversation would be like trying to ignore the Internet or color TV. World domination has already happened. Hip-hop is everywhere. Do we stick our heads in the sand and call it the "devil's music," or do we find a place for Christian rap in our worship circles?

Using Hip-Hop on a Larger Scale

Years ago, I was trying, with some difficulty, to get through to a Latino gang banger. While we were speaking, I got just the idea. I said, "Come see me tomorrow."

The next day, I was ready. I was armed with the brand new CD by T-Bone. Bone's dad was Nicaraguan, and his mother was Salvadoran. "T-Bone Corleone," as he sometimes calls himself, is not just one of the greatest Christian rappers ever to pick up a microphone, he is one of the greatest to do it – period. When I handed the kid my copy of "Gospelalphamegafunkyboogiediscomusic," his eyes spread wide as he took in the CD cover art. There was a quizzical look on his face. He said, "Rev, this guy looks like a pimp!"

And sure enough, with the white maxi coat and the wide brim hat with the feather in the band he did kind of look that part. Nevertheless, the young man took the CD from my hands. The next time I heard it, it was blasting louder than T-Bone had probably designed it to be played when he was in the studio. The young gang banger had it bouncing out of 15-inch woofers in his car trunk as he rode up and down the street. "Amazing grace/He took my place/And now I got all my sins erased, ..." T-bone testified.

The sad thing is that most of you have never heard of T-Bone. His music was shunned by mainstream Christian radio, and because it landed in the gospel bin, its target audience did not get the hearing that could have changed lives, like my young friend.

Here's a crazy idea. Why not become a champion for one of today's leading Christian hip-hop artists. Start a movement. Create a letter-writing campaign to your local R&B and hip-hop stations demanding that they play some of the Christian hip-hop artists you're supporting on Sunday morning. Write to your favorite Christian radio DJ and say that you want to hear that artist on his show. Host a gospel hip-hop throwdown at your church. Invest in bringing in one of the top acts, and give some stage time to local artists. Christian hip-hop has had some success, but it has never exploded. Demand that it explodes. Push it.

You could start that radio letter-writing campaign from a senior citizen home in Boise. Start seeking out web sites that give information about the top rappers in Christian hip-hop. You can even write to these artists. Put them on your prayer list. And if you are a member of a church, whether it's in the hood or a gated community in the hills, you can still host that Christian hip-hop festival.

You don't have to necessarily like hip-hop music to do this. I don't like opera music that much; however, if I found some Christian opera singer with a gift and a powerful message for people in the streets, I'd get behind that person and try to make sure they got heard by the people they could impact for the Kingdom of God. You can do the same thing with hip-hop artists. You don't necessarily have to like the style of music to let God use it for his glory.

Chapter 24

Evaluating the Voices That Can Impact the Streets

 People in church might tell you that O.G. means "of God" or something like that. But on the streets, O.G. means "original gangster." It's a term of respect and reverence. When I walk down the street, if a kid doesn't know me, he'll say, "What's up, O.G.?" In that case O.G. equates to "sir." Then, of course, there are O.G.'s who really are former gangsters.

Don't Ignore the O.G.s

I was counseling a young man who had relapsed some years ago. His head nodded like a sleep-walker as the heroin coursed through his veins. I began to talk to him about recovery, but he wasn't feeling me at all. In fact, he began to get smart with me. I have a very long fuse, but he was getting to the end of it. Fortunately for both of us, the door opened before the explosion came. In walked my next appointment, a former heroin dealer who had once stood high on the other end of the dope game. He wasn't someone on the corner selling balloons; he was a whole-saler, an infamous legend who had literally been profiled on television specials.

I don't recall that he knocked. He just walked into the room. The young fellow I'd been speaking with froze. His eyes nearly bulged out of his head when he caught sight of the hood legend. I asked the real O.G. to have a word with him. Before he complied, he looked into the eyes of the young fellow struggling with addiction and asked, "Do you know who I am?" I'll never forget his answer: "Everybody know[s]."

The O.G. didn't raise his voice or make threats. He didn't have to. His street cred was unquestioned. That day, the former drug lord laid hands on that victim of addiction and prayed for him.

Loose the O.G.s and Let Them Go

Back in seminary I used to wonder how someone who had never had to jump over a pee puddle in a housing project doorway could offer me insights into urban ministry. My views in many areas have changed a lot since those days, but not in that one. If you want to know something, ask someone who's been there. Don't be afraid to let a blood-washed believer who knows the streets lead the way into battle – or at least help you map out a strategy. In a lot of churches every other person is an ex-something or somebody. Plenty of O.G.s go to church. You've met some of them in this book. Sure, they raised pure, unholy hell on those blocks years ago. However, today they serve Jesus Christ, wholeheartedly and unashamedly. Some of them are the kind of Christians we might all hope and pray to be. In Luke 7:47, Jesus said, "Wherefore I say unto thee, Her sins, which are many, are forgiven; for she loved much: but to whom little is forgiven, the same loveth little."

Our O.G.s are reborn in Christ, and yet we silence them because they don't fit inside the box we call "respectability." We feel uncomfortable with their slang, the way they dress, and their taste in music. What those things have to do with Christianity, I have yet to figure out. I say, if this person can reach people in your community with the message of the gospel, USE THEM! And oh, don't make them put on a suit, a dress, or whatever cultural adornments might make *you* feel more comfortable. Make sure *they* can make your mission field comfortable. My friend, the O.G. wasn't wearing a suit the day he walked into my office, interrupting my counseling session, but the young man on drugs wasn't tripping on that. When O.G. said, "Let me lay hands on you and pray," the young fellow didn't dare say "no."

Born to These Streets

Joshua Mason is a Christian brother whom I respect. He has a Ph.D., not in theology but in hood life. He is a former street-gang and prison-gang member who was respected in the highest echelons of that lifestyle. Today, he heads HOMIE4Life, an organization designed to offer inner city young people tools to create better lives for themselves and their families. He lives in the San Francisco Bay Area.

There are some things that cause you to remember a person; sometimes it's a gesture, or maybe it's oft-repeated words. As I sat across the coffee shop table from Joshua Mason, I found one thing in our back-and-forth exchange that stood out. He was extremely gracious. He thanked me profusely for the coffee in front of him. "It's only coffee," I thought to myself, but he expressed a sense of profound appreciation that told me it was much more than that to him. When people have come from hard times, they tend to be grateful for even small kindnesses.

Joshua said, "I was born in Fresno, but my first day out of the hospital, Grandma brought me to live in Visitation Valley in San Francisco. My mom was young when she had me. She married my dad in Mexico at the age of 14. Dad was in his early 20s. They split up soon after I was born. I became a pawn between the two of them. My dad wound up getting custody of me. Mom was off the hook, getting loaded. She hooked up with a guy who was in prison."

Joshua started running away from home somewhere between the ages of 9 and 10. "I would run to San Francisco to visit my mom and uncles. I was this little kid walking around San Francisco's notorious 3rd Street, spending the night on the San Francisco city buses. The hood was comfortable to me. If I had been 15 years old walking around the projects there might have been problems. But at 9, I was so young, I was no threat to anyone. I just sat around with older men drinking Thunderbird wine.

"By the time I was about 11, I wound up in Juvenile Hall. I made friends. Some people we like, some people we don't. I bounced around and met people from all over: East Palo Alto, South City, and Redwood City. I could go anywhere and kick it."

Locked Down

Somewhere along the line, Joshua Mason got hooked by the lure of gang life. At age 19 he was arrested for attempted murder. He took a plea bargain offer. They gave him 10 years. He accepted his lot. "Like it or not, it was what it was," he says in reflection. "I was a byproduct of the lifestyle, so it was no big shock. I fit right in.

"I earned my G.E.D. I read a lot and was able to articulate myself well, where that came hard for some of my friends. I was fiercely loyal. The more disloyal someone would be to me, the more loyal I'd be to others. I got involved in prison politics."

As a result of his gang involvement he was bounced from prison to prison. Eventually, he was validated as a full-fledged prison gang member. He graduated to Pelican Bay, one of the most fearsome penal colonies in the world. He was locked down in the SHUE program, where the most serious offenders and gang shot callers are held. He said, "Through all of my time I had never planned on coming home. I never operated from the date of coming come."

Asking Questions of God

Though an active gang member, Joshua had many questions about God and God's followers. Mainly he wondered why, if all Christians followed the same beliefs, they were arguing with each other? Behind the iron walls, the incarcerated sometimes use the pages of the Holy Bible to roll up marijuana, since rolling paper is unavailable. However, when Joshua desired a Bible to study he called his mother and requested it. "That was the fastest mail I ever received," he says with a grin.

Joshua had no cell mate and plenty of quiet time, and so he read. He says, "I started at page one, which is what you do when you read a book." He found a pattern in the Old Testament stories. The children of Israel had an "idol problem," Joshua says. "They would get distracted. There would be a slaughter. It wasn't like God hated only the bad – they were all bad! God always had a remnant though. Eventually, I started reading about Jesus. I started believing in this God I was seeing. I started praying to this God. As long as you live you have a chance. It can eventually be too late, but it can never be too early."

But Joshua still had questions. "How come I got a release date when, technically, I didn't deserve one, and there are other people who will never leave prison? How come my brother died, and he wasn't even a gang banger. I mulled over those questions. Ultimately I came to realize that God, in His divinity, is the one who decides. He doesn't have to give an explanation."

Crossroads

"I gave my life to the Lord," Joshua explained. "Now, there's a big question in front of me. What's it going to be like to say that I'm a new being and still be gang affiliated. I sent a kite (a secret, coded letter, in this instance, to upper echelon gang members). It said, 'I'm not turning my back on you. I'm just turning to something different. I'm not debriefing. I'm not turning.'

"They came back with 'Go to God. Just don't come back.' A lot of them would like to do the same, but they're not coming home. They're stuck in there. I was facing a release date. Now, prison is not my whole reality. For them, why think about how life could be different? Left to my devices, if God isn't a factor in my life, I do crime."

Freedom

Joshua was in both feet. He studied the Bible. He wrote Bible commentaries. In December of 2005, he hit the gates a free man. Well, almost. He says, "I did 3 years on high-risk supervision. On paper I was a high-control individual. No matter, I had changed. I had committed to Jesus Christ. I held to asset-versus-deficit thinking. I wasn't looking at what I'd walked away from but what I was walking to.

"My mother was going to church with me now. I spoke at conferences and retreats. I had Bible study going on at my house with a bunch of knuckleheads. That sort of grew into God opening doors for me to doing unconventional ministry. I got into the nonprofit world. I was rough around the feathers. I have learned to be more tactful. I got married 11 months later to a lady who came from a crazy family. We were intent on breaking generational curses.

"Jesus solved the eternal issues but created a whole bunch of other ones. I've had to learn how to navigate in the world around me and to learn about myself. It's fun sometimes; other times it sucks. You can't have one without the other. If you pronounce that this is your journey and that it's the only road, then you'll face potholes and speed bumps."

Church for the Ex-Gangsta

One of the challenges people coming from the life have to face is finding a church where they can be completely accepted. Said Joshua, "Everybody wants to go to a church where they identify somehow with the pastor. In low-income communities, the pastors stay in the physical churches. They want the hood to look up to them and be more like them. It's easy when you see hood life to say, 'I'm good and you're a miserable criminal who's going to hell. You don't resemble me right now and you need to come to my church. If you're lucky you can be like me.'

"Ideally, the pastor and the church should be transformed by this reality of two cultures coming together. In other words, the pastor looks a little like the church, and the church looks a little like the pastor. But life falls short of the ideal. What we have here are two monologues. The streets are talking, and pastor is talking. Both are talking to themselves. There is no transformation.

Servanthood

"God is interested in us serving people, but God is also interested in the fruit of our service." Joshua equated Christian service to being a server in a restaurant. He made me laugh as he told the story of a waiter who walks into a restaurant sporting an apron and a name tag, and full of himself. Joshua says, "The folks in the restaurant are starving. The chef has prepared gourmet dinners for the customers. It's what they need – and then some! – it's literally life-sustaining food. Unfortunately, the waiter, distracted by the apron and name tag, isn't delivering the meals to the diners."

He breaks down the parable. "God has prepared the food. The streets are the people sitting at the restaurant. Unfortunately, they blame the chef for the lousy dining experience. They say, 'I went somewhere once to see God, but He didn't show up.' Perhaps, in reality, it was the servant who didn't show up. God (the Chef in the story) gets the blame, but it's the servant who has failed. It's a blessing to serve, but it's a huge responsibility. If the people are not getting fed, how well are you serving them? Reevaluate your role.

"God will never put you where you are not equipped. We put ourselves in roles all the time. Outsiders are juggling that reality. You feel bad for people in jail, so with the best of intentions you go in there and preach your pastoral sermon, but it's not for those men. You're not equipped."

Joshua tells the story of a friend who felt empathy for the incarcerated. "'I'm going to Juvenile Hall to minister,' my friend said. Before long, he came back and told me he was horrible! He couldn't figure out why things had gone so poorly. The answer was simple. He wasn't right for the audience," Joshua observed. Today the same man heads a very successful outreach to the homeless. He's equipped to serve there, and he's thriving.

Joshua encourages churches to ask questions. He told me, "You have churches who have no young people. If your preaching is so great, how come you haven't had a new member in 20 years?

"It's hard to do little barbecue stuff and small groups if you live far away from the people you're called to minister to. There's no new blood, no young folks. How can you have an effective ministry? In business, you have two angles: you want to keep your current customers and add new ones. Pastors and churches are called to do that. You still have to do outreach with that intent. You have the same 10 people there year in and year out. Are they growing? Has anyone on the outside ever wondered about the spiritual growth of the people inside and said, 'I got to go see what this is all about?'

"Some pastors are saying to themselves, 'I have enough people coming in here to sustain my budget. I don't need no children's ministry.'

Stay Connected to Those Streets

"The Bible says, 'Be in the world but not of it.' Too many of our churches get disconnected from the world. Pastors don't know what to do next. Here's a question for you: Do you talk to God? He might have some ideas. You claim to have an intimate relationship with the Creator of the universe. What's He saying to you?

Take a Real Stand

"Pastor, if the folks in your church are still hustling, selling dope, and shooting, you are part of the problem. Your presence here is not neutral. Take a stand! You can't be anointed and impotent at the same time!

"East Palo Alto has 52 churches within 2.5 square miles. Who's going to your services? Some 90 percent of the kids don't go to church. Why even bother? Give up the building and turn it into affordable housing. You're allowing people to do nothing and feel great. You say, 'They might leave if I challenge them.' I say, 'Let them leave! Somebody else might come and stay.'

"No church is meant to be just a church. If your church is not involved in outreach there's a problem. If your church is in the hood, at least some of your congregation should be from that hood. The congregation should be made up of people from there. If you don't have the capacity to reach them, you should get it. If I tell you, 'I'd love to have a job, but I don't know where to look so I'll just lay on this couch,' would you feel for sorry for me? Probably not. Imagine me saying, 'I don't know how to do this, so I'll just rest here in my ignorance.' If all of your members live in the suburbs, maybe you should just move your church to where the members live.

Draw the Line

"There are some churches where there is no accountability for gangsters. You need to say, 'Look dude, I heard you split that dude's wig last night.' (Shot somebody in the head.) Ask your congregants, why do you come? We stand on this, this is our value system, but you seem firmly rooted and comfortable. You've been coming here and haven't changed an inch. Why are coming here? Sleep in on Sunday mornings. Something must be happening for you here, but I'm not sure that's good. You come here because it makes you feel better about your destructive life style. You shoot somebody and then come to church to feel better about yourself. The gospel forces you to make a decision. Nobody is going to be confronted with the truth of the gospel and remain unchanged.

"Maybe they're not changing because they're not hearing the truth. Pastor, that's on you. Their hearts are so hardened because they've heard it every which way you can give it. These cats are still hustling, still shooting; they've fathered multiple kids with several different women. Cut these guys loose. They're going to die in that condition – but they'll be faithful church members to the end. Where's the profit for them in that? For folks who are knee deep in garbage this is the only way left.

"Pastor, take them aside and say, 'You are *not* entitled to come here. This is *not* a social club. These folks are in relationship with God and seeking to connect with each other and to grow spiritually. If you're a die-hard Oakland Raiders fan, why would you buy season tickets to the San

Chapter 25

The Minister's Map

 Some years back, I was invited to preach for an inner city church in search of a pastor. That summer Sunday morning, I preached from Luke, chapter four, verses 14-21. In the sermon I suggested that the church has to be more than a whooping and hollering station. I suggested that too often we sit in church, get fat off the sermons, then go home and belch (in a spiritual sense). I suggested that the thing to do might be to carry this word beyond the walls of the church, to help the addicted find recovery, to persuade gang members to stop warring, and to help single mothers get a break.

I thought it was a pretty good sermon. People were shouting. However, a few days later, I received a phone call from one of the church leaders. He said (and I quote verbatim), "So and So Baptist Church is not ready for the revolutionary Jesus you came here preaching."

What? Apparently, he and I had two conflicting understandings of Jesus. The Jesus I serve didn't die in his bed an old man who never made waves. No, the Jesus I serve died on a Roman cross precisely *because* he was a revolutionary. He came to upend injustice in the social order and to end slavery to sin. You can't be light in the darkness, as Jesus commanded, without being a revolutionary.

You can't read Jesus' teachings and apply them without seeing change in your life. You can't live out Jesus' teachings as a church within a community and not see the community change. Please find for me the scripture where Jesus says, "I have come to support the status quo. He who would challenge the systems of power, authority, and justice is not for me. I have come that you might take things easy and not make waves. Serving me should never make you go out of your way." The day you can show me that in the Bible is the day I will start watering down my sermons.

Years ago, my barber, who wasn't a church-going man, told me something as I sat back in his chair getting my bald-fade haircut attended to. He said, "Rev, if you removed most of these churches overnight and replaced them with delicatessens, nobody would know they were even gone." If you say that you serve the Jesus of the gospels and this is true of you, your church, or your non-profit, please note that something has gone desperately wrong. God calls revolutionaries, and revolutionaries rarely work incognito. I'm telling you what I know. I live in the San Francisco Bay Area, and I've met revolutionaries of every stripe, ideology, philosophy, and theology. Revolutionaries want change, and they're never secret about what they believe. They are on an eternal recruitment drive. It's time for you to get it popping, my Jesus revolutionary friend!

Lost in Preacher Land

"The harvest is plentiful but the laborers are few... ." So Jesus tells us in Luke 10:2. Few would doubt this theological point. And yet many mainstream churches are chock full of preachers sitting behind a lead pastor; preachers who labor at nothing but pulling off the cobwebs stuck to the seat of their pants. Instead of bearing fruit, they are frustrated, filled with dreams and talents that never come to life. Instead of preaching the word of God, they'll ride the pine benches until saddle sores force them to stand up and shout, "Amen! Say that Pastor!" This chapter is about the soldiers who want to go war but are waiting for one of God's generals to give the order. We need these people to be empowered. They are the silent army, the dormant power, the secret weapon that can save a city, a nation.

"… But the Laborers are Few"

Yes, Lord, the laborers *are* few. In fact, they are fewer than you would think, because not everybody in a clerical robe and shiny shoes is a laborer. A laborer is outside on the block kicking that gospel message to drug dealers. A laborer is offering to drive neighborhood kids to Sunday school. A laborer is in the back room of a coffee shop somewhere plotting how he or she can do God's will in the war zone. A laborer doesn't insist on comfort. They don't need their bag carried or their tea handed to them while they sit in the big chair. The laborer doesn't have anybody kissing their ring. The laborer can't walk past the lost without feeling a stirring inside. The laborer will walk in the direction of the gunshots to save the one. The laborer truly gives a damn, and anybody with eyes can see it.

Hard Truth for Preachers

The truth is that too many of our churches are filled with pomp and circumstance but not labor. Some of our churches are located right, smack dab in the middle of the ghetto gun-war zone, and yet people who actually live in the hood avoid our sanctuaries like the buildings are on fire. We've got more people driving in from 50 miles away than walking from 5 minutes away, and we're comfortable with that. We'll even go as far as to say God is blessing our church because we've got lots of people coming. Well, that may or may not mean that God is blessing. It may be that

He's just given us more rope to hang ourselves and greater distance to fall if we don't repent and do the first works. Is God going to bless your church if you ignore His command to go into all the world, starting with the community around your building? I'd have a hard time believing that. Without the blessing of God, your ministry will eventually crumble. It might seem as though it's thriving, but it's rotting deep down inside where you can't see the damage. Greed, corruption, and apathy are like an army of termites warring against the very foundation. Everything might look great above ground, but it can all fall in a day. What can change our destinies? We need to start with the foot soldiers.

Here's the hood truth. We really need to re-examine what it means to be a minister of the gospel. Today, our exposure to mega-preachers who preach sermons in stadiums causes us to define success in ministry as drawing a multitude. Our role models are ministers who live in villas, drive six-figure automobiles, and appear on reality television.

I believe that in our age, God has raised up ministers who can reach hundreds of thousands of people with a single sermon. However, I also believe that God has raised up preachers to reach one hundred people with a single sermon, even ten, maybe even just one. Does that make them any less successful than the mega-guy? No.

Are you one of the preachers struggling because you get no airplay? We have to redefine what it means to be a minister. Notice I used the term "minister" and not "preacher." Ministers bind up wounds, they speak hope in hopeless situations, they serve – be that setting up tables, or sitting on the curb praying for someone in the throes of drug addiction, knitting scarves, pouring grape punch at the after-school program, or helping some kid with his or her homework. Ministers serve, and they often do so without earthly recognition. Ministers bandage wounds and wash feet. The world may have enough preachers, but it will never have enough ministers. Orators may have denominational cred or pulpit cred. Real ministers in the hood have street cred.

Yes, someone may be able to stop you from preaching your sermon to the multitudes, but they can never stop you from serving sandwiches and water bottles to human trafficking victims on the corner. They might be able to stop you from whooping and hollering, but they will never be able to stop you from hosting a back-to-school clothing drive or mentoring some young person without parents.

Ministry is so much more than preaching. The community around you is hurting. It is starving for human touch and compassion. There are children literally dreaming of having an adult who truly, truly cares for them. (I'm not telling you something I've read in a book somewhere. I've met plenty of them.) There are unemployed people who have no one to show them how to complete a resume. There are sick people who have no one to show them the path to the hospital. There are senior citizens with no one to talk to.

And you sit in the front row of your church, Sunday after Sunday, boiling with anger and melting in frustration because the pastor won't give you the mic. You may not be able to find a sanctuary wherein to preach your three-point sermon in post-Christian America. However, that crowd in front of the liquor store may be dying to hear it. People behind bars and in senior citizen homes can't go to church. Imagine the blessing you could be if you simply went to them. No, you may never get rich doing this, but you'll please God, and isn't that what you really want?

Ministry is about so much more than fame and money. If Jesus was an itinerant minister who traveled the countryside on foot and more than likely owned only one garment, do you think He promises you great riches on earth in exchange for your faithful service? Do you think

Jesus would come to earth to die on the cross as a criminal but offer you fame and fortune if you but serve him? That doesn't make sense. Does it?

What Jesus does promise is life and life more abundantly. God gave you breath so your life would mean something to others, and I don't mean just the staff at the First National Bank. You are born to be a balm for a hurting world, Minister.

Study

One Sunday years ago, a friend invited me to visit his house of worship, the Cathedral Second Baptist Church in Perth Amboy, New Jersey. I was blown away. Bishop Donald Hilliard, Jr., was the "realest" preacher I had ever heard in my life. That Sunday he spoke about fornication and adultery. If you could cross the humor of Richard Pryor and piety of Billy Graham, you'd have an idea of what the sermon sounded like. Bishop Hilliard had a sermonic range that could reach from the Pentagon to the pool hall. I still list him among the "baddest" preachers on the planet.

When I first experienced the call to ministry, I called the pastoral offices of Cathedral Second Baptist Church to schedule a counseling appointment. Assistant Pastor Reverend Dr. Bernadette Glover, a spiritually minded intellectual, sat down and listened as I expressed what I was feeling. At the end of my monologue, she said three simple words that would change my life. She said, "Go to college."

I was in my 30s when I enrolled at Kean State University in Union, New Jersey, as a philosophy and religion major. I was off to a late start, and at times I felt lost. During my time of matriculation, the college hired an adjunct professor to teach a class on black religion. His name was Reverend Dr. Samuel DeWitt Proctor. I didn't know much about him at the time, other than the fact that he had once pastored historic Abyssinian Baptist Church in Harlem. Later, I found that he was one of the most respected African-American preachers ever and was considered so from Reverend Dr. Martin Luther King, Jr., on down. Dr. Proctor had your classic, deep baritone preacher's voice. He was warm and friendly, like the grandfather I'd never known.

Between classes, I would sit up in his office and just ask questions about faith and ministry. The public library had nothing on him. I'd sit at his feet enthralled. He was encouraging and full of counsel for a former rapper turned preacher who didn't have a whole lot going for him in the way of support. He told me that seminary would be a necessity. When I did write an application for admission to the American Baptist Seminary of the West in Berkeley, California, Dr. Proctor wrote a letter asking them to admit me.

Seminary challenged me, as Dr. Proctor said it would, but it also broadened my view of the world and deepened my faith. Not everyone agrees that theological education is necessary. In fact, some people think it's downright worldly.

I once accompanied the Reverend Dr. J. Alfred Smith, Sr., pastor emeritus of Allen Temple Baptist Church, to a church service in the Oakland community. The pastor of the host church was an anti-intellectual. He believed that if God called a person, the summons and the power of the Holy Spirit were all that were needed to fulfill the call. He believed that theological education was folly. Reverend Smith, on the other hand, has been a strong proponent of seminary-trained ministry for decades. Many, many preachers have completed college and graduate studies due to his prompting. I'm sure that the host preacher knew this and perhaps even resented it. In his opening remarks he said, "I am a God-called preacher. I have never been to the cemetery ... I mean seminary." An honest mistake? That's what I assumed ... the *first* time he made the remark. However, by the third time, I realized that he was doing it on purpose. In the car after service I asked Pastor Smith what he thought of the minister's rant against what he called the "cemetery." Dr. J. Alfred Smith, Sr., looked me in the eye and said, "At least the cemetery gave me some class." I fell out laughing.

I once heard a respected theologian say, "Seminary is not a greenhouse to grow your faith." He was right. It's not Sunday school, where everything you've been taught your whole life will be reinforced. On the contrary, everything you've been taught your whole life might be challenged in seminary. However, solid educational credentials can work hand in hand with street cred. You would probably have never heard of the Reverend Dr. Martin Luther King, Jr,. if he had not invested in a theological graduate degree. An education was the tool that helped him forge the concepts undergirding non-violent resistance and social justice.

Chapter 26

The View From the Pew

 Pastor, once you've prepared yourself, once you've been ordained, and once you've been installed, how far does your ministry extend? Is it limited to the members of your church, or does it extend to the community? This question is raised in one of my favorite black-and-white movies: *On The Waterfront* (1954).

The Awakening

One of the main characters in the Academy Award-winning film is a priest, Father Barry, who finds that his ministry is broader than the four walls of his church. Filmed in Hoboken, New Jersey, the film is a powerful period piece about waterfront corruption. It centers on a union local that has been taken over by a gangster named Johnny Friendly. We're introduced to the community by a scene where an innocent kid, a potential government witness, is lured to a rooftop and then tossed to his death by some of Friendly's goons.

As a crowd gathers, the priest pushes through the onlookers to administer last rites. If it's Friendly's intention to spread intimidation and fear throughout the community, he has succeeded. Onlookers cover the body with old newspapers.

"Father, who would want to kill Joey?" the dead boy's sister asks the priest.

Father Barry has no relevant answer. Instead he says to her, "Listen, I'm in the church if you need me."

She's appalled. "You're in the church if I need you?" she asks. "Did you ever hear of a saint hiding out in a church?"

Later, she apologies for her frankness. The priest counters with a question. "You think I'm just a gravy train rider with a turned around collar. Don't you?"

She says nothing. She doesn't have to. He has his answer. And here is the film's turning point. Circumstances force the priest to see his parish as broader than the handful of people who will journey into the safety of his church building. It's even broader than the people who belong to his denomination or even his religion. His calling is to the community that surrounds the building, a community he defines as a "parish."

After he's had this revelation, he once again approaches the murdered man's sister in conversation. He says, "I've been thinking about your question, and you're right Edie. This is my parish. I don't know how much I can do, but I'll never find out unless I come down here and take a good look for myself."

Oh, my. If but one of out of every ten pastors in America suddenly awoke to this reality, Lord, what would happen?

Along the way, Father Barry realizes that wandering outside the safety of the church and into the troubles of his parish members will prove a dangerous thing. But his faith mesmerizes him like a moth is drawn to the flames. At one time, he looks at the hardened but frightened longshoremen who shield the gangsters with their weary compliance and says, "How can we call ourselves Christians and protect these murderers with our silence?"

Father Barry has counted the cost, and there is no looking back now. Empowered by the Holy Spirit and in the name of Jesus Christ, he takes the stand he must take. One day he wanders down to the dock and ends up preaching a sermon about how Jesus sees the longshoremen being taken advantage of by the gangsters. He says, "Some people think the crucifixion only took place on Calvary. They'd better wise up. Taking Joey Doyle's life to stop him from testifying is a crucifixion ... and anybody who sits around and lets it happen and keeps silent about something he knows has happened is as guilty of it as much as the Roman soldier who pierced the flesh of our Lord to see if he was dead. He sees you selling your soul to the mob for a day's pay."

A gangster yells from the shadows, "Go back to your church, Father!"

Father Barry cannot be turned back now. He hollers back at the voice in the darkness, "Boys, *this* is my church! And if you don't think Christ is down here on the waterfront, you've got another guess coming!"

Believer, Where is Your Church?

If you define the people you are sent to as the card-carrying members of a faith club that meets inside a building, we're all done for. We might as well say, "Satan, you took the best. You might as well take the rest."

For if you define your church as merely those people who walk through your doors, you absolve yourself of any responsibility to the single mom struggling to put food on the table, the fatherless children with nothing to do after school but get in trouble, or the baby eating lead paint chips off the walls in her decrepit tenement apartment up the block. However, if you see them as an extension of your church, Christian, then their plight becomes *your* plight. And their ain't no runnin' from their pain!

If you want to see any real success in urban ministry, you must broaden your idea of "church." Your parish might encompass a three-block radius around your building site. It might be larger or smaller, but Pastor, you are the shepherd of not just your "church members" but of an entire community. Christian, you know those people standing in front of the liquor store that you drive past on Sunday morning on your way to church with your nose turned up? Guess what. They are also your church members.... . Uh-oh, that puts things in an entirely different perspective, doesn't it?

Chapter 27

Sharing with Shattered Families

Are you in a battle to build street cred for your ministry? Here's one way to do it. Reach out to the hundreds of shattered families: mothers and sometimes fathers raising children on their own under the weight of soul-crushing poverty. This issue is so pervasive, I could fill a library full of books this size with testimonies of parents struggling to make it. I will not. Instead, I will introduce you to one single mom. Her name is Gina.

Notes from a Single Mom

Gina is a long-time friend I've admired for years. She loves God and adores her children. She is the leader of a community of single parents struggling to keep a roof overhead and shoes on everyone's feet. They've found strength in banding together. Here, Gina introduces us to her story and the challenge of single parents inside the urban church.

The Family Breaks

"We had actually met in high school," Gina recalls. "We hung around with the same crowd. Then, one day he approached me and said he was interested in me. We had similar upbringings, both having been raised by our grandmothers. I didn't know my mother well. I didn't know my dad at all. From the time we were 16 until we reached our 20s, he and I continued to build our friendship.

"He was there when my grandmother kicked me out and disowned me. She was prejudiced. I'm Latino, and she didn't want me to be with an African-American. So, his family took me in at the age of 16. I felt understood by him. I felt heard and loved. We could share and talk. His family loved me. To this day they are like family to me. By the time I was 21, I was pregnant with my son.

"However, my relationship with my baby's father was unraveling. I got accepted to the University of California at Berkeley. At the same time, he was experimenting with drugs. I got more focused on school and work and, unfortunately, began neglecting my family. I was working full time and studying full time. He was uncomfortable with what I was doing. He was getting drunk and wanting me to pick him up at the bar. Tension escalated. We never saw eye to eye. By the time my son, Anthony, was 9 and my second child was 3, their dad's bags were packed and sitting out in the hallway. That was 2003; I've been on my own with the kids ever since.

"At one point, I wondered, 'How will I raise these kids, emotionally? How will I be able to work and take care of the kids?' God had me count the cost. There was no way I could both work and go to school full time. I had to drop out of Berkeley. Dropping out of school was like losing part of my identity. I felt as if I were losing myself.

"I remember praying, 'God, if you are real, and if you love me, put me in a church where you want me.' One of Anthony's friends invited us to his church. I was in that church for seven or eight years. I got baptized. I gave my life to God. I began living my life as a Christian. I went into a church that was very strict in their doctrine. Everyone in the church was married and had families, and people were asking questions about my divorce. Nobody there was single, or so I thought at the time. I felt guilty, ashamed, embarrassed, scared, and nervous.

Finding Community Within the Church

"I lost my car twice due to repossession. I had to ask friends for food. I lost my job. I was really losing myself. I went into a deep depression to numb the pain. Then I found some single moms. They were in the church after all, but they were hidden. I ended up leading them. We built a support network. We started cooking dinner for each other, helping each other clean. I no longer felt alone. My kids and I felt normal. We could relate to what other families were going through. There was a common bond.

"Since then we've built this single mom's network. We pitched in to provide childcare, toiletries, groceries, gas money. People were just there for each other. We would band together and talk about how painful and scary single parenthood is. All of the kids were without dads. We felt a lot of bitterness. The fathers had moved on. They had other kids now. But here we were struggling to keep a roof overhead.

"There was no child support for most of us. Still, we never bashed the dads. We prayed for them. We didn't want to turn our children against their fathers. God is in control, we reasoned. God is there to take care of the widows and orphans. By this time, my children's father had two other children with someone else. I became her friend. I invited her to my church. She was baptized. Her children have a relationship with my children.

Things Fall Apart

"The church was my anchor, but the role of single moms there was awkward. The church would ask the single moms to perform babysitting chores for the church as well as other things. Most of us were working full time, and many of the single moms were in college as well. The church commitment became overwhelming. If you called in and said you were sick, you were told to check your heart or adapt your schedule. They didn't understand. We were the ones raising the kids, going to the parent/teacher meetings, picking up and dropping them off, taking care of the finances, standing mentally/emotionally for our children. To give 100 percent to the church was mentally exhausting. The church people didn't understand what we were going through.

"If, in desperation, you reached out to the church for benevolence help, you were handed a 24-page form. They provided no help for back rent. If you came to them in desperate need of resources, their answer was, 'Put the child's father to work.'

"Somewhere along the line, they lost the focus of God's love and taking care of the widows and orphans. Struggling as a single parent and being less than perfect wasn't easy for any of us.

"Right now, I'm in the process of opening up a nonprofit for single parents. My vision is to have a formal network that provides support and understanding for people who have struggled as I have. It's tough being a single parent and having no one who can understand what you're going through, emotionally, physically, and psychologically. When my organization is up and functioning, therapists will be brought in to counsel some single moms who are open to it. Single parents will never feel alone, abandoned, or forgotten. When these parents walk through the door, they'll talk to someone who knows what they're going through. They'll know how to address your pain and stress and teach you how never to lose yourself."

The Single and Divorced in Your Midst

Do you value and treasure single moms like Gina? Do you know anyone like Gina, a single mom struggling to keep the ends meeting? Does she go to your church? Have you ever invited her to dinner with your family? Do you know her story? Have you reached out to her children? What kind of resources has your ministry set aside to help her? Do you preach sermons with her in mind? What ministry has your church created for single parents? How would you propose to help her if she came to you and said she didn't have enough food to last until the next payday?

Chapter 28

Saving Your Church from Extinction

 Do I think the traditional church will die? No. However, I do think that in the future the way we do ministry will change. We'll have to because young people like relationship. There are going to be more churches that meet in the back of coffee houses. Bi-vocational pastors will become more plentiful. They'll work at another career that finances their call to ministry.

Gentrification and black flight are going to challenge the black church. Eventually, there will be a generation who won't want to drive in from the suburbs to go to church in inner Detroit, Milwaukee, or Oakland. One day the church will no longer be the most segregated hour of the week. Our churches will be integrated. Hard decisions will have to be made.

One day awhile back, someone took me on a tour of West Oakland. They pointed to a crumbling church and said that was such and such a church where Reverend so and so was the pastor. The sign was faded. Weeds and tall grass flourished in the front yard. The church was long past its heyday. All around it was crack and crime, for which they had no answers and no outreach. The point of change – or death – was upon this congregation. Maybe it had already passed.

Gentrification: the Beast Without Conscience

In the park at Cole Street in San Francisco, a wayward Pacific Ocean breeze lifts the husky aroma of barbecue ribs high into the atmosphere. Old friends stand, laughing in the smoke, some reunited after decades of separation. Lionel Ritchie croons from the DJ's speakers. A pair of senior citizens dance to the applause of a small gaggle of teenagers.

"Come get in this picture, homeboy," a gray-headed man in a black and orange Giants hat beckons. I'm not a part of this gathering. I just happen to be passing through, but they don't know that. Like each of them, I'm black, and they just assume I belong. Why spoil the fun? So, I jump in between two brothers who could be my age and flash the peace sign. I imagine that later they'll sit around arguing about whose cousin or brother I am.

These brothers lived in this neighborhood when the line between neighbor and family was as thin as a well-worn thread. The Haight-Ashbury District in San Francisco will long be remembered for the hippies who made it a landing zone in the 1967 Summer of Love. However, long before that and long after it, the area was home to many, many African-Americans. And then realtors began to see it as a desirable location. Posh tea shops began to go up where Mom and Pop soul food restaurants once existed. The rents also went up. The price of the average house began to pass what the average person could pay.

None of the people dancing and laughing in the park can afford to live here now. The apartments and condos around the park are now occupied almost exclusively by white and Asian people. They walk by us with their dogs on a leash, gawking. They do a double-take as they stroll by this gathering of blacks in an area where black people no longer live. In a few hours, the picnic will be over. The exiles will pack up and go back to the four corners of the Bay Area where they have been dispersed, and the new residents will have the land back to themselves.

Exile and Displacement

The term "gentrification" was originally coined by a British sociologist. It takes place when people of economic means identify a neighborhood populated by poor people, often people of color. They begin to move in to take up residence in the community. Housing prices soar. Eventually, the marginalized people are pushed out of the community. Bike lanes and dog parks appear on what might have once been a desolate landscape. City services, once nearly absent from the area are now readily available to the neighborhood. The housing stock is restored. For years, residents might have begged the city for streetlights and better trash collection services. Those things will now appear in time to serve the new residents.

Gentrification is ripping the soul out of San Francisco. It was once the city where people came to gain a new start. Its melting pot of eclectic people made it an unusual and unique place. The tech industry is now headquartered in the San Francisco Bay Area. Its high-salaried employees want to live in proximity to their jobs, and they have the money to do it.

Today San Francisco is the most expense city for renters in the United States, outstripping even New York City. San Francisco also has the second smallest percentage of African-American people of any major American city. Some say it's hovering around 3 percent and decreasing rapidly. Evictions are up 115 percent.

In a *Newsweek* article, entitled "Tech Boom Forces a Ruthless Gentrification in San Francisco," writer Joe Kloc reports: "Between 2010 and 2012, more than 13,000 technology sector jobs were created in the Bay Area. When, in the last few years, Twitter and Facebook went public, they created thousands of millionaires." The Brookings Institute reported that San Francisco has the fastest growing income inequality rate in the entire country.[1]

The purge hasn't stopped with the black community. The San Francisco Mission District has been targeted, and the bulldozer is moving fast. Latino families who called the Mission home for generations are being squeezed out by spiraling out-of-control rents. On a Saturday evening stroll through the community, one will more likely walk past white hipsters out for a latte than a Mexican-American family headed toward Saturday evening mass.

There is a huge difference between integration and gentrification. Integration takes place when people of different cultures or class strata create a melting pot in a given location, each working together for the common good. Gentrification's paradigm re-creates a community in the best interests of the newcomers. Businesses go up that the traditional residents can't afford to patronize. Housing values skyrocket, making it impossible for many of the longtime neighbors to remain in the community. At a point, the gentrifiers might even change the name of the community altogether.

Sometime back, I visited Harlem, New York. When I got out of the subway at West 116th Street and Frederick Douglass Boulevard, I was amazed. The only thing left from the days when I lived there was the street sign. An outdoor establishment called the Harlem Tavern sat in the middle of my former hood. White folks blew the foam off their cold beer as they bathed in the rays of the sun. I walked over to the after-hours joint that once stood on the corner of West 115th Street and Frederick Douglass Boulevard. It was gone. In its place? A ritzy upscale condominium. I wondered what had happened to the older folks who used to sit in front playing dominoes and telling jokes, the ones I used to wave to on the way to work. On Malcolm X Boulevard, a bagel stand occupied the corner, and the new neighbors purchased scones and Danish pastries from a young, blond girl who looked like she was on summer vacation from Yale.

And then there were the stately, gothic churches that once housed the black multitudes. Once the gentrification of Harlem is complete, what will happen to them?

Noted Black Leader Addresses Gentrification

A week after I'd flown back to the San Francisco Bay Area, I sat down with the Reverend Dr. Amos Brown, pastor of the historic Third Baptist Church and president of the local NAACP. His church is located in the Fillmore district, once an African-American enclave in the city of San Francisco. That evening, I got off the bus at the wrong stop and had to walk about 10 blocks to reach the church. In that time, I did not pass a single black person. I mentioned that to him.

Reverend Brown said, "When I first arrived in this community, blacks owned Victorian houses up and down this street. Many of the owners were my members. On Fillmore Street, when I came here in 1976, there was the fallout of the redevelopment, which was really black removal.

"During World War II white folks didn't trust black folks on the front line. They even told the lie that we couldn't fly airplanes. So who was trusted on the front lines of the segregated army? White men. That meant that white men were not here to build the ships or unload the ships. Kaiser, the shipbuilder, sent recruiters to Louisiana, Mississippi, Alabama, and Arkansas to recruit the necessary labor. For the first time, ship builders of color were hired and black longshoremen got jobs unloading the ships. Then the black population began to grow.

"See, until 1940 there were only about 4,000 blacks in this city. After World War II, the black community mushroomed from 90,000 to 100,000. There were black businesses, theaters, restaurants, barbershops, and jazz clubs. Duke Ellington, Nat King Cole, Ella Fitzgerald and a host of other jazz and blues greats performed in the Fillmore. The San Francisco Fillmore district became known as the Harlem of the West.

"They thought we were all going to go back to the South after the war, so they built temporary units, which later became public housing. After we didn't go away, they had to find a way to get rid of us. When we moved from the manufacturing and industrial age to the information and computer age, they found a way to get us on another front. They wouldn't teach us in the schools. The high tech folk are white. Folks are coming here all the way from India. Now the area has become gentrified.

"Church attendance around here is down. My prediction is that if there is no focused intentional effort made by this administration to stop this hemorrhaging of the black community, 20 years from now there weren't be 20,000 blacks left in San Francisco." [Today, there are around 800,000 people living in San Francisco.]

The Curious Mystery of the Sunday Sermon

Too few preachers are engaging the crisis of gentrification. On Sunday morning, pastors deliver spirited messages on how God used Esther to deliver the children of Israel or how He used Moses to lead the Hebrews out of Egypt. Few have anything to say about how God wants to save his children in the 21st century from the evils of foreclosure and displacement. If God cared enough to deliver Shadrach, Meshach, and Abednego from the fiery furnace in ancient times, does he care enough to deliver poor people in America from the iron jaws of displacement and homelessness today? Or has God changed over the years?

Believer, just as the leaders of the Civil Rights movement rose up to fight against segregation, we need you to rise up against the sin of gentrification. The people whom you say that God has entrusted into your hands need you to make this do-or-die stand – now!

Before I left Reverend Brown's presence that day, he said, "We're people of the Way. If you follow the Jesus way, you have to be involved in the hood. You have to be involved in the liberation gospel. You have to challenge the status quo. You have to work to set the captives free or else you are counterfeit."

After the End Has Come

They called New York City's hottest nightclub the "Limelight." Party-goers snorted pearl white cocaine in the same balconies where worshipers had once knelt to pray. Rappers grabbed their crotches and mouthed loud but barely decipherable obscenities from the stage – a stage that had once been a pulpit. That's right. At one time the Limelight had been a thriving Christian church.

The pews had been pulled out. The new worshipers did the grind and gyrated on the same floor where hymns once rose to heaven. The great-grandchildren of the church members smoked pot and gave themselves to casual sex with absolute strangers in the bathrooms.

The original worshipers at the Episcopal Church of the Holy Communion sacrificed to pay for that structure. They had dedicated that building to God, for God's use, so that souls might be brought into the kingdom. But one hundred years later, souls were being ushered into the kingdom there, but it was the wrong kingdom.

What happened? At some point, the community where the church building was located changed. Housing structures were replaced by industrial buildings. The church could not foresee the shift and was ill-equipped or perhaps not ready to address the changing times. The old families that had once been the backbone of the church moved away. Perhaps children who grew to adulthood were attracted to the magnetic pull of more charismatic pastors or churches that had better nursery facilities. Whatever the case, the Episcopal Church of the Holy Communion one day became the Limelight.

Would God Allow My Church to Collapse?

Many of you reading this are saying to yourself, "That couldn't happen to my church. God wouldn't let it happen." But the scriptures say differently. I like how the King James Version phrases I Corinthians 3:9. It says, "For we are laborers together with God: ye are God's husbandry, ye are God's building." That's right. God is *not* in this all by Himself. God has partners in the work.

If my cousin and I own a gas station together and it's my responsibility to pay the mortgage, what happens if I neglect to do so for eight months? My cousin might be as angry with me as he can be, but truth be told, at the end of that eight-month period, we would both be sitting on our cans out on the cold sidewalk. The fact that I am a co-laborer means that I have a powerful say in the outcome of our enterprise. The local church is a joint venture between God and the members of the body.

At the risk of bruising your feelings, I have to tell you that there are churches all over America's inner cities that are going to end up like the Limelight. Gentrification, aging congregations, and disinterested children will eventually turn these once-vibrant church buildings into skeletons. Charles Darwin is the most controversial and, dare I say, hated name in church circles, but he wasn't wrong about everything. For the man once uttered the words, "It is not the strongest species that survive, nor the most intelligent, but the ones most responsive to change." Apathy, laziness, and blindness will cause some of you to scoff at these words. Those of you who can see, however, have a responsibility. Don't sit there like a knot on a log while your church crumbles and the numbers dwindle down to nothing. Don't wait for the day the board decides the electric bill can't be paid. Change now, while change is still possible.

Welcome Table in the Hood

I have been told the late poet Maya Angelou invited visitors from all over the United States to her palatial North Carolina home. By all accounts she was a fantastic cook, and she loved to entertain guests over Southern cuisine served at what she simply called "the table." Here, the guests would tell their stories. They would discuss the world's problems and propose solutions.

Such a thing would be a futile waste of time, you say? I think not. Think of the kinds of people – the movers and shakers – the late poet would have been able to draw to her table!

My last, and perhaps most important, suggestion is that you create a table of your own. It doesn't necessarily have to be a space in your home. It could be in the back room of your favorite coffee house. It could be in the church fellowship hall. It should be in a space where you can imagine with others another kind of future. Your table should be a place where members of your family, church, or community-based organization will be able to think and speak freely without fear of reprisal or retribution, where no idea is belittled. The table is a space for equals, not demagogues and minions. It is the place where hope is planned and not where long-held grudges are unleashed.

Is your church dying? Does it lack street cred? Do you think that your outreach ministry could be more effective? Even if everything seems to be firing on all cylinders, isn't there something that can be tweaked or improved. The table is the place where we ask, "What's working? What can be improved or jettisoned completely. How do we define Christ's Great Commission? Where do we live that out right here? What is our common vision? Where are we in the plan? What needs to happen for this all to work? What does success look like? What should be done now?" The table is where the elephants in the room get talked about.

I was in a church service once when one of the pastors announced an upcoming church-wide meeting where church expenditures would be discussed. He ended his remarks with a warning: "You're going to have to bring some to get some." Those are words that precede a street fight. It means, "You may give me some lumps, but you won't be able to do that without catching a few lumps yourself." That's not the message you want to convey here. You are teammates on a common mission, not enemy combatants. Remember, a house divided against itself cannot stand. However, if you get just two or three people together focused on doing the will of God, how can you be stopped? Fight for agreement. Get on the same page. Go forward in prayer, submission to God's will and one another, and work in line with God's word.

Remember, this is spiritual warfare. The enemy knows that greater is God within you than he that is in the world. God can't be defeated, so the enemy's age-old strategy is to divide God's troops and then get them fighting each other. You can't let that happen if you want to see God's power manifested in these streets. That means there is going to have to be some cheek-turning and some trespass-dropping within the ranks.

Release the past offenses. Drop the grudges. You're on a mission now. Present a united front and a common mission when you go do what it is you're called to do. Feel me?

Here's a suggestion. Offer this book as a church-wide study project. Ask people to make notes and jot down ideas from this book that trigger thoughts and emotions for them, and then plan for an event called "The Table." The Table will be a proactive place where all can be boldly honest (in fact, ought to be). Tell them that The Table is where we will engage in real talk about the direction of our church or faith-based organization.

Can This Work?

A handful of people sat down in a room and designed a rocket ship that would hurl human beings into space and then bring them back again. A group of people that were focused on one goal sat down and designed New York City's famed Empire State Building. Jesus changed the entire world with just 12 disciples. Often, He used just three of them, and none of them had any money. Imagine what a group of people committed to the Kingdom of God could do if they stepped out in faith with a common vision and dared to truly fulfill the Great Commission? I shiver to think.

Imagine for a moment that a boiler fire caused your cruise ship to sink. Before the huge, iron hulk disappears beneath the surface, you and a couple dozen passengers are able to escape into a lifeboat. You have no map, no compass, very little food, and only one oar. I imagine there would be many serious conversations about the direction the little boat needed to travel, especially after the first raindrops began to fall. Now imagine that there's one guy in the front of the boat, paddle in hand, who has been declared the leader but refuses to discuss the direction of the lifeboat because he feels that God has made him captain. What would you say to him?

In the church world, often the pastor's word, lifestyle, and decisions go unquestioned because no matter what he or she does, people have been taught that it is a sin to hold pastors accountable. After all, they are God's anointed and the questioner might be destroyed. But is that truly what the Bible says?

Old Testament scholar and Academic Dean of American Baptist Seminary of the West, Dr. LeAnn Flescher says, "In the Bible, the anointed of God most often refers to the King, although it also refers at times to another leader raised up by God to lead the people. In the OT the Hebrew word is Mashiach = messiah. This word is translated into the Greek as Christos = Christ. The messiah in the OT, most often the king, was the one that led them into battle for victory; in other words led them to deliverance from their enemies. The NT writers apply this term, in the Greek (Christos) to Jesus – understanding him as the ultimate and final messiah... .

"1 Chronicles 16:22 references the period before the establishment of Israel as a nation where God protected God's chosen people from malicious acts by foreign kings as they travelled through their lands. This verse harks back to the Genesis stories. In this instance the term 'anointed one' refers to the chosen people and their leaders – broader than a reference to the king, priest, or prophet, because all of those positions had not yet been established. Israel was not yet a nation. These were the called out ones. The verse references physical harm.

"If you remember in the books of Samuel and Kings, David and Saul were in conflict and David had a chance to kill Saul, but would not because Saul was an anointed one by God. Over and over again the command comes/is referenced not to touch the anointed by God, in other words, do not lay a hand on them. However, the prophets were called to speak truth to the king (the anointed one). They were not called to physically harm the king, but they were called to speak truth about the need for reform and they were called to address their message to the king. It was the king's role to lead the people to be faithful to the covenant. If the covenant was violated then the prophets spoke a message of truth to the king and called for reform.

"So, contrary to some modern interpretations, the text is actually describing prophets called to critique the kings, and to critique them severely, but to never physically touch or harm the king (the anointed one). I would conclude that pastors and religious leaders that are violating the covenant (as we would understand that word today) should expect to be critiqued and critiqued severely by prophetic voices from their communities, e.g., inappropriate use of funding, sexual misconduct, abusive behavior, etc. But, we ought never physically touch or harm them. God is at work in every generation calling prophets to speak out against the social and religious ills of the time. Pastors ought not assume they can hide behind their sense of being called to "anointed leadership" as protection against critique. "If they are being irresponsible or unethical leaders they will be critiqued and rightly so. But, we must also be clear that disagreements about leadership styles and directions do not constitute irresponsible and unethical behavior. We might disagree with a leader's choices and need to bite our tongue so as not to create trouble for the directions the leader is taking the group, but when the 'anointed leader' crosses the ethical line, then the prophets need to speak out for the sake of all."

The Second Table

Luke 14:12-14 is a precursor to Jesus' parable of the great banquet. It reads, "Then Jesus said to his host, 'When you give a luncheon or dinner, do not invite your friends, your brothers or sisters, your relatives, or your rich neighbors; if you do, they may invite you back and so you will be repaid. But when you give a banquet, invite the poor, the crippled, the lame, the blind, and you will be blessed. Although they cannot repay you, you will be repaid at the resurrection of the righteous.'"

Subsequent verses talk about a great banquet where the poorest of the poor are treated to a sumptuous feast. I'd like you to prepare such a feast for the people in the hood or the trailer park close to your church building. Host a community meal and sit down with the people to converse the way equals do.

Quite recently, someone loaned me a credit card so that I could take some homeless youth to lunch. It is one thing to sit across a sterile desk and converse as social worker and client. It's another thing for six people, all dressed in jeans and sneakers to sit down over burgers and fries. One fellow sat at the luncheon table with last night's blanket draped around his shoulders.

I had eaten in this two-star eatery several times. The kids with me had walked past it hundreds of times and never been inside. It's the kind of joint that has plastic tablecloths and serves your soda in the bottle. Yet, the kids acted as though they had been taken to a five-star tux and tails restaurant. They savored the dignity with which they were being treated by the wait staff. The sense of honor twinkled in their eyes.

These kids live in a world of secrets. They are strangers even to each other. They drift over county and state lines in search of an amorphous thing called "freedom." Some are running from something or somebody. All of this necessitates that they master the illusion of cordiality without actually extending friendship. They live out in wooded areas or in homeless shelters, but they are kind. I have watched them share the last cookie with a fellow traveler. They are also brilliant. They are philosophers and theologians who explain the world using eastern religious concepts. Yet, they do not give away much about themselves. The first time I saw them walk out from behind the shadows which hide their true selves was over a meal.

How can you minister to people you don't know? How can you create an engaging sermon for people whose very world is unfamiliar to you. More important still, how can you design ministry for people without actually sitting down with them to find out who they are and what they actually want and need? Bring the folks in the hood to the table with you if you are a suburbanite. Sit down together as equals and then listen to their hearts. Make them partners in their own deliverance.

The Streets are Calling

A few months ago, I walked through what appeared to be a drug transaction in the middle of the San Francisco Tenderloin district. Nothing new there. The T.L. is an open-air drug bazaar, and parts of it are as active as the McDonald's drive-through at lunch time. Here's what caught my eye. The deal was going down between a crack dealer and three soccer moms with an edge. He wore a San Francisco 49ers ball cap, mirror shades, and a denim jacket, outer stuff that he could take off in a hurry if he ever had to make a run for it. In ten seconds he'd be completely unrecognizable to anybody but his mother. The soccer moms all wore ripped blue jeans and jack boots. Three children, the oldest perhaps 11, were with them. One blond haired tyke was in a baby carriage.

One of the moms was begging for a price break. "C'mon man. I haven't been out here in awhile, and we just spent a lot of money with you." The man in the ball cap gave them each what appeared to be a white pebble.

My heart went out to the children. The things their young eyes have seen in this neighborhood: people smoking rock cocaine everywhere, defecating in the streets, on their hands and knees in a state of psychosis chasing that lost, invisible ghost rock, fist fights, shootings, robberies, and now here's mama negotiating diaper and milk money for a hit. By the end of the month, that might not be all that mama is willing to negotiate for an extra hit, and these kids have seen it all. By the time they reach their adult years, what impact might all of these experiences have on their futures? It's something you'll want to think about (and I hope lose some sleep over), because these kids walk past the front door of your church every day.

The Beatles might have said it best, "All the lonely people, where do they all come from?" I've shaken hands with people swallowed up in trouble and without another human being in the world who genuinely loves them. Will you love them?

The New Gentiles

In the early days of the Christian faith, believers saw the church as an extension of Judaism. They were reluctant to receive gentile (non-Jewish) believers into their gatherings. Gentiles were considered unclean outsiders. Even after God spoke to Peter in a vision about the inclusion of gentiles, Peter bristled against the idea. In the book of Galatians, Peter and Paul clashed openly over the matter. What is to be done with the outsiders? Even if we let them in the doors, will they be our equals, or will they be second-class saints? Will they be eligible for church leadership at some point, or will they be forever pigeonholed as beneficiaries of our prideful benevolence, second-class members good for little more than the opportunity to grovel for the crumbs from our table? Do we plan to drive in from the suburbs to be the voice of the voiceless, or is our plan to find ways to give the voiceless their own voices?

SAVING YOUR CHURCH FROM EXTINCTION | 375

It All Comes Down to How Much You Care

Often the precursor to a miracle was the phrase, "Jesus was moved with compassion." Jesus would look at a suffering or lost person, and compassion would swell up in His bones. It was more than sympathy. Compassion is a deep, deep sense that encircles the soul. Jesus would look at a hurting person and be moved in His guts. Jesus felt the weary anguish and physical torment of other people as though these things were happening to Him.

Is that what you feel when you see snotty nose kids running around your church block who are not a part of anybody's Sunday school anywhere? Is that what you feel when you walk past homeless people huddled in doorways on a rainy winter's night?

The Holy Spirit uses compassion as a hand on your back pressing you forward through the haze of a dark world thirsty for light. Let compassion be your beacon. It will lead your way to street cred. In the hood, everybody respects a soldier. Are you ready to get down with this?

How much do you care? Put down the book now, and let's see.

Notes

CHAPTER 1

[1]C. Eric Lincoln and Lawrence Mamiya, *The Black Church in the African American Experience*, Duke Press, Durham; 1990, pg. 384.

CHAPTER 6

[1]Stanley Tookie Williams, *Blue Rage, Black Redemption*, Pleasant Hill, Damamli, 2014, p. i (foreword).

[2]Monique W. Morris, *Black Stats*, The New Press, NY, 2014, p. 106.

[3]David Simon, Bill Moyers, www.billmoyers.com, April 17, 2009.

[4]Rakim, "Man Above," from the album *Seventh Seal*, Ra Records, 2009.

[5]Monique W. Morris, p. 121.

CHAPTER 7

[1]Curtis Snow, My Name Is Curtis Snow And I'm A G, Over The Edge Books, Los Angeles, CA 2007, Act 2, p. 9

CHAPTER 12

[1]Bobby Seale, A Lonely Rage, New York Times Books, New York, NY, 1979, p. 157

[2]Michelle Alexander, *The New Jim Crow*, The New Press, 2010, p. 97.

[3]*The Last Poets*, w/Melle Mel et. al., Rykodisc, New York, 1993.

[4]Michelle Alexander, p. 97.

[5]www.sentencingproject.org

CHAPTER 13

[1]*The Mack*, New Line Cinema, 1973.

CHAPTER 15

[1]E.P. Sanders, *The Historical Figure Of Jesus*, Penguin Books, New York, 1993, p. 1.

[2]Sanders, pp. 268, 269.

[3]Robert B. Cootes, *Amos Among the Prophets*, Prentice-Hall, Englewood Cliffs, 1981, p. 26.

[4]Ron Sider, *One-Sided Christianity*, Zondervan, Grand Rapids, 1993, p. 148.

[5]John Perkins, *Notes From An Economic Hit Man*, Plume, New York, 2005.

CHAPTER 17

[1]Samuel Reed, Call And Response On The State Of The Black Church, New York Times, April 16, 2010

CHAPTER 18

[1]Plies, "God I'm Tired Of Lying To You" from the "Lost Sessions" album, 101 Distribution, Phoenix, 2010

CHAPTER 19

[1]Joe Darion and Mitch Leigh, "The Impossible Dream (The Quest), Alfred Publishing Belwin Division, Van Nuys, CA 1965

[2]Pirates Of Silicon Valley, TNT Studios, Atlanta, Georgia, 1999

[3]James Alfred Smith, Sr., and Harry Williams, II, Title, InterVarsity Press, Downers Grove, IL, 2004.

CHAPTER 22

[1]Michael J. Feeney, Rapper Rick Ross Poaching Mob Boss John Gotti's Nickname "Teflon Don" For New CD, New York Daily News, New York, NY, July 21, 2010

CHAPTER 28

[1]Joe Kloc, Tech Boom Forces A Ruthless Gentrification In San Francisco, Newsweek Magazine, New York, April 15, 2014

Acknowledgements

Much love and thanks to Tam, Tom, Erin, Dick, and the entire TLC Graphics crew, some of the most astounding people I have ever met. Book design does not even begin to cover what they do. Wow! Thanks to Lea Baker, my neighbor from East Oakland who was there for me when gentrification took my home. Thank you Reggie Jones of the Allen Temple United Men's Fellowship; you were there with a pickup truck and an ocean liner full of patience. Blessings to the wonderful young people whom I served in Berkeley, California, John and Kim McGlothen, David Aron, a.k.a. Dave Dizzle, and the People's Bible Study at Glide Church, SF. Platinum thanks to Dr. Dianne Budd and Mr. Tim Pearson, two incredible people who taught me that not all angels have wings. Peace to all of my Facebook friends. Platinum thanks to Matt Beardsley, Leena Bakshi, Mike O'Donal, a.k.a. M.I. (Money's Involved), Ellen Dahlke, Ms. Irma McDaniel (my second mother), all of my people back in Asbury Park, NJ. Angela and Smiley back in Harlem, NY, John and Helene Camacho and everyone who showed me kindness along the way (too numerous to mention). Gratitude to The De Ida Spencer Mission Society Circle, Allen Temple Baptist Church, Oakland, CA, Dr. Regina Brown, Phd., and Reverend Dr. Wynnetta Wymberley, Phd. In memory of Pastor Ron Christian, Christian Love Baptist Church, Irvington, NJ. Many thanks to everyone who agreed to be interviewed for this book; some are named, and some remain unnamed for obvious reasons.

Photo by Matt Beardsley

Bring Reverend Harry Louis Williams, II
to your church, conference, revival, retreat, etc.
Contact him with questions and comments:
streetcredmanual@yahoo.com.

Learn more about the author and his mission, gather
new insights, and continue the conversation online at
www.RevHarryWilliams.us.

 Follow him on Twitter: @Revharry1

Download the official *Street Cred Study Guide*
free by writing to streetcredmanual@yahoo.com.

Made in the USA
Middletown, DE
27 December 2016